Complete Aikido

AIKIDO KYOHAN:

*The Definitive Guide
to the Way of Harmony*

**Roy Suenaka
and Christopher Watson**

First published in 1997 by Tuttle Publishing, an imprint of Periplus Editions (HK) Ltd., with editorial offices at 153 Milk Street, Boston, Massachusetts 02109.

Library of Congress Catalog Card Number: 97-61864

ISBN 0-8048-3140-8

DISTRIBUTED BY:

USA	*Japan*	*Southeast Asia*
Tuttle Publishing	*Tuttle Shokai Ltd.*	*Berkeley Books Pte. Ltd.*
RR 1 Box 231-5	1-21-13, Seki	5 Little Road #08-01
North Clarendon, VT 05759	Tama-ku, Kawasaki-shi	Singapore 536983
Tel.: (802) 773-8930	Kanagawa-ken 214, Japan	Tel.: (65) 280-3320
Fax: (802) 773-6993	Tel.: (044) 833-0225	Fax: (65) 280-6290
	Fax: (044) 822-0413	

First edition
05 04 03 02 01 00 99 98 97 1 3 5 7 9 10 8 6 4 2
Printed in Singapore

TABLE OF CONTENTS

ACKNOWLEDGEMENTS

To all those people who have in one way or another contributed to the making of this book: through your constant encouragement, patience and understanding, you supported me and helped me to clear my mind and focus my energy.

To Founder Morihei Ueshiba, the creator of aikido. Undeniably the greatest martial artist the world has ever known, he taught us that we are the Universe and that through the virtue acquired from devoted practice, we can perceive the principles of heaven and earth. I thank him for sharing with us this impeccable martial art.

To Master Koichi Tohei, my mentor, the teacher who first showed me the way of *Aiki,* and who taught me the very important fundamentals of proper aikido waza. I will always be grateful to him.

To Christopher Watson, Shibu-cho, my co-author. I am deeply indebted to him, especially for his insight in preparing this book. His tremendously focused thinking and writing skills have brought aikido into a new dimension. His patience, encouragement and love of the wonderful philosophy of aikido, and our close friendship, will always be appreciated.

To Mark S. "Sonny" Roobin—Shibu-cho, Orlando, Florida—who has on many occasions listened to my stories with a very attentive ear. He has accompanied me on many adventures abroad and has proved to be a valuable asset in our growing organization. I will always be grateful for his loyalty and interest in maintaining continuity in our cause.

To Jackie Watson, of whom I affectionately think of as my little sister. I thank you for your unselfish time and love, your total involvement in the growth of our aikido, the preparation of this book, and especially your loyalty and devotion to me and my quest.

To Randy Sherman—senior instructor, Aikido of Richmond, Virginia—for his unselfish support and enthusiasm in providing the design and layout of this book.

To Fenwick Ackerman—Shibu-cho, Atlanta, Georgia—for his time and valuable suggestions, and especially for his inspiring thoughts and confidence in me. Special thanks to him for his hospitality in opening his *dojo* to us for the photography sessions that yielded the photos in this book.

To Chad Taylor—Dojo-cho, Clemson University—who in the past six years has been such a devotee to the development and growth of our aikido style and organization, and for serving as my primary uke for the techniques demonstrated in this book.

To Yoko Heffner—senior instructor, Hombu *dojo*—who provided the wonderful and artistic Japanese calligraphy for this book. *Domo arigato gozaimasu.*

Finally, to Sean and Laura Chartier go my deep appreciation for their time and professionalism in the production of the photos that appear in this book.

Special thanks go to the following students for their support and assistance: Steven Steele, Shibu-cho and chief instructor, Aikido of Richmond; Ed Parent, David Isgett and Ray McClain, senior instructors, Hombu *dojo*; Scott Hager, Aikido of Greenville, North Carolina at East Carolina University; Tom Manson and Leigh Manson, Aikido of Key West, Florida; Michael Hawley, Aikido of Buffalo, New York; Tim Ackerman and Eric and Derric Glenn, Atlanta *dojo*; and Frances Melfi, Tony Eustis, Christina Giles, and Perry Lambert, Hombu *dojo*.

To my Dad, Warren Kenji Suenaka, who was the first teacher in my life. He was always there for me with care and support. He taught me the meaning of life, and how to be a survivor.

To the most wonderful girl in my life, my wife, Kanako. My guardian angel, she was always at my side through thick and thin. She taught me the meaning of true love. Also to our children, Valerie and John, and my energetic grandson, Atao, for their loyalty, total commitment, strength and love. You are my closest friends.

To Michael A. DeMarco, Editor-in-Chief, *Journal of Asian Martial Arts,* for publishing our first major magazine article, and for his support in providing the resources and opportunity leading to the publication of this book.

Lastly, but not least, my deepest appreciation to Mark Wiley and his staff at Charles E. Tuttle, Co. (in my opinion, *the* authoritative martial arts publisher) for his enthusiastic work in making this book a reality.

ROY SUENAKA

For their early support and belief, well-deserved thanks go to editor Mark Wiley at Charles E. Tuttle, Co., and Michael DeMarco, publisher of the excellent *Journal of Asian Martial Arts*.

While all members of the Wadokai were unfailingly supportive during the genesis and creation of *Complete Aikido: Aikido Kyohan,* certain people deserve particular mention: Richard Shainwald, for his hospitality during the initial interview sessions; Christopher Caile, for his assistance in the interview process, particularly in matters of karate; Sonny Roobin, for his rock-solid faith and blunt, on-target assessments; Fenwick Ackerman, for his insight and common-sense counsel; and Michael Hawley, a exemplary *aikidoka* and human being. Thanks as well to the Wadokai *aikidoka* who patiently posed for the photographs at their own expense, some of whom drove literally halfway across the country to be a part of this enterprise.

Randall Sherman of *Cook Sherman Inc.* selflessly gave of his time and considerable talents in the design and layout for *Complete Aikido: Aikido Kyohan.* His crisp professionalism and unflagging support were invaluable in making this work a reality, and is reflected in every page. Thanks as well to Mr. Sherman's partner, Ken Cook, for his design contribution and support of the project. Likewise, photographers Sean and Laura Chartier put their lives on hold for one intense Atlanta weekend during which over 800 *waza, taiso* and *ukemi* photographs were taken, from which those that appear in this book were selected. Their superb work was the final element that pulled together over three years of labor.

Yoko Heffner kindly provided the kanji that begin every chapter— *gokuro sama deshita, Yoko-san.*

Special thanks to my wife, Jackie, for her proofreading, suggestions, support, encouragement, and belief, and to my parents, Charles and Betty Watson, for raising me to walk the Path.

Finally, my heartfelt thanks to Roy Yukio Suenaka Sensei for inestimably enriching my life, and for affording me the honor of assisting in this enterprise. Your friendship and tutelage are true blessings for which I shall be forever grateful. May this work serve as a humble gift of thanks for everything you have unselfishly given to me, and to us all.

CHRISTOPHER WATSON

Not that long ago, aikido books were scarce. You might have found a few classics at a decent martial arts supply store, but not many. Aikido schools were scarcer still—unless you lived in or near a large city, your chances of finding one were slim. Today, however, things are different. Aikido has enjoyed a meteoric rise in popularity over the last twenty years or so. You can find books on aikido at the bookstore in your local mall, and a check of the *Yellow Pages*™ will undoubtedly turn up at least one school within reasonable commuting distance.

Part of aikido's rise in popularity can quite simply be attributed to time. In the almost thirty years since the death of aikido founder Morihei Ueshiba O'Sensei, his many students have spread his philosophy and vision across the world, passing it on to a new generation of students who continue to sow the seeds of his legacy. More recently, aikido's appearance in popular films and on television has exposed O'Sensei's teachings to a worldwide audience, inspiring many to seek out more information and, ultimately, to study. Aikido's fundamental philosophy of non-violence is one that today's increasingly more violent society seems eager to embrace. In addition, aikido's non-reliance on physical strength or size for effectiveness arguably invites a broader range of students than other martial arts.

Whatever the reasons, aikido's rise in popularity has come at a cost. Aikido is now subject to the same broad misconceptions that first greeted more established and familiar (at least now) arts such as karate, judo, kung-fu, taekwondo, and so on, perhaps even more so. Because of aikido's emphasis on non-violence, some people characterize it as more of a spiritual pursuit than a practical means of self-defense. Others argue that aikido will work only if regressed to its more brutal Daito-ryu jujutsu roots, and that spirituality is secondary, at best. These schools of thought are very much like the parable of the four blind men feeling an elephant for the first time. One feels the trunk, and says an elephant is like a snake. Another touches a leg, and says it is like a tree, and so on. While these observations contain some truth, it is an incomplete truth. It is for this reason, among others, that *Complete Aikido: Aikido Kyohan* was written.

Roy Yukio Suenaka Sensei has devoted his life, beginning at age four, to martial arts study, and has learned at the feet of some of the world's most celebrated martial masters. His primary instructors include judo's Kazuo Ito and Kyuzo Mifune; Kodenkan (now Danzan-ryu) jujutsu's Henry Seishiro Okazaki; Kosho-ryu kempo's legendary James Masayoshi Mitose; kendo's Shuji Mikami; Matsumura Seito and Hakutsuru Shorin-ryu karate grandmaster Hohan Soken; and aikido's Yukiso Yamamoto, Koichi Tohei, Kisshomaru Ueshiba, and founder Morihei Ueshiba O'Sensei. Roy Suenaka is ranked *nidan* (second degree black belt) in kendo, and *sandan* (third degree black belt) in judo and jujutsu. He was awarded a *rokudan* (sixth degree black belt) in Matsumura Seito karate by Hohan Soken, an *okuden* certificate of advanced Shin-Shin Toitsu aikido proficiency by Koichi Tohei, and a *menkyo-kaiden* certificate of aikido mastery from Morihei Ueshiba O'Sensei. He is recognized as *hachidan* (eigth degree black belt) in aikido by the International Black Belt Federation and the Dai Nippon Butokukai. Suenaka was also the first person to open a successful aikido school in Okinawa, and one of the first to teach aikido on the United States mainland. In addition to his martial pedigree, Suenaka has a wealth of street-fighting experience, and as a former military man, he saw active combat duty in Vietnam, and taught unarmed combat to Army Special Forces, Navy SEALs, and other personnel stationed there.

Suenaka Sensei's rich, extensive experience makes him uniquely qualified to comment on what aikido is and is not, and to dispel the many misconceptions which plague its history, philosophy, and martial technique. Nothing makes him angrier than to hear people disparage the art to which he has devoted his life, or to read uninformed or inaccurate accounts of events in aikido's history of which he was a part. Because of this, Suenaka's students have urged him for decades to put his thoughts and experiences down on paper, but he had always declined. He is a humble and modest man, content to teach, not desiring fame or recognition. It is only to address the misconceptions noted earlier that he has finally consented to write this, his first book.

Complete Aikido: Aikido Kyohan is divided into two sections. The first, A Martial Biography of Roy Yukio Suenaka Sensei, is a recounting of Suenaka's early martial arts training, with a focus on his introduction to and study of aikido, and his martial philosophy. Here you will find a wealth of entertaining and illuminating personal anecdotes from his life, particularly his studies with Hohan Soken, Koichi Tohei, and O'Sensei. This section also contains details of many controversial incidents in aikido's history, some of which have never before appeared in print. As such, it is acknowledged that there may be some who also were involved whose recollection may differ.

The second section of *Complete Aikido: Aikido Kyohan* focuses on Suenaka-ha Tetsugaku-ho aikido philosophy and technique. It is possible to skip to the second section without reading the first, but it is not advisable. Only by reading Suenaka's martial biography will you truly understand the wealth of experience he brings to his technique, and the authority behind it.

Finally, a note on the narrative style. *Complete Aikido* is the result of over twenty hours of tape-recorded interviews with Suenaka Sensei, and countless hours of casual conversation with him over the past ten years. It is not written in the first-person, at Suenaka Sensei's insistence, for no more mysterious a reason than he does not feel comfortable writing about his own experiences and achievements. Instead, his biography has been summarized from his discussions and dictation, and is highlighted throughout by dozens of first-person narrative passages taken verbatim from the interviews with him. The entirety of the second section was written from Suenaka Sensei's personal notes and under his direct instruction, and it is Suenaka himself who demonstrates the techniques. He personally reviewed each successive draft of the text, and made changes as he saw fit. Despite this writer's byline, you may rest assured that *Complete Aikido: Aikido Kyohan* is Suenaka's work alone, and his spirit and authority underlies each and every word. Also, rather than adhere to a strict chronological retelling of events, many of the events and stories Suenaka relates in the biographical portion appear out of sequence, which will appear obvious as you read. This was done to preserve the flow of the narrative, and to group stories and events of like significance.

"Complete" and *"kyohan"* have similar meanings. *Kyohan* means master text, or canon. Nevertheless, this book is not meant to be a complete encyclopedia of aikido. It is, rather, a distillation of Suenaka Sensei's martial history and aikido teaching. It is a canon as it relates to Suenaka Sensei's life in aikido. On behalf of Suenaka Sensei, I hope you enjoy *Complete Aikido: Aikido Kyohan,* and that it becomes a valuable and permanent addition to your martial library, and your life.

Christopher Watson
May 14, 1997

For many years, martial artists of varying degrees of expertise have written books on aikido. Recently, more and more books have been written, but only a select few of these books have some genuine value. Aikido theory can be very sophisticated and complex, in turn making the physical aspects, the techniques, seem extremely difficult and varied. As in all things, over the years aikido has changed, evolved or, in some cases, regressed. To have any significant value, a good book should demonstrate consistency within aikido, and have a systematic purpose. The purpose of *Complete Aikido: Aikido Kyohan* is to provide this consistency.

Aikido is often defined as a peaceful martial art, an art of love, spirituality and mental discipline. While this is correct, the true and legitimate historical aspects, martial and practical applications of aikido have oftentimes been grossly misrepresented. This compels me to address the current state of aikido. Some styles teach aikido primarily as a philosophy of life and as a means of spiritual development and social intercourse, ignoring the defensive or martial aspects, treating them as a means of exercise. Still other styles teach aikido solely to vanquish an adversary as quickly as possible, ignoring the spiritual aspects. While all of these motives are valid reasons to study any martial art, separately, they are not conducive to the understanding and continued integrated development of the total martial art form aikido was meant to be.

Further, as a result of these differing conceptions, aikido has often been described as an ineffective martial art, a formerly effective art that has been "watered-down," a martial arts dance form, and other derogatory definitions. The truth of the matter is, if aikido is practiced diligently and sincerely, with emphasis on its original martial traditions and standards, it is one of the most effective means of self-defense in the world. The techniques in aikido are extremely potent, and can cause crippling or even fatal injury. However, if practiced under ideal conditions with a knowledgeable teacher, one can learn how to apply aiki principles in everyday life. It is this integrated approach that defines true aikido, and one should seek out an aikido style that teaches self-control, humility, confidence, and discipline, emphasizes spirituality, and yet is ultimately street-effective.

While this book is titled *Complete Aikido: Aikido Kyohan,* it is considered the canon, or master text, of Suenaka-ha Testugaku-ho aikido, and is meant to provide an overview of this style, as well as a grounding in the basic principles of all aikido styles. I have also attempted to systematize and simplify the practice of aikido in general; to provide an integrated approach by explaining the philosophy, history and evolution of aikido, so the reader may understand the many often confusing or misinterpreted aspects of this martial art.

I have been very fortunate to have studied many different martial arts in my life. My initiation took place as a child in Hawaii, studying with my Dad, and continued under other highly-acclaimed teachers there. In 1958, I opened one of the first aikido schools in California and the continental United States. The Air Force then sent me to Japan and Okinawa, where I met and studied under many of the foremost martial arts teachers in the world. My life has been a quest to learn as much as I can, to become the best I can be as an integrated human being. It is my hope that *Complete Aikido: Aikido Kyohan* helps you to do the same. As the saying goes: Perfect Practice Makes Perfect.

In memory of my mother, Ruth Masako Suenaka. She gave me life, supported me in all my endeavors, and provided me with strength, wisdom and inspiration. She guided me through all the challenges of life and showed me that no boundries exist in the quest for success. She taught me how to love, and that all humans were from one family, and to this day I continue to cherish this very valuable lesson. I loved her dearly. She passed away peacefully on November 28, 1995.

"One does not need buildings, money, power or status to practice the art of peace. Heaven is right where you are standing, and that is the place to train."

—Morihei Ueshiba O'Sensei

PART ONE

THE MARTIAL BIOGRAPHY *of* ROY YUKIO SUENAKA

CHAPTER ONE

EARLY EDUCATION

It is the eleventh century. The formidable mounted warriors of Khubilai Kahn have swept out of the steppes of central Europe on a campaign of conquest that will ultimately bring most of Western Europe, China, and all of Korea under Mongol rule. In November of 1274, the Kahn sought to expand his empire by sending an armada of 450 ships bearing some 15,000 troops from conquered Korea southeast across the relatively narrow Korea Strait to the latest object of his desire, the mountainous island chain of Japan. His intent: to take the southernmost island of Kyushu, then sweep northward until the entire chain was under his dominion. Expecting a repeat of his earlier victories, he was to be disappointed. After a day's fierce fighting on the shores of Kyushu, the Mongol fleet limped home, unexpectedly repelled by the determined samurai forces they encountered.

Angry and humiliated, Khubilai Kahn spent the next seven years assembling what remained until modern times the largest sea-borne invasion force in history. In June of 1281, the Kahn tried again, with ten times the troops. On June 23, the Mongols landed at several spots along Kyushu's northwest coast, mounting a series of relentless attacks in an attempt to penetrate the island's coastal defenses. However, though boasting superior weaponry and proven tactics, the forces of the Kahn were no match for the legions of samurai once again awaiting them.

Some of the most fierce fighting took place outside the walled city of Hakata, overlooking Hakata Bay. Over the next fifty days the samurai, brandishing their cherished, razor-edged *tachi* (swords), held the Mongols to within a few miles of the coast. On the shore, samurai boldly boarded the lumbering enemy warships in daring "mosquito raids," cutting down the crew before slipping away in their small skiffs to attack anew. By the end of August, the valor of the samurai, with help from a massive typhoon (known from that day on as *kamikaze,* or "divine wind"), which splintered and sank the Mongol fleet, the Japanese had once again successfully repelled the forces of the Kahn.

Although many written accounts exist, there is but one detailed pictorial record of the second Mongol invasion. The samurai Takezaki Suenaga, who was also a veteran of the first invasion attempt, commissioned a series of scroll paintings to record his prowess during the battle of Hakata Bay. Known as the *Moko Shurai Ekotoba,* they today reside as part of the private Imperial Household Collection in Tokyo.

The defeat of the second Mongol invasion marked the beginning of the end of Imperial rule in Japan and the rise of the samurai warrior class. Whereas before, court nobility and aristocrats wielded power, under the Shogunate the samurai ruled supreme, guided by the strict tenants of *bushido,* the way of the warrior. Samurai families flourished, the Suenaga clan not excepted, for the next five-hundred years.

Although Suenaga's fame for his exploits at Hakata Bay spread far, it was not enough to keep his creditors from his door. Heavily in debt from his war expenditures, he was hounded incessantly, to the point that he took the drastic step of changing his name, to Suenaka. A minor alteration, certainly, but evidently enough to avoid further financial persecution.

The year 1867 marked the end of Japan's feudal period, as the Emperor Meiji took advantage of growing dissent and factional fighting among regional shoguns and ascended the imperial throne, beginning the Meiji Restoration the following year. Rebellious samurai were ordered to lay down their arms, cut off their prized topknots, and turn to more peaceful pursuits, or face the Emperor's punishment. Such was the case with the Suenaka clan, who gave up the sword in favor of the hoe and plow. Although the clan's lineage was well-known, this simple vocation change was sufficient to placate the authorities, appearing as it did a renunciation (at least on the surface) of their martial tradition. Privately, however, the Suenaka clan continued to pass down the martial traditions of their ancestors from father to son, particularly jujutsu and kenjutsu.

In 1878, dissatisfied with farming and with other jobs scarce, Yoshigoro Suenaka, wife Uta (nee Maemoto) and his two elder brothers, Denkichi and Shokichi, emigrated to Honolulu, Hawaii, in search of a new beginning. Yoshigoro and his brothers worked in the sugar cane fields by day, and continued to practice their ancestral *budo* (warrior arts) when the day's work was done, striving to keep their heritage alive in their new home. In November of 1913, Yoshigoro's youngest son, Warren Kenji, was born, and it was into this proud, centuries-old samurai tradition that Roy Yukio Suenaka, the first of four sons, was born to

Warren Kenji and Ruth Masako Suenaka (nee Iwahiro) on June 25, 1940.

From the moment of his birth, Suenaka's survival was in doubt. He was a "breach baby," born feet first; a difficult enough birth in a hospital, made even more hazardous by his home delivery by a midwife. The family physician, Doctor Yamamoto, was quickly summoned and, working with the midwife, was able to deliver the baby. Still, newborn Suenaka would not breathe. Knowing they had but a few minutes before oxygen deprivation would result in irreparable brain damage, the midwife, Yamamoto, and Suenaka's maternal grandfather, Tsurujiro Iwahiro, worked feverishly to revive the infant: the physician using the accouterments of Western medicine, while Grandfather Tsurujiro applied his decades of skill in *reiki*— the projection of *ki* (vital life energy) through the laying on of hands. Finally, almost five minutes after his delivery, technically long enough for brain damage to occur, Roy Suenaka took his first breath.

Though he suffered no permanent damage as the result of his difficult birth, Suenaka's youth was plagued with related health problems. He was barely months old before he was diagnosed with bronchial asthma. Attacks were frequent, sudden, and severe, his respiratory tract becoming clogged with mucous, often to the point where he would stop breathing altogether. Tsurujiro would immediately begin performing *reiki* while Dr. Yamamoto, who fortunately lived but minutes away, was summoned. Eastern and Western medicine again worked together to handle the crisis.

Despite his condition, Suenaka began physical training, under the apt tutelage of his father, almost as soon as he was able to walk.

Young as he was, Suenaka was introduced to the basics of weight training, doing his best to imitate his father as he joined him in his daily workouts. Though Suenaka no doubt considered these sessions more like play than work, his father was consciously laying the foundation for what was to become a lifetime of physical and martial study.

Clockwise, from top left: Calvin, Greg and Wesley Suenaka, Warren Suenaka, Roy Suenaka, in front of their home in Honolulu; 1966

This early education was accelerated at age four, when Warren Suenaka introduced his son to the family arts of jujutsu and kenjutsu, as well as judo, having begun his study of this system during one of his many

5

trips back to Japan, and continuing upon returning to Hawaii.

Warren Suenaka also introduced his son to the fundamentals of Western boxing and wrestling, skills that served the boy well in countless schoolyard brawls and neighborhood street fights. Throughout his youth and early adulthood, young Suenaka and his peers would constantly challenge one another to see who was tougher, more skilled, or simply the most stubborn. While adolescent brawls are a common rite of passage for many young men, in Suenaka's case these constant challenges served as an early crucible in which the efficacy of martial technique learned on the mat was put to practical test on the street. This ultimate proof was to become one of the guiding philosophies behind Suenaka Sensei's *waza* (martial technique) throughout his life: in short, if a technique doesn't work "on the street," regardless of how impressive it may look on the mat or how commonplace or accepted its practice, then that technique does not work, period, and so has no place being taught at all.

It is interesting to note that one of Suenaka's earliest schoolyard sparring partners was Paul Fujii, a good friend from, as Suenaka puts it, their *"hanabata"* days (literally, "nose butter," or runny-nosed toddler days) through high school. Suenaka recalls brawling with Fujii "practically every day," beginning in kindergarten in 1945, though less, of course, as they grew older. Eighteen years later, Fujii defeated Sandro Lopopolo of Italy to win the world junior welterweight boxing title. Even at such an early age, Suenaka's training was world-class.

This early training also had an unexpected, though very welcome, additional benefit. As Suenaka grew older and his training increased in frequency and intensity, his asthma attacks decreased until, at age twenty-one, they ceased entirely, never to return. Although puberty no doubt played a role, Suenaka unhesitatingly credits his training with the cure, particularly the constant *ibuki* breathing exercises and intense *misogi* (ritual purification and meditation) sessions.

As Warren Suenaka saw to the martial education of his son, so too did he attend to his own continuing education. Already a black belt practitioner of judo, jujutsu, and kempo (and, later, aikido) and an experienced, respected local street fighter ("He was a bit of a brawler," says Suenaka), the elder Suenaka made certain he was well-familiar with all martial styles and systems taught in the area. With a trained eye discriminating and demanding, he visited every area school, carefully observing both style and instructor before ultimately choosing three systems that were to constitute his son's first formal martial arts training. It is because of this, combined with his personal tutelage, that Warren Suenaka's influence on his son's martial education cannot be underestimated.

In 1948, when Suenaka was eight years old, his father deemed him ready to begin training in Kodenkan jujutsu under founder Henry Seishiro Okazaki. For young Suenaka, there was no choice: "(My father) said, 'You ought to study this . . . you will study this, too!' And of course, I really enjoyed it." Suenaka recalls Okazaki Sensei as "an intimidating man, burly. His voice was real gruff, but yet you could see that he was a very kind person. He wasn't very mean; he just looked mean." While his personality might have been forgiving, Suenaka found Okazaki Sensei physically intimidating: "He was a fairly big man, I would say around five feet six inches or five feet seven inches. To us, he was very tall. He weighed around two-hundred pounds, with big, solid muscles and huge arms. A very, very powerful man."

While no stranger to jujutsu even at that early age, Suenaka found Okazaki-ryu jujutsu somewhat different from the more traditional Daito-ryu style learned under his father. "He (Okazaki) had other jujutsu styles . . . that were incorporated or combined with the Okazaki system, even a lot of techniques from lua, the Hawaiian martial art. He also studied Western boxing and wrestling. He studied everything that he could." Other than his father, Okazaki Sensei would become one of Suenaka's most influential pre-aikido martial arts instructors, and Suenaka studied Kodenkan jujutsu from 1948 until Okazaki Sensei's death in 1952. Kodenkan jujutsu is still taught and practiced in Hawaii and elsewhere, including the mainland United States, although it is now more commonly known as Danzan-ryu ("the Hawaiian style") jujutsu.

One year later, in 1949, Suenaka was introduced to his second most influential pre-aikido teacher as he began instruction in Kosho-ryu kempo under James Masayoshi Mitose. One of kempo's most renowned practitioners, Mitose Sensei, a Buddhist priest and later an ordained Presbyterian minister, was the man who introduced kempo to the United States. The name *Kosho-ryu* translates as "old pine tree style," and is a unique family style, a combination of Japanese jujutsu and traditional Chinese Shaolin boxing, which is itself the largely the progenitor of present-day Okinawan karate.

Soft-spoken yet stern, powerful yet kind, Mitose Sensei remained one of Suenaka's primary instructors until his move to Los Angeles in December of 1952 (some say early 1953), at which time Thomas Young, a Chinese-Hawaiian and then Mitose's senior student, assumed his master's teaching duties in Hawaii. Like Henry Okazaki, James Mitose had a profound influence on young Suenaka, so much so that when Mitose departed Hawaii, Suenaka gradually decreased his study of Koshu-ryu. "We were so used to learning under Mitose Sensei," Suenaka recalls. "I really loved him; he was a good teacher. Like Jesus Christ, he was the best."

In 1950, Warren Suenaka introduced his son, now ten, to judo, the third and final martial system Suenaka was to study prior to his introduction to aikido. As stated earlier, Warren Suenaka was himself an experienced *judoka,* and so he took especial care in selecting a school for his son to attend. Luckily, judo was perhaps the most widespread martial art in the area at the time, with a number of quality schools available. Suenaka ultimately studied judo at two different schools under three instructors: Higami Sensei at Honolulu's

Left to right: Tanaka Sensei, Warren Suenaka, Roy Suenaka, "Ike" Ikehara Sensei, at the YBA (Young Buddhist Association) hall in Honolulu; 1954

Shobukan ("We called him 'Rubber Man,' because he was so limber"); Yukiso Yamamato, who taught at the local YBA (Young Buddhist Association) hall; and Matsumoto Sensei ("I never knew his first name," Suenaka says. "We just called him 'Sensei'."), a member of Japan's Kodokan, who taught at his own local school. Suenaka at first studied primarily with Higami, though he soon found himself drawn more to study under Yamamoto. Personality and not quality of instruction was the reason. Suenaka remembers Higami as being "too hard. When we got something wrong, he would whack us with a stick!" Eventually, Suenaka's judo instruction took place exclusively under Yamamoto and Matsumoto, with Yamamoto the primary instructor. Of course, Warren Suenaka was always there to offer his son additional instruction and advice.

As one can imagine, Suenaka's childhood was extremely active, with little time for the carefree play normally associated with youth. The young martial artist would rise just in time to make it to school by 8:00 am. When classes ended at 3:00 pm, and his fellow classmates would spend the rest of the afternoon playing sports or hanging out with friends, Suenaka would spend a brief time in exercise, usually running or working out in the school gym, before heading to Okazaki's *dojo* to train. Once study under Mitose began, there was no longer time after school for free exercise. Suenaka would leave school and immediately walk or hop a bus the three miles or so to the Okazaki *dojo* in downtown Honolulu, where he would spend anywhere from ninety minutes to two hours in hard practice. Around five o'clock or so, Suenaka would dash home, staying there only long enough to change and grab a quick bite to eat before heading off for Mitose's *dojo* for another hour or two of study or, when his judo study began, a couple hours at the YBA. Finally, at around seven-thirty in the evening, Suenaka would return home for the day, leaving him with just enough time to bathe, eat, do his homework, and go to bed. Weekends were not much different, with his training augmented by lessons under his father. Of course, there were those rare free moments where he could relax with his friends on the beautiful beaches of his home, but in all, young Roy Suenaka spent an average of thirty hours a week in hard training, an incredible schedule for a boy barely into his teens.

By the age of thirteen, Suenaka already possessed the martial skills and discipline of a man twice his age, forged by nine years of hard study under his father and many of the world's most celebrated contemporary Japanese martial masters. While he was to augment his skill in these and other arts with later training, his early years perhaps only set the stage for his introduction to the art to which he would ultimately devote his life: aikido.

By 1953, Suenaka's training reached a turning point. Henry Okazaki was now gone, having passed away a year earlier, while James Mitose had relocated to Los Angeles not long after. Both events strongly affected Suenaka: "Both my great teachers were gone." Somewhat disillusioned, and without the constant impetus of his accustomed teachers, twelve year-old Suenaka cut back on his jujutsu and kempo training, although his judo study continued as usual. Still, there existed a void—more emotional than physical—created by the absence of the two men who, other than his father, exerted the greatest influence in shaping him physically and spiritually. In retrospect, however, it appears that the departure of Okazaki and Mitose merely signaled the end of the first stage of Suenaka's martial evolution; it could be said these two teachers were made a part of his life in order to lay the foundation for his first meeting with a man who would later become more important to him than either of his former mentors.

In February of 1961, aikido founder Morihei Ueshiba O'Sensei was invited to Hawaii to preside over opening ceremonies of the first aikido *dojo* established there. At a farewell party held in his honor just before his departure, O'Sensei briefly addressed the assembled well-wishers, summarizing his feelings thusly:

"The reason I am going to Hawaii is to build a "silver bridge" of understanding. I have been building a 'golden bridge' within Japan, but I also wanted to build bridges overseas and, through aikido, to cultivate mutual understanding between East and West. I want to build bridges everywhere and connect all people through harmony and love. This I believe to be the task of aikido." (*The Spirit of Aikido, Kisshomaru Ueshiba*)

Although O'Sensei's first and only visit to Hawaii did not occur until 1961, construction of his "silver bridge," or *shinbashi,* began with another man's earlier visit. Katsuzo Nishi, a wealthy local businessman and owner of the Nishi Kai health club in Honolulu, extended to O'Sensei a formal invitation to send a representative to Hawaii to demonstrate the art that had impressed him so much during an earlier visit to Japan. In response, in February of 1953, O'Sensei dispatched Koichi Tohei Sensei to Oahu as his ambassador.

Born January 17, 1920, Koichi Tohei had just turned thirty-three years old at the time of this historic first visit. Having begun his study of what was then known as aiki-budo in 1939, by 1953 Tohei was ranked *hachidan* (eighth degree black belt) and was *shihan bucho* (chief instructor) at the Aikikai Hombu headquarters *dojo* in

Suenaka Sensei with Shin-Shin Toitsu Aikido founder Koichi Tohei at a party in Punaluu honoring O'Sensei's Hawaiian visit; March, 1961.

Tokyo. This, understandably, made him a natural choice to introduce this relatively new martial art to the Western world. Not surprisingly, the Hawaiian martial arts community was buzzing with anticipation of Tohei Sensei's visit. As Suenaka recalls, "Everybody got all excited and said, 'Hey, this is a new martial art, they say it's better than anything around.'" Also not surprisingly, Warren Suenaka learned early on through Nishi-san of the impending visit and made a point of attending Tohei's first Hawaiian demonstration. Naturally, he took his sons with him.

Tohei Sensei's first Hawaiian aikido demonstration took place at the Nishi Kai and was attended by the Nishi Kai membership and invited guests, which included many of the area's prominent martial artists, among them Yukiso Yamamoto; *karateka* "Koa" Kimura (who would later shift his study to aikido and ally himself with Tohei's Ki no Kenkyukai before breaking away to found his own organization): *judoka* Kazuto Sugimoto; noted *kendoka* and respected local business-man Isao Takahashi; and *judoka* and Okinawan Olympic Greco-Roman wrestler Oki Shikina. Suenaka has vivid memories of this important event:

"[The demonstration observers] took part in the demonstration and, naturally, they resisted, they tried to really, really overthrow [Tohei Sensei], and they couldn't do it; he threw those guys around like nothing. Tohei Sensei was a bear. He was about five-feet three-inches tall, and at that time probably weighed about 180 pounds, so he was a bear—a big, little man—extremely powerful, and these guys could not hold him down. Even . . . Oki Shikina . . . he was thrown around, and said, 'My, this guy is phenomenal.' His demonstration was very impressive. But, at the same time, everyone who stepped onto the mat with him was very respectful of who he was, and why he was there. They tried hard to throw him, but they didn't come at him full-force, as in a street-fighting situation. It was a very controlled situation."

Warren Suenaka throwing Roy Suenaka sayu-nage in their back yard in Honolulu, Hawaii, just before Suenaka Sensei's departure for Japan; March, 1961.

Suenaka and his father followed Tohei to several of the demonstrations he gave on Oahu, with the exception of a private demonstration given for the benefit of the local police. Tohei even gave a demonstration in the auditorium of Suenaka's school, McKinley High, before traveling to the other islands in the Hawaiian chain to stage further demonstrations and establish schools. By this time, though, Warren Suenaka had no doubts. He immediately made aikido the new focus of his studies, and Roy Suenaka, though he needed no persuasion, was told to do likewise.

Warren Suenaka wasn't the only man impressed by aikido's uncommon power and efficacy. Tohei Sensei's first visit to Hawaii lasted one year—long enough to establish a firm foothold, during which time many of the island's ranking martial artists rushed to study under him. Among these early U.S. aikido pupils were many who attended the first demonstration at the Nishi-kai, including Yukiso Yamamoto, at the time fifty years old, Kazuto Sugimoto, "Koa" Kimura, and Isao Takahashi. For lack of a private *dojo*, aikido classes were conducted at the YBA hall in Honolulu on Tuesdays and Thursdays, and at the Kompira-san—a Buddhist temple which already doubled as a *dojo* for numerous martial arts, including judo, jujutsu, kendo, sumo, and kyudo—on all other days except Sunday. Suenaka studied every chance he could, alternating between classes at the YBA and the Kompira-san, training in aikido five days a week, almost to the exclusion of his judo training. As Yamamoto was also studying aikido, this potential conflict of focus caused no problems. Indeed, upon his departure a year later, Koichi Tohei appointed Yamamoto chief instructor of the brand-new Hawaii Aikikai, the parent organization for aikido in the Hawaiian islands, the headquarters of which was, naturally, at the

YBA. Tohei awarded the judo *godan* (fifth degree black belt) the aikido rank of *sandan* (third degree black belt) and did the same for Takahashi and Sugimoto, naming them assistant chief instructors to Yamamoto. All three rotated among the YBA, Kompira-san, and other area schools, teaching aikido, though at the time Yamamoto had not totally forsaken his judo study and instruction.

Although Suenaka would later develop a close and lasting personal relationship with Koichi Tohei, he had little contact with his future mentor during these early days of study, other than the normal contact one of many students has with his sensei (of course, Tohei remained in Hawaii but a year during this first visit, and Suenaka had left Honolulu by the time of Tohei's subsequent visits). Suenaka studied hard and learned quickly, in large part because of his prior experience in other martial arts. His skills in *ukemi* (falling and tumbling techniques) were already honed through his judo study, while aikido's similarities to jujutsu enabled Suenaka to readily assimilate aikido technique. "I just sort of

Honolulu's Kompira-San Training Hall today.

melded or fell right into aikido," he says. "It was almost natural for me. (These other arts) were building a foundation for me, so when I went into aikido it was second nature."

It should be noted that even though aikido was now the primary focus of Suenaka's study, in 1955 he somehow managed to find time to begin the study of kendo under Shuji Mikami, at the time the highest-ranking kendo master in the Western world. Suenaka studied under him for just short of three years. And a year earlier, in 1954, Suenaka also became involved in amateur boxing, and fought competitively until 1958.

By the age of eighteen, Suenaka Sensei had already received *dan* (black belt) ranking in three arts. His high school graduation, though, as it does with anyone, marked yet another turning point in his life. While he could have found a job and remained at home in Hawaii, continuing his martial studies as before, Suenaka opted instead to see the world. Accordingly, on September 26, 1958, Roy Suenaka enlisted in the United States Air Force.

We all have a point where our earliest memories begin. For most, it is perhaps our third or fourth year; for others, it might be earlier, recollection triggered by some momentous event that burns itself into our consciousness. For Suenaka, his earliest memories are of December 8, 1941, when he and his family were returning home from an outing and suddenly the skies over Honolulu were filled with Japanese Zero fighter planes dancing with American aircraft during the attack on Pearl Harbor. Though just eighteen months old, his memories sketchy at best, Suenaka can recall the day. One image stands out in his mind— the sound of machine gun fire as he watched from a bunker two planes engaged in a dogfight overhead. "For some reason, I remember seeing fireballs. It's something a person doesn't forget."

It might have been this unforgettable early glimpse of air combat that led Suenaka to investigate becoming an Air Force fighter pilot. However, his initial enthusiasm was cooled somewhat by the gradual realization of the lengthy study necessary to attain that goal. First, he would need a college degree. Then, he would attend Officer's Preparatory School. And then, if he made it that far, he would move on to actual pilot training. Nevertheless, he was determined to give it a shot.

After completing boot camp at Lackland Air Base in San Antonio, Texas, in December 1958, electrician and Airman 3rd Class Roy Suenaka was assigned to Mather Air Force Base, the ATC (Air Training Command) and SAC (Strategic Air Command) base in Sacramento, California. After enrolling in Sacramento College to study electrical engineering, top priority was finding a place to practice martial arts. Just a few months after arrival and with Yamamoto Sensei's blessing, Suenaka began teaching aikido at the Mather Air Base gym. He also landed a part-time job with the San Juan school district teaching judo, plus some aikido, at Encino High School two hours a day, three days a week, for which he was paid the handsome sum of ten dollars an hour. For a young man in the early 1960's, it was excellent money, especially since the Air Force already paid for his housing and medical care on top of his base salary.

As aikido was in its infant stage in the United States, Suenaka's aikido classes, modest though they were, made him one of the first people to teach organized aikido on the U.S. mainland. While it seems logical that there may have been other *aikidoka* who opened earlier schools on the mainland, probably U.S. servicemen who began their studies in Japan, documentation is scarce. Eugene Combs, who was introduced to Yoshinkan aikido at the Army's Camp Drake outside Tokyo in 1955, opened the American School of Aikido in Lawndale, California in 1956, making him one of the first to teach the art on the U.S. mainland. In May of 1953, about four months after his initial arrival in Hawaii, Koichi Tohei traveled to San Jose, California to conduct an aikido demonstration there, while Kenji Tomiki traveled to the U.S. mainland one month later at the invitation of the U.S. Air Force (more on this later). However, these latter two events were demonstrations only. Besides Combs, the first wave of *aikidoka* to teach on the mainland were born of Koichi Tohei's 1953 Hawaiian visit, and included not only Suenaka, but Tokuji Hirata, who began teaching aikido in San Diego around the same time Suenaka arrived in Sacramento, and Isao Takahashi, who moved to Los Angeles in 1959, becoming chief instructor at the Los Angeles Aikikai. Other Hawaiian *aikidoka* who subsequently emigrated to the mainland include Roderick Kobayashi, Clem Yoshida, Harry Ishisaka (who commenced his aikido study after moving to Southern California), and Ben Sekishiro, all of whom commenced their aikido studies after Suenaka's departure from Hawaii (with the exception of Kobayashi, who began his study in 1957).

Much like his father, Suenaka took every opportunity he could to investigate and, in some cases, study as many different arts offered in the area as he could. In particular, while in Sacramento, Suenaka developed a brief friendship with noted tang soo do instructor Mariano "Cisco" Estioko, and occasionally studied with him on an informal basis as time allowed. Studying different arts, no matter how briefly, whenever the opportunity presented itself was a conscious practice for Suenaka, meant to provide him with as broad a martial reference base as possible. Just as his street-fighting experience, both during his youth in Hawaii and his later days as a serviceman in Japan and Okinawa, provided him with "real world" proofs for his primary disciplines of aikido and karate, Suenaka's constant study of other systems and styles enabled him to judge with authority the worth of a given technique, to say with authority, "This might work in this situation, but not in that one," or "This technique from style A could be countered with this technique from style B." It is due in large part to his extensive experience that Suenaka Sensei later came to discount so-called "advanced" techniques, regardless of system (including aikido), modifying or casting aside those techniques vulnerable to *kaeshi* (countering) and concentrating instead on proven fundamental methods. To him, the simpler and more direct a technique, the broader its potential applications and the fewer the chances for failure. It is out of this conviction that one of Suenaka Sensei's guiding philosophies was born: "Advanced techniques are merely the basics performed better."

In addition to teaching in Sacramento, Suenaka gave several demonstrations in the city and surrounding area, including one in San Francisco's Veteran's Hospital. It may have been at one of these demonstrations that Suenaka came to the attention of actor and producer Ben Alexander, perhaps best-remembered by most as Sgt. Frank Smith in the early seasons of the *Dragnet* television series. Alexander hosted a local television talent show. One day, Suenaka received in the mail an invitation to appear on the show to discuss this new and strange martial art, aikido. The appearance went well, and several months later, Suenaka received another invitation to appear on the program, this time to demonstrate aikido technique.

Suenaka opted to perform the demonstration with his *uke* (demonstration partner) using a "live" (or sharp) blade, a bayonet from an M1 Garand (minus the rifle, of course). After the first few techniques, Suenaka's *uke* came charging in with a *munetsuki* attack (a thrust to the belly). Suenaka turned to the side, preparing to execute *kote-gaeshi* (a wrist-cutting throw). The *uke,* however, anticipating what Suenaka Sensei was about to do, "choked" his attack, changing the angle and following Suenaka's turn, thrusting the foot-long blade full-speed directly at Suenaka's abdomen. Suenaka was able to pivot out of the way of the altered thrust, though just barely—the blade penetrated his *gi,* barely missing his flesh as Suenaka captured the *uke's* wrist and, reflexively, delivered a *kote-gaeshi* so powerful, the wrist was fractured. The *uke* collapsed to the floor, writhing in pain, the studio audience burst into wild applause, and Alexander quickly cut to a commercial, ending the demonstration. Suenaka was not invited back. Though gratified that his training saved his life, Suenaka is not proud of the incident, stating: "We were young."

In late 1960, twenty year-old Suenaka reluctantly gave up his dreams of becoming a pilot, his early fervor quelled by the long years of study necessary to achieve that goal. More significantly, he was realizing that the time necessary to achieve that goal was time he would much rather spend furthering his martial education. More and more, he found himself entertaining thoughts of traveling to Japan, to immerse himself in its rich martial tradition. However, he felt the likelihood of someone as low on the ladder as he receiving such a plum assignment was slim, at best. As luck would have it, however, around the same time Suenaka was beginning to have second thoughts about pilot school, Air Force SAC Commander General Curtis LeMay happened to visit Mather, one of many stops on a tour of North American SAC bases. Suenaka was in one of the base's flight simulator rooms, inspecting the equipment, when LeMay popped in for an unannounced, informal inspection.

At the time, LeMay, himself an experienced *judoka,* was actively promoting and encouraging martial arts study for Air Force personnel (the Air Force invitation extended to Tomiki Sensei, mentioned earlier, was the result of this program). He and Suenaka managed a moment or two of conversation, during which Suenaka mentioned LeMay's infant program, his own aikido study, and how much we was hoping to be transferred to Japan to continue his education:

"He told me to go ahead and submit my transfer request to the CBPO (Central Base Personnel Office). So I said I would, and that was the end of the conversation. Not too long after that, around the end of 1959, I submitted my 'dream sheet,' my list of preferred assignments, to the CBPO, and almost immediately, I was told I was being transferred to Tachikawa Air Base, about thiry miles outside of Tokyo, in sixty days. I don't know for certain if LeMay or his program had anything to do with it or not, but I was very happy."

Immediately, Suenaka quit Sacramento College and headed back to Hawaii to spend a little vacation time with his family before heading overseas. Upon arriving home in February, however, he was stunned to discover O'Sensei himself was in Honolulu; incredibly, Suenaka had received no news of the Founder's historic visit. Suenaka arrived the day after O'Sensei's blessing of the newly-constructed Hawaii Aikikai. Although he was unable to attend, his family did; his father, mother, and brother Greg can be seen in many frames of a film, available on video, of the event.

While in Hawaii, O'Sensei was gracious enough to teach a few classes and give several lectures. Naturally, Suenaka took full advantage of the situation, attending as many classes and lectures as he could, as well as those conducted by Tohei Sensei who, having spent some seven years planting the seeds of aikido in America, had accompanied the Founder there to see the seeds bear their first fruit. Suenaka's first glimpse of O'Sensei was at one of these lectures, during which the Founder demonstrated first-hand the heart of aikido, manifested in the spiritual power of *ki.* Suenaka vividly remembers the demonstration:

"O'Sensei stood there and put his hand, straight-armed, on this guy's head, like he was blessing him, and then, boom!, the guy just crumbled, straight down to the ground. Then O'Sensei put his finger on the side of the guy's head there on the mat, and the guy couldn't move. Then he turned the guy over on his stomach and laid the back of his head on the middle of this guy's back, like he was laying on a pillow. He told the guy to get up, and the guy couldn't move! Now, I looked at that and I thought, 'This is awesome!'"

On about the third day of his visit, a banquet was held in O'Sensei's honor at the Rainbow Garden Teahouse, a local inn where he was staying during his time in Honolulu. Among the invited guests were those martial artists who found themselves drawn to this new art of aikido, Suenaka included. Following the feast, O'Sensei retired early, as was his habit. Not long after his departure, Suenaka decided to get a closer look at the mysterious, diminuitive master, unaware that just a few minutes later, he would unexpectedly have his first face-to-face meeting with the Founder.

After a few moments investigation, Suenaka identified O'Sensei's bungalow and quietly crept closer, not wanting to betray his presence and risk angering Ueshiba. Finally, he got close enough to see inside:

"He was sitting in his room—the sliding shoji screen door was slightly open, as he really liked the natural surroundings, the breeze. . . . I was standing approximately fifty feet away, in the trees behind some bushes, just watching him, just to see what he was doing in there. He was sitting in seiza, reading a book."

Suddenly, O'Sensei began to speak:

"I understood Japanese vaguely then. I couldn't speak very much, but I could understand that he was saying something like, 'Hey you, out there!' His back was turned toward me, and he said, 'Why don't you come in here, don't stand out there.' Of course, I looked around and didn't see anyone else there but me, so I approached the door, and I said, 'Boku?,' which means 'me' in Japanese. And he said, 'Yes, you!' So I went in and sat down and faced him on the other side of the table.

"I was very intimidated. He didn't even look at me. He continued to read, and I looked at him. I had never thought what I'd feel like (meeting O'Sensei). I guess I'd never expected to feel like a dumb fool, just sitting there—and I sat there for a good long period, ten or fifteen minutes. That's when he wet his finger and reached back behind him, without looking, and brought out a little baby cockroach—he had caught him on his back and his little legs were waving in the air—and I looked at it and said, 'Oh, yeah.' And he put it down and let it run away. He never killed things, never even flies or mosquitos."

The small incident with the insect may not seem like much, but it sent Suenaka's mind reeling. How had O'Sensei known the little cockroach was there? Even more, how had he known Suenaka was there? Was O'Sensei sending Suenaka a subtle, even comical message? Not certain what to do, whether to stay or leave, speak or remain silent, Suenaka remained seated, watching the Founder as he read. To say he was nervous would be an understatement, and he wondered if the Founder was angry for being spied on. A few minutes later, O'Sensei again challenged Suenaka's perception.

"After the cockroach incident, I just continued sitting there and watching him as he was reading. There might have been a breeze or something, I don't know, but . . . I was watching the page just turn by itself, and I was thinking, 'My God! Such power!' I was really impressed! But I really don't know if it was a breeze or not that did it. He didn't touch the page at all . . . To this day, I don't know.

"We didn't converse at all. Only when he said,' See, look at this,' and I went 'Uh hum.' But after a while, he looked up at me and looked me straight in the eye and said, 'Okay, you can go now.' Then he smiled, and I left."

As may be expected, this first face-to-face meeting with O'Sensei had a profound effect on Suenaka, who in the days to follow observed O'Sensei even more intently than before. For his part, O'Sensei obviously remembered his unexpected evening visitor. Several days after their initial meeting, Suenaka paid another, more formal, visit to O'Sensei at his bungalow, this time as part of a group which included his father, brothers, and others. During the visit, O'Sensei made a point of asking Suenaka if he planned to attend yet another luau in his honor, an upcoming weekend affair organized by Dr. Wakatake, an *aikidoka* and respected local physician (who was later president of the Hawaii Aikikai), and held at his country home in Punaluu, on the other side of Oahu. Naturally, Suenaka answered yes.

The luau was a grand affair, featuring professional musicians, dancers, and other entertainers, as well as an seemingly endless supply of food. Rather than travel back and forth from home to the party, Suenaka and others stayed on Wakatake's estate. One night, after O'Sensei had gone to bed, several of the older *aikidoka* dared Suenaka to slip into O'Sensei's room and leave a note on his nightstand without being detected. The note itself contained a message to the effect of "Gotcha!," meaning someone had managed to sneak up on the preternaturally perceptive Founder without his knowledge. As Suenaka stealthily entered the room, he saw O'Sensei had his back turned to the door and was facing the wall, apparently asleep. Carefully, he lay the note on the nightstand and hastily made his exit. "The next day, after he got up," recalls Suenaka, "O'Sensei handed me the paper and said, 'You forgot this on my nightstand last night.' Everybody laughed and thought it was funny; I was just dumbfounded."

The second day of the luau passed much as the first, with demonstrations and classes during the day, and Saturday night filled with food and entertainment. With festivities still in full swing, O'Sensei again decided to retire early, and called for his *otomo* (valet) to assist him. However, his *otomo* was nowhere to be found; it was soon discovered he had instead elected to enjoy the Honolulu nightlife. Suenaka recalls his first glimpse of O'Sensei's formidable anger:

"He was enraged—he was yelling and carrying on and everybody was scared. Everybody just spread out, nobody wanted to be around him—they thought the world was going to explode! . . . [But] he got right over it. That's the way I am now, and maybe it was something he ingrained in me. I told O'Sensei later I had learned that from him—he said, 'Well, you maintain that frame of mind!'"

His *otomo* absent, O'Sensei changed his mind about retiring and instead decided to take a walk along the beach to enjoy the cool of the early evening. Even though O'Sensei didn't even know the name of the young Hawaiian who had just recently unceremoniously invaded his privacy, to his delight, Suenaka was invited to join him:

"We walked across the street—the beach was right across the street from the country home. So we were walking along the beach on the sand, and I was on the outside, the road side, and O'Sensei was walking on the inside. We walked probably a half-mile or so down the beach. We were walking in silence—I couldn't converse with him, because I didn't speak very good Japanese then. So we walked, and it was enjoyable because just standing next to O'Sensei gave one the feeling of exhilaration. Just being next to him, the energy coming from him made my hair stand up! He was right beside me, brushing arms as we were walking, and that's when I felt it, like a high-voltage transformer . . . that kind of energy. And that's when I looked at him and thought to myself, 'My God, such a little man—I bet I could really hit him and knock him out."

What happened next shook Suenaka to his very core:

"As soon as I thought that, he stopped me and said, 'Thinking thoughts like that is not good for you. You always have to think positively.' Well, I just collapsed right there, my legs turned to rubber and I just fell down on my knees, right there on the beach. I thought he was going to kill me! I began to apologize, over and over, and he said something to the effect that, 'One apology is enough—more apologies make you look more like a fool. . . . There's no need to apologize more than one time for any mistake; therefore, make one mistake at a time.' I thought that was a wonderful philosophy.

That was my first experience with enlightenment.

"So then I got back up [and] we contined to walk, and then we turned around and went back to the house. He thanked me and I thanked him. It was the most exciting experience of my life, to that point, the most exciting thing that had ever happened to me!"

Of course, the enlightenment of which Suenaka spoke is O'Sensei's enlightenment; the experience of being in the presence of one who has attained that state of higher knowledge and perception to which all earnest *budoka* aspire. It was Suenaka's first personal, incontrovertible proof that, in his words, "there was a force, a God-like force, that all humans could achieve that level of energy. I believed in his philosophy then—I said, 'There's no doubting such a thing.'"

Although Suenaka related his experience to his father and a few close friends, he generally kept it to himself. He knew there were those in the community who might resent the fact that he, still basically a kid at twenty-years-old, was granted a rare private moment with the Founder. In the weeks to come Suenaka would play the walk on the beach over and over in his mind, pondering the apparent impossibility of what he had experienced, yet finding his doubts time and again swept away by the undeniable reality of the event. Just as the arrival of Koichi Tohei in 1953 marked the end of the first stage of his martial development and the beginning of his aikido education, Suenaka Sensei's experiences with O'Sensei, culminating in this extraordinary occurrence, marked the end of his days in Hawaii, and set the stage for the next steps in his martial development, which would begin less than a month later, upon his arrival in Japan.

Several weeks after his walk on the beach with Suenaka, O'Sensei returned to his homeland. Suenaka and his family joined others in bidding their formal good-byes to the Founder, seeing him off at Honolulu International Airport the day of his departure. Although Tohei Sensei remained in Hawaii for a short while, once again guiding the development of the local *aikidoka,* Suenaka had little time for practice, occupied as he was with preparations for his imminent move to Japan. And so it was that in early March of 1961, less than a month after his first meeting with O'Sensei, Airman Suenaka found himself, duffel in hand, standing on the tarmac at Tachikawa Air Base.

The first thing one does when arriving at a new military station is to report to one's immediate command, receive one's housing assignment, and get settled in. This, of course, is assuming your command is aware of and anticipating your arrival. Upon reporting to the Tachikawa HQ Squadron CBPO (Central Base Personnel Office), Suenaka was told there was no record of his assignment there—for some reason, his orders were nowhere to be found. Straightening things out would take days, perhaps weeks, and Suenaka was placed on a list of "surplus airmen" and told to find something to do in the interim. The choice was easy. After taking only as much time as necessary to drop off his bags at his barracks and pack a few essentials, Suenaka hailed a cab and told the driver to take him to Tokyo and the Aikikai Hombu.

With Tachikawa AFB a good thirty miles outside the city limits, the driver was somewhat reluctant to make the journey. However, after assurances that he had enough money to pay for the trip ("It cost me about 3,000 yen, which was only about $8.50 then; I think today it would cost about $300!"), Suenaka was on his way.

Even today, Tokyo's labyrinthine streets and haphazard addresses make navigation difficult, so much so that even natives have a tough time finding their destination. It was no different in 1961, as Suenaka recalls:

"The taxi driver said, 'Well, where's the dojo?' And I said, 'Shinjuku-ku,' which is a district in Tokyo, one of the largest. He said, 'We are in Shinjuku-ku—where in Shinjukuku?' And I said, 'Wakamatsu-cho,' which is like a borough, or part of a town. And he said, 'Wakamatsu-cho?' So we drove around for what seemed like an hour, until finally he said, 'This is Wakamatsu-cho.' Then we had to find Nishi Okubo, which is in Western Okubo, which is a neighborhood there in Wakamatsu-cho, like a subdivision, and it's also the name of the main street in Nishi Okubo. We kept driving and he asked around—we finally found Nishi Okubo, the street, and we drove and drove and drove looking for Nuke-Benten, which was a store or supermarket near the Hombu on Nishi Okubo . . . [The driver said], 'This is the town, but where's the house?,' and so about another half-an-hour or so, we were driving around and I looked at a telephone pole right on the side of the road with a little sign with 'aikido' calligraphy on it and an arrow pointing down the lane. I yelled, 'This is it! We found it!' The taxi driver was elated . . . It took about an hour-and-a-half to drive thirty miles and find it."

Although Suenaka told O'Sensei in Hawaii that he would soon be in Tokyo, he hadn't called ahead to inform the Aikikai of his arrival. Consequently, when he walked into the Hombu *dojo* and announced he wished to see the Founder, the staff afforded him a polite, yet understandably cool reception:

Morihei Ueshiba O'Sensei in his Iwama dojo; Aiki Festival, April, 1964.

"I walked in; there were secretaries there, and the office manager, and they said, 'Who are you?' I said I had just arrived from Hawaii, and they said, 'Oh! O'Sensei just returned from there!' I said, 'Yeah, I know, I saw him there.' So I said, 'Can I see him?,' and they said, 'Well, we don't know, we can't bother O'Sensei.' Apparently, though, somebody had gone back (into the *dojo*) and said there was a visitor from Hawaii. So I sat in the office, and they served me tea.

"There were Dutch doors that led from the outer office to the *dojo*—the bottom part was open, and the top was shut. As I was sitting there, I could see partially into the *dojo*, under the door . . . I saw O'Sensei walking. Suddenly he stopped, and then he bent over and peeked under the doors and saw me, and he ducked under the Dutch door and came into the room. He couldn't remember my name, so he said, 'Hawaii Boy! How are you, how are you?,' and he came up and hugged me. He was really happy to see me, and I was even happier than he was! [There were] all these stories that we heard about him that he was untouchable, he was unapproachable, you had to get permission from his chief disciples to even get close to him, let alone talk to him, so when he came in and hugged me, I thought, 'Hey! This is real special!' And, of course, that's when our relationship began."

The office staff was dumbfounded at the reception the usually formal and reserved O'Sensei afforded this young man from Hawaii. Suenaka recalls the staff telling him later that they had never before seen O'Sensei embrace anyone, and Suenaka himself cannot recall ever again seeing the Founder greet anyone in that way. Yet that warm encounter set a precedent between the two. "Every time I would see him, I would run up to him and say, 'O'Sensei!,' and hug him, and he just loved that!" Indeed, to this day, at all of Suenaka Sensei's schools, at the end of class all students embrace each and every fellow *aikidoka* before leaving the mat. The tradition is as essential to *dojo* etiquette as bowing to the *kamiza* before and after each practice session, and is a direct result of that first Hombu encounter. One may also consider it, as Suenaka Sensei does, another demonstration of O'Sensei's guiding philosophy that "The true nature of *budo* lies in the loving protection of all things." When new students, at first uncomfortable with the practice, ask why they must embrace at the end of class, always Suenaka Sensei's reply is, "Because O'Sensei hugged me."

Suenaka Sensei with O'Sensei at Iwama, home of the Aiki Jinja (shrine); April, 1964.

At O'Sensei's invitation, Suenaka remained at the Hombu that day. Nobuyoshi Tamura, at the time one of O'Sensei's *uchi deshi* (live-in disciples) and whom Suenaka had briefly met with O'Sensei in Hawaii, was kind enough to give him a tour of the Hombu and to make arrangements for Suenaka to stay the night, seeing to it he had a room and could find his way. After managing to squeeze a bit of practice into what was already a very full day, Suenaka was preparing to retire when O'Sensei happened by and extended an invitation to join him at breakfast the next morning. Suenaka went to bed a happy man.

What was originally intended to be a brief afternoon visit turned into a three-day stay. Suenaka rose the next morning, making sure he was at table by seven o'clock sharp for breakfast with the Founder. "I was overwhelmed by the honor," Suenaka recalls. "I don't remember much about it other than that. The fact that my Japanese wasn't all that great kept me from really carrying on a conversation, but I did ask him many questions. It was just a very honorable event to be there."

Breakfast concluded, Suenaka headed off for the day's first class. As the years passed and their relationship progressed, O'Sensei often invited Suenaka not only to breakfast, but dinner as well, a pattern that began during this first visit and continued throughout all of Suenaka Sensei's stays at the Hombu in the years to come. "Naturally, I was always there. I never missed out having breakfast or dinner with him!" Suenaka usually sat with others at the same table as O'Sensei, rather than the separate table reserved for *deshi,* while O'Sensei's wife Hatsu, as per custom, took her meals in the kitchen with the domestic help.

O'Sensei at Iwama during the Aiki-Matsuri (Aiki Festival); April, 1964.

The first full day at the Hombu unfolded predictably enough. Sometimes O'Sensei would teach the first class, although often, at his father's discretion, the first class of the day was taught by Kisshomaru Ueshiba Doshu, known then as *wakasensei,* a title given to the son of a system founder before he becomes the successor (today, Moriteru Ueshiba, son of Doshu, bears the title *wakasensei*). Afterwards, Doshu would usually turn his attention to administrative duties, leaving the day's instruction in the hands of a *shihan.* At that time, Koichi Tohei was still in Hawaii, but when at the Hombu the responsibility of teaching the next few classes was his, though he would often designate various students to teach throughout the day. Instruction commenced at around 6:30 a.m., and ended just before 9:00 p.m. Suenaka attended as many classes as he could, and enjoyed dinner with the Founder before retiring that night. The third day proceeded as the first: breakfast with O'Sensei, then classes all day long, and dinner before falling into bed.

For more than the obvious reasons, Suenaka found his first aikido instruction at the Hombu, and his study there in the ensuing years, a singular experience. When one studies an art or style of art, no matter what it may be, under one instructor or group of instructors for a long period of time and then visits another *dojo* teaching the same art or style, quite often the student notices differences in technique— sometimes subtle, sometimes significant—that can make it seem as if he or she has studied an entirely different art. There is always a degree of pride at stake, of wanting to acquit oneself and one's teachers well in a familiar, yet foreign environment. It was no different for Suenaka; indeed, if anything, the responsibility he felt was even greater. He had spent eight years studying aikido in Hawaii, thousands of miles away from where he now stood, under the watchful eyes of the Founder. He was one of the first fruits of the seed Koichi Tohei planted in Hawaii in 1953, and very much represented the outcome of that maiden effort. And there was another source of pressure as well. Though Japanese by blood, Suenaka was American by birth. While completely Japanese in appearance, English was his native tongue; as Suenaka has noted several times earlier, though he could make himself understood, he was at the time by no means fluent in Japanese. He was, in many ways, a foreigner, as much as any American serviceman stationed in Japan, though in his case his native hosts' expectations of his behavior were immeasurably higher.

It was with a mixture of confident anticipation and wariness that Suenaka first stepped onto the Hombu mat. The other students were friendly, but distant, and were obviously testing him with each and every technique. Despite his credentials, learning aikido under Tohei Sensei and his designated instructors, Suenaka realized he would have to prove himself. It is a tribute to his skill and tutelage that he was not found wanting:

"The *waza* at the Hombu was somewhat different, in that there were several other *shihan* teaching, so the style of aikido, so to speak, was a little different from what I had learned in Hawaii. Everybody had his own interpretation of what aikido was, under O'Sensei, so it wasn't really drastically different, but I noticed little differences here and there, which made it interesting for my study. My aikido fit in pretty well, because at that time, or course, Tohei Sensei was the chief instructor, and so everybody pretty much followed suit; his particular style of aikido was reflected in all the other instructors' aikido."

During his years at the Hombu, Suenaka noticed one major difference between the way O'Sensei taught and the way Koichi Tohei taught, a difference that prophesied Tohei's later split with the Aikikai:

"O'Sensei never really emphasized *ki*. He talked about *ki*, but more than, you could say, 'instructing' *ki*, he demonstrated *ki* in his *waza*, whereas Tohei Sensei really stressed *ki* development and using *ki* in aikido techniques. O'Sensei would give lectures on *ki*, but not while he was demonstrating aikido. He would mention specific techniques during his lectures, and demonstrated using *ki* in techniques as part of the lecture, in a lot of different ways. But Tohei Sensei stressed *ki* a lot more while he was teaching *waza* than O'Sensei did."

Though he needed no further convincing after his private experiences with O'Sensei in Hawaii, it was during one of O'Sensei's lectures that Suenaka received a forceful demonstration of the power of *ki:*

"O'Sensei was demonstrating what true *ki* was supposed to be like or feel like, and he used me as *uke*. He was holding a chopstick in his hand, but he didn't say what he was going to do. I was kind of skeptical, but I trusted him. I never hesitated to attack him. I knew he wasn't going to kill me or really hurt me badly. He didn't tell me how to attack him, he just said, you know, 'Come get me.' As I attacked him, he struck me in the forehead with the chopstick and knocked me down. He knocked the heck out of me! I almost lost consciousness, very close to it. Everything went white for a few seconds, then I got up and went back to my place and sat down, and I asked someone there 'What happened?' They said, 'Man, he knocked you down with a chopstick!' I had a big welt in the middle of my forehead from where he'd hit me with this chopstick! He knocked me silly!"

As Suenaka says, while O'Sensei never lectured about *ki* during *waza,* the strength of his *ki*—as well as his considerable physical strength, despite his advanced years—was apparent:

"There was another time, when we were doing *katate-tori,* where I would go in and grab O'Sensei. He would grab my wrist as he countered the attack and throw me across the room. And when I got up, there would be a bruise already forming on my wrist from where he'd grabbed me. [O'Sensei] didn't like it when the *uke* didn't give him a strong attack; some-times it would seem like he would throw you even harder if you didn't attack him hard. And then he would hardly ever use you as an *uke* again. [O'Sensei] used me as an *uke* a lot, because I always came in and attacked him hard! I knew he would wipe me out when I did, but again, I knew he would throw me even harder if I didn't! Anyway, I didn't care; I loved it!"

Despite his prodigious martial skill, the ease with which he tossed his ardent *uke* about the *dojo* and his uncanny command of *ki,* Suenaka Sensei remembers O'Sensei more than anything as a gentle man, kind, and forgiving. Though quick to erupt into awe-inspiring anger when provoked, sending his students immediately to their knees in respectful *seiza* (sitting posture), his anger disappeared almost as soon as it surfaced. For O'Sensei, it would seem as if anger was a tool, serving to get the offending party's attention; though no doubt genuine, it was put away as soon as it had served its purpose. Again, this is in keeping with the guiding philosophy of aikido, as expressed by the Founder.

Suenaka recalls an incident during one of his evening meals with O'Sensei during his first visit, which echoed their first encounter in O'Sensei's hotel room in Hawaii a month earlier. The event impressed on him, in an unexpected and almost comic way, aikido's guiding philosophy; that O'Sensei, martial master though he was, literally wouldn't even harm a fly:

> "As we got ready to eat, he noticed a fly on his bowl of rice. There were some other *uchi deshi* eating with him as well, and we all noticed the fly and were ready to chase it away, and he stopped us. 'The little fly won't eat too much,' he said. 'We'll just let him eat his fill and then let him go away, happy.' We tried to tell him about flies carrying diseases and all that, but we all ended up just sitting there watching the fly eat until it eventually flew away."

On his fourth day in Japan, Suenaka realized it would probably be in his best interest to report back to his duty station before the MPs began searching for him. After taking his leave of O'Sensei, Suenaka hopped a cab back to Tachikawa Air Force Base and again reported to the CBPO. This time, he was sent to his squadron for assignment. It was there that Suenaka met Captain Rausch, his squadron commander and the man who was to unwittingly play a pivotal role in Suenaka's continuing martial education.

Captain Rausch was young, barely ten years older than the twenty-one year old Suenaka. In answer to Rausch's query, Suenaka said he was supposed to report to Civil Engineering, whose primary responsibility it was to keep the base's physical plant in good repair, but that there was no record of his orders. "What's your AFSC (Air Force Specialty Code)?," Rausch asked. As luck would have it, he was frustrated with CE's slow reponse to his repeated requests for service: whenever he needed something fixed, it took them days to attend to it. "I can't even get them to come by and change my lightbulbs!," Rausch lamented. When Suenaka informed him he was an electrician, Rausch asked, "Would you take care of my lightbulbs, electrical switches, everything? Can you repair things?," he asked. "Oh, I can repair anything!," Suenaka responded. That's all the answer Capt. Rausch needed. Before the day was through, Suenaka found himself assigned directly under Rausch, charged with the awesome duty of pretty much killing time until a lightbulb burned out. He was issued his own supply card to requisition supplies as needed, and was left alone.

Opportunity was banging on the barracks door. Suenaka wasted no time in approaching the barracks houseboy, Yama-san, who made about forty dollars a month to see to the household chores of all the airmen on Suenaka's floor: shining shoes, cleaning house, laundering clothes and uniforms. Would Yama-san be interested in earning an extra 2,000 yen (at the time, $5.60) a month to change lightbulbs and electrical switches? For Yama-san, it was close to a week's extra salary, so naturally, his answer was yes.

As long as his light bulbs and switches were changed whenever needed, Capt. Rausch cared little who changed them. Suenaka left his supply card and the Hombu phone number with Yama-san and headed for Tokyo. He stayed at the Hombu for weeks at a time, checking in occasionally with Yama-san to make sure everything was okay, and returning about once a month to meet with Capt. Rausch in person to ensure he was satisfied. "Very satisfactory," Rausch would say. 'You're doing a good job!" And so Suenaka would thank his CO, pay Yama-san his 2,000 yen, and return to the Hombu. Paid by Uncle Sam to study aikido under the Founder; it was a pretty sweet deal.

Even with his near constant study at the Hombu, Suenaka from time to time took a few days to travel from *dojo* to *dojo* to observe and study other styles, both familiar and foreign. Suenaka visited *dojos* not only in Tokyo, but in Shizuoka, Nagano, Beppu, Osaka, and other cities. Many of these visits were part of his travels with O'Sensei, Tohei Sensei, and

Suenaka Sensei with judo Meijin (10th dan master) Kazuo Ito at the Kodokan in Tokyo; Winter, 1969

other *uchi deshi* as part of teaching assignments, both during his time at Tachikawa and during his subsequent years in Okinawa (discussed later), but just as many were undertaken alone. (Note: Many of the events described hereinafter occurred over a period of several years, for reasons which will also be addressed later.)

One of the first places Suenaka visited was the Kodokan, established in 1882 by judo founder Jigoro Kano, the Mecca for *judoka* worldwide as much as the Aikikai Hombu is for *aikidoka*. It was there that Suenaka met Meijin Kyuzo Mifune, one of the world's most celebrated *judoka,* and Meijin Kazuo Ito, under whom Suenaka studied whenever he was at the Kodokan. Suenaka had the great honor and good fortune of occasionally practicing with Mifune Sensei: "He threw me around quite a few times!," recalls Suenaka. "It was very pleasurable being thrown around by him; it was like being used as an *uke* by O'Sensei." Suenaka also studied from time to time under Ito contemporary Sumiyuki Kotani, but it was Ito Sensei with whom he spent most of his time. The judo and jujutsu master, at the time in his early sixties, took the young Hawaiian under his wing, and the two soon developed a relationship much like Suenaka's relationship with O'Sensei, with Suenaka serving as Ito's *deshi* whenever he was at the Kodokan. One might think O'Sensei would have discouraged Suenaka's study of other arts, but the contrary proved to be true. It was precisely because of Suenaka's pre-aikido experience in judo, kempo, and jujutsu that the Founder gave his blessing to Suenaka's extracurricular studies. Indeed, O'Sensei made a point of discussing Suenaka's outside studies with him whenever he returned to the Hombu: "He would ask me how they were teaching, and what I thought about them. Of course, he was very happy when I told him that nothing compared to aikido!" Ultimately, in his position as president of the Kodokan promotional board, it was Ito Sensei who, in 1970, encouraged Suenaka Sensei to request promotion to *sandan* (third degree black belt) in judo and jujutsu, and who personally awarded him those ranks; his dual certificate is signed by Ito Sensei and Risei Kano, son of Jigoro Kano.

Less frequent but no less educational were Suenaka's occasional visits to Masutatsu Oyama's Kyokushin-kai karate *hombu,* his first introduction to that rather brutal and unforgiving martial art form. All three of his brothers had studied Kyokushin-kai in Hawaii under Edward "Bobby" Lowe, one of Mas Oyama's chief pupils, but Suenaka himself had been too busy with his other martial studies to join them. Fit and experienced as he was, Suenaka was forced to limit his study to a maximum of two hours a week, lest he risk injuries that would interfere with his judo and aikido studies. Still, he relished his time there, and the hard lessons learned.

Despite his outside studies, Suenaka's heart remained true to aikido, and the more time he spent with O'Sensei, the more their relationship grew. The Founder seemed to have a distinct fondness for "Suenaka-kun" (*kun* is an affectionate term; roughly, "Young Suenaka"), perhaps because of their unique first meetings. Regardless of the reasons, Suenaka found himself spending a lot of time with O'Sensei. He often served as his *kaban mochi* (personal valet) when O'Sensei traveled; carrying his bags, holding doors open, or assisting the vigorous but nevertheless aged Founder up and down stairs. Often, O'Sensei personally requested that Suenaka accompany him. Other times, Suenaka was chosen by Tendokan founder Kenji Shimizu, a favorite *uchi deshi* of O'Sensei. Suenaka was also lucky enough to be invited to join O'Sensei from time to time as the Founder visited area temples to meditate, or traveled to the Aiki Jinja (aikido shrine) at his country home in Iwama, for practice and meditation. (Morihiro Saito Sensei, at the time in his early 30s, was the assigned caretaker of the *jinja,* a duty he maintains today.) Though an enviable honor, traveling with O'Sensei was pretty much a formal affair, as Suenaka recalls:

"[O'Sensei] never really talked too much. He was very private, very busy. The only time we really talked was when he was relaxing, or while we were eating. Usually when he traveled, he never talked too much. You couldn't really go up to him and engage him in conversation, not from your side. If he asked you to come sit with him and talk, that's when you talked. Otherwise, in our travels, he would spend his free time resting or sleeping."

There are stories of O'Sensei, particularly in the early days of aikido, putting his attendants to the test; for example, changing his mind about boarding a train at the last possible moment, sending his valets scrambling to retrieve his bags and arrange new transportation. However, Suenaka never experienced any of this:

"It might be true that in the old days O'Sensei did that, but he wasn't like that while I was [in Japan]. He never really tested us or tried to fool us like that. He might have done that before, playfully, or maybe just decided to change his mind for whatever reason, but it was all pretty straightforward when we were with him. He was a real serious guy."

As Suenaka's relationship with O'Sensei grew, so did his relationship with the man who first introduced him to aikido, Koichi Tohei. Thanks to the Air Force, Suenaka was one of the few original Hawaiian *aikidoka* who was able to spend an appreciable length of time studying at the Hombu, and so developed a relationship with Tohei perhaps unrivaled by those whose aikido practice began as his did, with Tohei's first Hawaiian visit in 1953. Just over forty years old at the time of Suenaka's arrival in Japan, Tohei was entering into his physical and martial prime. Handsome, charismatic, and boasting powerful technique, he was a commanding and popular presence on the mat and off, and had an equally powerful personal effect on young Suenaka. Tohei Sensei recognized Suenaka from his many trips to Hawaii, and upon returning to Japan about a month after Suenaka's arrival there, Tohei took the younger man under

Suenaka Sensei with Koichi Tohei at Iwama; April, 1964.

Kisshomaru Ueshiba and Suenaka Sensei, at O'Sensei's Iwama dojo; April 1964. The figure seen in silhouette in the doorway behind them is O'Sensei.

Suenaka Sensei with Kisshomaru Ueshiba at the Aikikai Hombu; December, 1993.

his wing from the very start: "My relationship with Tohei Sensei was, I guess you would say, like a father and son . . . we had a lot of respect for each other, a lot of love for each other . . . . And even today, [I] have a lot of love and respect for him."

As their relationship grew, Tohei took Suenaka with him on his frequent travels throughout Japan as his personal *deshi,* teaching aikido and lecturing and, after the day's work was done, spending the night on the town. "We did a lot of things together," Suenaka recalls. "We went out together, partied together, went nightclubbing together, ate together. . . . He had a lot of friends, and was a very popular person all over Japan." In his position as chief Hombu instructor, Tohei Sensei pretty much set his own schedule, arranging his own demonstrations and lectures, departing and returning to the Hombu as he wished.

Where his relationship with Tohei Sensei was close, Suenaka's relationship with Kisshomaru Ueshiba Doshu was more formal. This was not so much a function of temperment as it was position. As the son of the Founder, Doshu was charged with the day-to-day administrative duties necessary to run the organization. Suenaka describes his relationship with Doshu as ". . . business-like. Knowing that Tohei Sensei and I were very close, and I was one of his *deshi,* Doshu didn't ignore me, but he left me to Tohei Sensei's guidance." Still, there were many times during the years Suenaka studied at the Hombu during which he accompanied Doshu to the Aiki Jinja in Iwama to meditate and say prayers. Whenever he traveled to the Hombu, Suenaka would formally request permission to spend a few moments with Doshu, both out of respect for Doshu's position and out of curiosity and a sincere desire to get to know him better. "He always had time to talk to me," Suenaka says. "Of course, I would bring gifts. In Japan, you have to bring gifts . . . they bring gifts, you bring gifts. I brought real good gifts—Napoleon brandy and Henessey cognac—so they were very appreciative! But I wasn't buying favors, and they understood that. He gave me his time, and I respect him for that. Whenever we got together, [Doshu] was such a warm person. He is reserved, but very humble, self-effacing. He is a very gracious person."

With Koichi Tohei, Suenaka also found the opportunity to practice *misogi* (ritual purification) with disciples of Shin-Shin Toitsu Do ("Way of Mind and Body Coordinated"), the spiritual development system founded by Tempu Nakamura and based on elements of yoga and other spiritual disciplines, as well as swordsmanship. Suenaka and others would make pilgrimages into the mountains, kneeling in meditation in the snow, then plunging shirtless into an icy mountain stream, kneeling in the water up to their necks, then running back to kneel in the snow once again and continue meditating. "After a while, the water felt warmer than the air!," says Suenaka. "But it really focused you, and made you tough."

Nakamura's teachings had an even greater influence on Tohei. When he ultimately severed relations with the Hombu in the years following O'Sensei's death, Tohei Sensei christened his new organization Shin-Shin Toitsu aikido (Aikido with Mind and Body Coordinated), and gradually shifted his teaching emphasis from physical *waza* to *ki* development almost exclusively (discussed later).

The arrangement at the Hombu was too good to be true, and so perhaps too good to last. In May of 1961, about three months after his arrival in Japan, Airman Suenaka unexpectedly received transfer orders. He was still considered a surplus airman, remaining in Japan only until the Air Force could find room for him elsewhere, which they did—in Korea. Suenaka was shocked. Regardless of its close geographic proximity, it might as well have been on another planet. But having just tasted what it was like to study with O'Sensei, he wasn't about to give it up without a fight. Fortunately, he had a cousin who was assigned to the 5th Air Force, the regional command. Suenaka pleaded with him to do whatever he could to allow him to remain in Japan. "He said, 'The best I can do for you is Kadena Air Base in Okinawa." The U.S. government was constructing a missile base there to help defend the Japanese mainland, Okinawa and nearby smaller islands against possible attack by the Communist Chinese, and servicemen possessing electrical engineering skills like Suenaka were in high demand. Still, at the time, Okinawa seemed to him no better than Korea. It was even more distant from Tokyo, and the likelihood of being able to spend weeks at a time studying at the Hombu, as he was then, seemed remote at best. On the other hand, Okinawa was obviously more akin culturally to Japan than was Korea, so Suenaka would feel more at home, especially considering that while his Japanese was still rusty, he spoke no Korean. And while travel to the Hombu might be difficult, it wouldn't be impossible. Okinawa was clearly his best alternative, and he accepted the assignment. Once again, though, it seemed as if divine providence was guiding Suenaka's life; far from being a disappointment, his stay in Okinawa was to become one of the most significant periods in both his martial development and his personal life.

CHAPTER FIVE

OKINAWA AND ELSEWHERE

As it turned out, Suenaka Sensei's fear that moving to Okinawa would seriously curtail his study at the Hombu was unrealized. The air force was still actively encouraging servicemen and women to pursue the martial arts, as part of fitness and survival training for air crews and related personnel. When Suenaka arrived at Kadena in May of 1961, he found more sympathy than resistance from his command when it came to furthering his martial education. Again, because of the nature of his duties, Suenaka was able to take what is known as "permissive TDY" (temporary duty), meaning he was given permission by his CO to take occasional personal leave; granted, not as frequently as when he was stationed in Tokyo, but still, he managed to visit and study

Tendokan aikido founder Kenji Shimizu and Suenaka Sensei at Iwama; April, 1964.

with O'Sensei four or five times a year, for several weeks at a time, serving as an *uchi deshi* and, later, a personal *deshi* to Tohei Sensei. Suenaka recalls one of his more humorous experiences with O'Sensei from this time, involving Tendokan aikido founder Kenji Shimizu:

"It was in the spring of 1964. It was the Aiki-Matsuri, the Aiki Festival, which was held every year in Iwama, at the aiki shrine. People came from all over the world to pay homage to the Aiki-Jinja and O'Sensei. There were about two or three hundred people there—Robert Frager, Robert Nadeau, Terry Dobson, several

Shimizu Sensei and Suenaka Sensei at Shimizu's dojo in Setagaya, Japan; Winter, 1993

instructors from the U.S., although I can't remember anyone from Hawaii being there. But anyway, Kenji Shimizu and I went there early in the morning, around eight o'clock, to wait for O'Sensei. I think he arrived at about noon, by car, and all the *uchi deshi* were waiting around for him.

"The car pulled up right in front of the dojo, and as it happened Shimizu and I were standing right there. So when the car door opened and O'Sensei stepped out, we reached forward and each of us took one of his hands in ours, to help him, and walked him up the stairs to the dojo. By that time most everyone besides the *deshi* were waiting for O'Sensei inside the dojo, and it was a small dojo, too, even smaller than it is today, so the place was packed, the walls were lined with people. So Shimizu and I helped O'Sensei to the middle of the mat, and when we got there we continued to hold his hands. I don't know why; maybe we were nervous or something. But O'Sensei looked around at all the people there, and then he slowly looked over at me, then at Shimizu, and he had to be thinking, 'What are these two idiots doing still holding my hands?' And then suddenly, wham! He executed a double *sayu-nage,* his arms came up and back and Shimizu and I flew backwards. I mean, our feet came up off the mat and we somersaulted and slammed into the *tatami.* It hit us like a freight train! And there was O'Sensei looking down at us, and he said, "Why were you holding my hands? What, do you think I'm a useless old man, I can't stand up on my own?" He wasn't really angry with us, but he wasn't really joking, either. He was scolding us, 'What's the matter with you two?,' that sort of attitude. Of course, Shimizu and I were bowing: *'Hai O'Sensei! Gomen nasai!'* ('Yes, O'Sensei, I'm sorry!'). We hopped right back up and took our places by his side again, but we didn't hold his hands! And then he told us, 'Now, go sit down.' It was pretty funny."

Immediately upon his arrival at Kadena, Suenaka began teaching aikido in the base gymnasium, gradually accumulating students from base personnel. He did this with O'Sensei's blessing, secured prior to his departure from Japan, as the Founder was eager to introduce aikido to Okinawa. Twice before, *aikidoka* had traveled to the birthplace of Japanese karate to promote the art there, only to quickly be sent packing by the local *karateka;* literally, challenged on the mat and defeated in single combat. Each time, the instigator of these long trips home to the Hombu was Fusei Kise.

Born in 1935, Fusei Kise first began studying martial arts at age twelve, augmenting his primary training in later years with instruction in Shorinji kempo and Shorin-ryu karate under many of Okinawa's greatest living masters, including Shorinji-ryu founder Zenryo Shimabukuro, and the late Hakutsuru Shorin-ryu and Matsumura Seito Shorin-ryu Kobudo Grandmaster Hohan Soken. By the time

Sueneka Sensei with Shorin-ryu Kenshinkan karate founder Fusei Kise in Jacksoneille, N.C., July, 1997.

Suenaka arrived in Okinawa, Kise was well-advanced in these and other karate styles. Today, he is one of the art's most celebrated and respected practitioners, and continues in Okinawa to teach his own style of Shorin-ryu Kenshinkan karate, which he founded upon the retirement of Soken

from active teaching in 1978, and also has numerous schools in the United States. A short, powerfully-built, and somewhat gruff man, Kise Sensei cared little for words when it came to expounding the virtues of any given style, preferring instead to see how it fared in *kumite* (sparring), or direct hand-to-hand combat. The test was simple. If you could beat him, your style was worthwhile. If not, shut up and go away.

Though unforgiving, such a test is undeniably fair. The first aikido practicioner, a *yondan* (fourth degree black belt) in both aikido and karate who had traveled from Japan specifically to introduce aikido to Okinawa, was unable to weather the trial, nor was the second, an even more celebrated *aikidoka*. In their defense, it should be noted that both men, though skilled and sincere, boasted little experience outside the controlled strictures of the *dojo*, and so were perhaps as much mentally ill-prepared as they were physically to meet Kise's blunt challenge. Consequently, it's not surprising that, at the time of Suenaka's arrival in Okinawa, the local opinion of aikido was poor, at best. This, however, would soon change.

Fusei Kise was what the air force termed a "third country national," or indigenous worker, and was employed as an electrician on the air base. Given that Suenaka was an electrician as well, it was inevitable that the two would eventually meet. In fact, Suenaka found himself assigned to the same shop in which Kise worked. Suenaka remembers

Kise as "a sort of real stand-offish guy, almost arrogant, at least during our first meeting." The two exchanged little beyond the usual pleasantries during their first meeting. Neither knew that they would soon become friends, brought together by the very disparity in martial styles that had thus far made Kise the bane of aikido on Okinawa.

Suenaka Sensei taught aikido in Zemke Gymnasium, one of two gyms on Kadena. Zemke Gym had two levels, and he taught on the upper floor. Not long after he first met Kise Sensei, Suenaka was in the middle of teaching a class when he heard a disturbance on the lower floor:

"I heard some shouting downstairs, and I went to look,' recalls Suenaka. There was a big group of karate students, about fifty people in the class. I had my students continue training and I walked downstairs; it was Kise Sensei. I said, 'Hey, what are you doing?,' and he said, 'This is my karate class—what are you doing up there?' And I said, "That's my aikido class.' He said, 'Aikido, eh? Hmmmm.' He didn't say very much then. So I went back upstairs and continued."

Perhaps it was because Suenaka was a fellow employee in the electrical shop that Kise opted not to challenge him that very night. Perhaps it was because he liked Suenaka personally, brief though their acquaintance was at that point, more than he had the previous *aikidoka*. Later, it may have been because both found they shared common experiences in their study of the martial arts; beginning study in a variety of styles at an early age, a preference for deeds over words, and a sincere (and no doubt purely professional) love of a good street fight. Whatever the reasons, Kise Sensei never formally challenged Suenaka to physically defend his art. Indeed, after their meeting in the gym, they found themselves spending more and more time together, both on the job and socially, becoming fast friends. Still, there were implied challenges, as Suenaka recalls:

"There were a lot of times that he commented negatively about aikido. There were many times that he indirectly challenged me, and of course, I took the challenge and said, 'Let's do it!' And he would say, 'No, we're friends.' We never got into a real fight. We got into verbal confrontations many times, but never a physical confrontation. We were really just teasing each other."

Let it not be said, though, that Fusei Kise wasn't prepared to fight when pressed—or insulted:

"We were in the squadron day room. There was a pool table there, snack bar, people were playing cards. We were sitting down, watching television. I was in uniform, but of course Kise Sensei was a third country national, so he was in street clothes. This great big guy walked in the room—he recognized that I was a GI, from the uniform, even though I looked Japanese, but he saw Kise, and he said 'You goddamn gook! What the hell are you doing in here?' Kise Sensei heard him, but he didn't understand a lot of English, he just looked up and said, 'Huh?' And the guy said 'You deaf? I said what are you doing in here?' So I said to the guy, 'Hey, what's your problem? He's the night electrician. He belongs in here, he works here!' And the guy says, 'What the hell they got a gook doing that job for?' By that time Kise Sensei knew something was up, and he asks me, 'What did he say?' I said, 'He called you a gook. I think he wants to kick your butt.' And Kise said 'What?!' Then he got up, his eyes got small and he turned red as a beet, and I thought, 'Uh-oh.' So I turned to the guy and I said, 'You better get out of here, now. He may be small, but he can kill you and me right now, just like that.' And then the guy's eyes got real big, and he said 'No shit?' And voom!, he was out the door. Later on I saw the guy again, and he asked me, 'Who was that guy?' So I told him. I said, 'If that man had gotten ahold of you, you would have been lying in little pieces. And by the way, I'm Oriental, and I don't like the word gook either.' And he said, 'Oh, man! I'm sorry!' And he went back and apologized to Kise Sensei, and Kise accepted. He was pretty good about stuff like that. He could be pretty mean when he wanted to, but he knew his limits as to what he could and couldn't do on the air base. Now, had it happened in town, the outcome would have been very different!"

By this time, Kise was familiar with Suenaka's aikido, as Suenaka was familiar with Kise's karate, both men having observed the other's classes and technique with an educated, critical eye. Though neither man's machismo would allow them to openly admit it, both were impressed with the other's prowess and technique. Of the aikido Suenaka taught at the time, he notes: "It wasn't like the aikido we have today; fairly similar, but probably a lot harder, a little more violent, so it impressed him."

21-year-old Suenaka Sensei demonstrating ikkyo on student Allen Wagstaff in Zemke Gym, Kadena Air Force Base, Okinawa; Fall, 1961.

As the months passed, Suenaka's student body outgrew the space available in Zemke Gym, forcing him to begin another class at Kadena's second gym, McConnell Gym. At the same time Suenaka began entertaining thoughts of opening a *dojo* off-base, in town. For this, he would need O'Sensei's blessing, which he secured upon his first return trip to the Hombu, less than a month after his move to Okinawa ("I didn't waste any time. . . . I think then maybe I had more guts than brains."). Again, the Founder was eager to introduce aikido to Okinawa, more so after the previous failed ventures. Ironically, it was a *karateka,* Shorinji-ryu karate founder Zenryo Shimabukuro, who guided Suenaka in this pursuit.

Suenaka first encountered Shimabukuro Sensei through Kiyotaka Nema, owner of the local sporting goods store where Suenaka purchased his *gis* and other supplies. (Although Fuse Kise was a student of Shimabukuro's, as noted earlier, Suenaka hadn't met him.) Suenaka mentioned to Nema his desire to open a *dojo* in town. "Nema said, 'Oh, you don't want to do that.' He warned me. He said, 'I don't think aikido is going to go over very big in town. You want to stay on the base.' But I told him I did, and he said, 'I know a person who can help you.'" Nema took Suenaka to Shimabukuro's *dojo,* about five miles outside of the air base. After observing a class, Nema introduced the two and told Shimabukuro of Suenaka's plans. It's remarkable that Shimabukuro, one of a scant handful of *judan* (tenth degree black belt) in the area, in addition to being one of Okinawa's most highly regarded *karateka,* was so willing to help. "He was a great master. For someone of his stature to say, 'Okay, young man, I'll help you,' was really something," Suenaka says. "He could have just as easily said 'Look kid, why don't you come and learn under me?' But he respected me for wanting to teach aikido, and we became good friends. I had a lot more respect for him than he did for me, I'm sure, because of what he did for me."

Shimabukuro Sensei called on a friend who was vice-president of a local bank and learned of a building in nearby Nakanomachi that would suit Suenaka's needs, and his modest income. The low concrete structure housed a laundry in the left half, with the right half empty. There was a sliding, wooden warehouse-style door, four windows, no bathroom ("We went outside in the back of the building. All the plants there grew nice and green!") and fifteen-hundred square feet of space; not a palace, but it would do, especially since rent was just fifteen dollars a month. Suenaka signed the lease.

Now that he had a building, Suenaka needed mats to make it a *dojo.* Again, Shimabukuro was there to help, putting Suenaka in touch with a local *tatami* (rice straw mat) maker who was a good friend of his, and from whom Shimabukuro purchased his mats. The *tatami* maker was more than willing to provide Suenaka with the mats:

"He said, 'They're special made . . . how many do you need?' He was selling the mats for about five dollars each, which was an incredibly low price even then, but he said he'd give them to me for about two-fifty apiece! Today, a standard residential *tatami* is about two-hundred fifty dollars, each. The *tatami* maker was selling residential *tatami* for two-and-a-half dollars, and the thick judo mats for five, so he was giving them to me for half price, and it took him the better part of a day to make just one, because he made them all by hand. But I didn't know any of this. I said, 'Boy, I'm gonna need about forty mats . . . that's a hundred dollars!' All he said was, 'Please, come in, watch.' And I watched him make a mat from scratch. I watched him gather the straw and bundle it, twist it, compressing it down, all by hand. After about two hours of watching him, he hadn't even begun forming the mat yet. And that's when I bowed and said, 'I'm very sorry. Please forgive me. I should pay you more!' But he said, 'No, I'll give you a discount, that's okay. You're a friend of a friend.' I felt so humble, so small. They were exceptional mats, and I learned another lesson."

Although Suenaka was grateful for Shimabukuro's help, he had little time to further their relationship. He did attend several classes at Shimabukuro Sensei's dojo, both out of curiosity and respect, and Shimabukuro observed one of Suenaka's aikido classes. "He liked aikido. He said, 'Aikido has nice, flowing moves.' I think he was being straight with me. He was a very respected man in the area, so he had no need to lie."

Building and mats secured, there was still one final obstacle standing in the way of Suenaka's plans. He would need approval from the Okinawan government before he would be allowed to formally open his school in town, and in order to secure this final, essential consent, Suenaka would need a formal, written teaching license. Discouraged, he returned to the Hombu with the news. To his astonishment and delight, O'Sensei cleared the way by presenting him with a rare *menkyo kaiden* certificate, granting not only license to teach aikido, but certifying Suenaka Sensei's mastery of the art. Suenaka was excited, but more because he now would be able to open his own *dojo*. It wasn't until years later that he fully realized the depth of the honor O'Sensei had bestowed upon him. As such certificates were recognized by the Japanese Ministry of Education, it was all he needed to unlock the final door. Thus armed, he returned to Okinawa and secured in short order official government permission to open his school, which he dubbed the Okinawa Aikikai.

Once he had his mats, the Okinawa Aikikai was ready for business. But teaching aikido in the secure confines of an American military base is one thing; teaching it on the home turf of the local *karateka* was quite another. Like Nema, Shimabukuro had warned Suenaka earlier that he might run into problems with some of the local karate toughs, and indeed, the challenges began just days after the Okinawa Aikikai opened:

"We were met with a lot of resistance by the local karate community, and there were many challenges. Almost from day one,

43

there were challenges—they'd walk in the door, with their arms crossed or hands on hips, really belligerent, making comments and asking what it was I was teaching. When I told them it was aikido, they laughed and made fun. They had heard about aikido, and called it many names. But we held off their attacks. Many times, I threw the first punch! They came into my school and threatened me in my school! They were the ones who initiated the attack by threatening me, so we knocked them out and threw them out the door! Some of them came back—with more people! But we always held them off; I had a lot of tough guys in my class!"

The significance of these early challenges cannot be under-estimated, for there was more than personal pride and loss of face at stake. As stated earlier, two previous attempts to introduce aikido to Okinawa had failed utterly. As a result, aikido's reputation on the island at the time was, at best, laughable, with some refusing even to call aikido a martial art. If they did, they considered it ineffective, certainly not a worthwhile means of self-defense. All it would take was word on the street of just one defeat at the hands of a roughneck to further destroy aikido's already poor reputation. Plus, Suenaka was a seasoned street fighter, and simply wasn't about to back down from a challenge. As a result, those who came to the Okinawa Aikikai expecting to put another notch in their belts were dealt with harshly:

"These two guys came in . . . almost all of the challenges began the same way. They'd walk in, crossed-arms . . . most of the time they wore *gis,* trying to intimidate me or impress me, with black belts, red belts, red-and-white belts. Very few came in wearing street clothes. I was standing in the corner, and one of these guys was standing in the doorway, the other was standing beside it. The guy in the doorway said something like, 'I think you guys are all sissies." And I said, 'Oh, you do? That's good. Thank you. Good-bye.' But he wouldn't leave, he said, 'No, I think I'll beat you all up tonight.' Just like that, matter-of-fact. He had moved in and was standing really close to the wall, so I moved in fast, *irimi,* and hit him in the temple and his head hit the wall, and I grabbed his head and turned it and smashed his face into the wall a second time. It was rough concrete, and his face scraped down it . . . oh, he was a mess. Of course, by that time he was out cold, and the other guy jumped out of the dojo into the middle of the street. We had a *benjo* ditch, an open sewage ditch, which ran right in front of the building along the street—it was covered with concrete in front of the door so you could walk over it, but to either side it was open. I picked up the guy from inside the dojo and deposited him into the ditch, then I turned to the other guy and said, 'Take him and get out. Tell everybody about this, will you?'

"Word got out, and more people came to challenge. After a while, I let some of my students handle them. Someone would walk in, and I would say 'It's free time! Who wants him?' By then my students had realized most of these guys weren't that tough, and they'd handle them. Nobody ever beat us, and so after a while the challenges stopped."

Not all challengers exited so unceremoniously:

"There was this one local guy who came in, wearing street clothes, and said he studied Kobayashi-ryu, which I was familiar with, because it was a system founded by Chibana Chosin, who was a very great teacher. That's all he said, 'I study Kobayashi-ryu.' He didn't even give his name. So I said, 'Well, okay . . . what are you trying to tell me?' Then he showed me a big cut on his hand, he said, 'We punch rocks, stick our hands in glass . . . that's how I got this cut.' And I said, "That's really stupid, you know? There's other ways to get tough.' So he said, 'Well, then, what's this? This doesn't look like it works. You guys move like you're dancing.' I said, 'Well, we can take care of you if we have to.' And he said, 'You mind showing me?' It was an outright challenge, and you don't walk into a dojo and do that, not at that time. So I said, 'What do you want me to show you?' I was ready to just blast him then, but he was a fairly young guy, maybe just a little older than me, and he looked pretty crisp, pretty sharp. He said, 'Why don't I punch you and see what you can do?' I knew my *ma-ai* . . . he came in with a punch and kicked at me, real fast, and I pivoted out of the way and boom!, I hit his face, broke his nose, and grabbed his hand, executed *kote-gaeshi* and broke his wrist. So he got up and I said, 'What would you like to see now?' He asked me then if he could be a student of mine, and wound up studying with me for about a year, as soon as his wrist healed. He was one of the few Okinawan students I had, and he started out by challenging me. He was a good kid after that, and we became good friends."

If the reader gets the impression from these stories that Suenaka Sensei was a bit of a roughneck during his Okinawa days, they're only partially correct. While a self-confessed scrapper, he wasn't a bully. He was, however, deadly serious about defending aikido's reputation in this new and often unfriendly environment. His love for and devotion to O'Sensei was beyond question, short though their association was at that point. While a defeat by a challenger would have caused him to lose face locally, such humiliation was nothing compared to the shame he would have felt were he forced to tell O'Sensei he had failed to acquit himself and O'Sensei's art in the face of a challenge.

It may also appear that Suenaka's unforgiving responses to the challenges he encountered flies in the face of aikido's basic philosophy of love and compassion—that is wasn't very *"aiki."* Many times challengers were dispatched not with a well-executed aikido technique, but, as in the first example, basic, hard *atemi* (vital point strike); rough, but effective. It could be argued that Suenaka might have dealt less harshly with challenges than he did, perhaps even without physical force. In fact, that's what happened more times than not. People who entered his *dojo* with respect, regardless of however poor their opinion of aikido might have been, were treated with like respect, whether they remained as students or not. Even if they did not, as in the second example above, an apology was all it took for Suenaka to forgive a challenger, after which they were always welcome to remain and study in the true spirit of *aiki*. All challengers were first given the opportunity to leave without a fight. It was only when it became clear that a challenger was determined to cause trouble—again, as in the first example above—that Suenaka responded in kind:

> "Being in Okinawa during that period and trying to teach aikido there was like being behind enemy lines, surrounded by the enemy. I don't mean to say that the local *karateka* were enemies, but it was a real 'put up or shut up' atmosphere. Oftentimes after a challenge was issued, it was the challenger who initiated the attack, who made the first move, or threw the first punch. You had no choice but to react accordingly when you were challenged this way. Very often that's the only response they would respect. And, ultimately, it worked."

The bottom line is that there was a point to be made. Given the prevailing opinion of aikido at the time, spreading the word that anyone who challenged the *sensei* at the new aikido *dojo* wound up getting tossed into the street simultaneously accomplished the primary objective, that of spreading the word that aikido was indeed an effective and valid martial art. One might consider it a direct, *irimi* response, rather than a circular, *tenkan* one. Whether a challenger's ejection from Suenaka's *dojo* was the result of a well-executed aikido *kokyu-nage* or a kick to the backside was, at that time, irrelevant. What mattered was that everyone realize that: Suenaka is tough, Suenaka teaches aikido, therefore aikido is tough. Ultimately, this simple formula proved effective. Where previous attempts had failed, twenty-one-year-old Suenaka Sensei had succeeded. O'Sensei now had an aikido *dojo* in Okinawa.

It soon became apparent that trying to teach aikido in three separate locations, on top of working for Uncle Sam, was just too demanding, and so Suenaka discontinued teaching his class at Zemke Gym and cut back on the time he spent teaching at McConnell, focusing the bulk of his energy on making the new *dojo* successful. While he lost many of his on-base students in the process, enough followed him to establish a solid student body from the start, and he attracted a number of new students from the local native population, including some *karateka* who switched to aikido. However, the greater part of his student body was comprised of American military personnel: airmen, marines, navy Seabees, and army Green Berets. Building a solid student body at this time was important for reasons more than pride, as there was now rent and power bills to be paid.

Cutting back on teaching hours also freed Suenaka to explore the local martial arts scene. As he introduced many of the local *karateka* to this new and different style, so did they introduce him to their world. Given his already solid grounding in karate, Suenaka was an enthusiastic participant. One of the first people to assist in this further education was Seijin Inamine, at the time a *godan* (fifth degree black belt) in Shobayashi Shorin-ryu karate, and a student of Eizo Shimabuku, who was himself a chief student of famed Sukunaihayashi Shorin-ryu founder Chotoku Kyan. Suenaka was somewhat familiar with this style, as he had already found time to study with some regularity with Chibana Chosin, a chief student of Kyan Sensei, in the historic city of Shuri, the traditional Okinawan capital (Today, Shuri is an historic district within Naha, the present Okinawan capital city). Like Kise Sensei, Inamine Sensei was a third country national, and worked in the base laundry, which is where Suenaka first encountered him. Inamine often invited Suenaka to train with him, the two journeying into the nearby hills or performing *kata* on the roof of Inamine's home. A few months after their initial acquaintance, while the two were taking a break from a training session, Inamine commented, "You know, I think I know where Master Soken lives," referring to Hakutsuru Shorin-ryu founder Hohan Soken. This brief mention was all it took; a few moments later, the two were off to see the famed master.

Grandmaster Hohan Soken; Summer, 1970

At the time, Hohan Soken was widely regarded as the greatest living *karateka* in Okinawa. Born in 1889, Soken was the nephew of the famed Nabe Matsumura, who was himself the grandson of Bushi Matsumura, considered by many to be the originator of present-day Okinawan karate. As Soken is said to have been Nabe Matsumura's only student, beginning his training at age thirteen, he was indeed fortunate to have been born into such a rich heritage, as it ultimately made him the sole, direct living link to the Matsumura *seito* (orthodox) karate tradition, which

Soken Sensei in later years officially dubbed Matsumura Seito Shorin-ryu.

At age twenty-three, Soken commenced instruction under Nabe Matsumura in the techniques of the *hakutsuru* (white crane) style of karate, techniques which emphasized grace and balance. Those who have seen the film *The Karate Kid* will have witnessed a bit of this style, as the film was partly inspired by *hakutsuru* technique. Work on Okinawa being scarce, Soken emigrated to Argentina in 1924, where he remained until 1945, at which time he returned to Okinawa and began accepting a limited number of carefully-selected students (including, as previously noted, Fusei Kise), teaching Matsumura Seito Shorin-ryu kobudo and also Hakutsuru Shorin-ryu for a few hours each day at his home. At the time Suenaka moved to Okinawa, Soken's reputation as the island's pre-eminent *karateka* was firmly established.

Suenaka was already familiar with Soken, both by reputation and from having witnessed Soken in action at a demonstration conducted by Kise at the air base, at which Soken was both honored guest and featured celebrity, giving a brief demonstration of his considerable skills. Ever since that time, Suenaka had vowed to someday meet the master face-to-face. Naturally, he jumped at the chance to accompany Inamine Sensei to Soken's home. Eager and hopeful, Suenaka and Inamine knocked on the door and were greeted by Soken's wife, who politely but firmly informed them that the master was not home. So ended the great excursion, and the day. Suenaka, however, was not so easily dissuaded.

Since he now knew where Soken lived, Suenaka was determined to gain acceptance as his student. Day after day he traveled to Soken's home, usually in the early evening, after his day's work was done. And so, the dance began, as Suenaka recounts:

"I wasn't turned away, but now (Soken's wife) said, 'Just wait here.' So I waited and waited and nobody came out, so I left. I would get there at about seven o'clock, and at about nine o'clock, I would see these guys leaving—I could hear them in the back practicing as I waited—and then they would be leaving, and I was just sitting there, and I thought, 'Well, I guess I'd better go, too.' I returned to his house almost every night for about three weeks, because I really wanted to meet this man. So every night I would knock on his door, and his wife or one of his *deshi* would come out. . . . 'Oh, well, he's in the back, you have to wait.' So I was patient. I thought, 'Oh heck, if this is the way it's done, I'll wait.' Finally, after about three weeks—there wasn't a class that night—his wife said, 'Well, come on in.' I thought, 'Finally!'

"So I sat and [Soken] came into the drawing room and sat down and introduced himself, and I introduced myself. He said, 'You're not from these parts, are you? You look like us, but you don't talk like us. Where are you from?' I told him, "Hawaii," and he said, "Oh! You must know my nephew!" He had a nephew in Hawaii; I can't remember his name. I said, 'No, I don't know your nephew.' Then he said, 'Well, if I had known you were from Hawaii, I wouldn't have had you wait so long!' And I said, 'Well, if I had known that, I would have told you!'

'Well, no matter,' he said. 'What do you want?' So I told him I would like to be one of his students and learn under him. And he said, 'Well, we'll see. What have you studied?' So I told him . . . about my background, and aikido, and he said, 'Oh, aikido! Very good martial art!' He knew about aikido, and knew about O'Sensei, though they had never met. We discussed several things, and then he said, 'Let me see what you have learned so far.' So I showed him a few *kata,* and he corrected me. Finally, he said, 'You need a lot of help! I'll take you on as a student."

Elated, Suenaka returned to the air base. Although Suenaka told Inamine about his meeting, and Inamine accompanied Suenaka to his first training session with Soken, Inamine did not study with the master beyond that first encounter. When Suenaka returned for his second training session, sans Inamine, Soken reqested he attend all subsequent sessions alone. Although Suenaka at the time didn't question Soken's judgement ("I never questioned him, not then."), Soken later admitted his decision was based on a perceived difference in style, philosophy, and attitude. It seems the two, for whatever reasons, simply did not "hit it off." Though Inamine was eager to return, it speaks to his martial cultivation that he, too, did not question Master Soken's decision. Despite being the reluctant bearer of bad news, Suenaka and Inamine remained good friends. Though he and Suenaka ultimately lost touch, Inamine today continues to teach karate in Okinawa, and is one of the founders of Ryukyu Shorin-ryu karate.

Although he inquired about dues, Soken seemed disinclined to accept money in exchange for instruction, at least from Suenaka:

"I asked him how much I should pay him for instruction, right after I started I asked him. But he replied, 'I don't want to talk about monetary payment for classes.' That's the way he would say it. So I never asked him again, because I think it would have made him angry. But I would always put some money in an envelope and give it to his wife, and I would always bring them several bags of groceries, about once a week. Soken Sensei knew, of course, but he never said anything. Plus, I would always help out around the house whenever I could, you know, cleaning the house or the yard, sometimes with the cooking. Which, of course, is the way it should be."

One might think that, being the venerated master that he was, studying with Soken Sensei would be a very formal, traditional affair. But as Suenaka discovered from the start, Soken didn't seem to bother much with formality:

"Soken Sensei only had a handful of students at the time, most of which studied sporadically. He really didn't conduct classes per se. If you were to go to his dojo, maybe with somebody else, he would say, 'Oh, good, let's do something!' But it wasn't a real structured class environment. He would show us a few things, then say, 'Let me see your *kata,*' and I'd show him a *kata;* then, 'Now let me see yours,' and you'd show him a *kata.* Then he'd say, 'Let's do it together,' and he would say, 'You're messing up here and here.' He'd show us the finer points, correct us, then say, 'Okay, good-bye.' And he'd go into the house while we stayed in the back and worked on what he'd shown us. That's how he taught.

"When I arrived, we'd sit and have some tea, very informal. Usually he would be watching TV when I got there . . . he loved to watch TV. He liked samurai movies, gangster movies, and some of the old Japanese family-type shows. Sometimes he'd just say, 'Hello. Go in the back and I'll be there shortly.' So I'd go in the dojo and start working on *kata* or something on my own. Then he'd join me and say, 'Okay, I just saw you make a mistake, let's work on this form,' and that would be the beginning of class. Of course, we'd bow before we started, even though he didn't have a *kamiza* (position/object of respect; a scroll, altar, etc.) or anything. His dojo was about four-hundred square feet, maybe, very small, in the back of the house. Nothing fancy, no *tatami,* all wood with a wooden floor and with *makiwara* (striking post) outside lining the left side of the dojo, facing the courtyard, buried in concrete. Traditional *makiwara,* no

Suenaka Sensei with Matsumura Seito and Hakutsuru Shorin-ryu karate Grandmaster Hohan Soken at his dojo in Okinawa; Summer, 1970.

canvas or rubber—just twisted straw, all different sizes. I think he may have had one light bulb inside the dojo, but no air or heat, of course."

As the *kobudo* designation declares, weapons skill was an essential part of Matsumura Seito Shorin-ryu kobudo karate. It wasn't long after Suenaka began studying with Soken that Suenaka got his first taste of the master's exceptional skill in this facet of the style, as Suenaka recalls:

"It was maybe during my third or fourth class with Soken Sensei. We were practicing that night and he was showing me some techniques with the *bo*—empty-hand defenses against the *bo*, against a *bokken*, things like that. I was doing some *suburi* (individual movements) with a *bokken*, and he asked me if I'd ever worked with *kama*, which is the sickle, of course. I had seen him working out with *kama* before, during his demonstration on the base with Kise Sensei. So I said no, I hadn't worked with the kama before. I said that I had been very impressed with his demonstration on the base, but I told him that I was afraid of the *kama*—too sharp (laughs). He said, "Well, if you're careless you can get hurt, you can damage your eye, like I did." I think it was his left eye that was partially blind. He'd been doing a *kama kata* once—this was well before I'd met him, of course—using a *kama* with a long chain attached to the bottom of the handle and with some big fish hooks attached to the far end of the chain, shark hooks, sort of like a *kusari-gama*. He showed me the *kata* once . . . he'd swing the *kama* around him, back and forth, and throw the *kama* up into the air and catch it by the fish hook end of the chain, wrap it around his neck and his body and then throw the fish hook end out, you know, snapping it straight out. He said one time when he was spinning the chain around his arm, one of the hooks nicked his eye. So I said, 'Well, apparently you're not afraid of the *kama!*,' and he said, 'No. It can be dangerous, but now I can teach you how to be careful!' He said something like, you know, if you fall off a horse you have to get back on, because that's the only way you can get better.

"Anyway, he told me, 'Strike my head with the *bokken*.' And I said, 'Oh, no, I don't want to hit you, Sensei!' And he said, 'Don't worry; you won't! But I want you to try.' I wanted to be a good student, so I took an easy *shomen* strike at his head, and he said, 'No, no. You must strike me hard.' I was looking at those sickles in his hands, and I said, "You're not going to cut me, Sensei?' He laughed and said, 'Don't worry, I'm not going to cut you. Swing it hard.' I didn't give it everything I had, but I came down hard, you could hear the *bokken* cut the air, and then whaaaang! It stopped cold, and my whole body shook with the impact up my arms. And I looked and there was the *kama*, just an inch away from my hands—he was holding it with the handle down along his forearm, with the blade curving outward and up, and he'd caught the *bokken* on the inside curve of the *kama,* against the edge, and the other *kama* was just a few inches from my face.

"I said, 'Wow! That was impressive! I'd end up with my head split open by the *bokken* if I tried that!' And then he said, 'Now . . . try it again.' So I came down again, even harder this time, and whaaaang!, he stopped the *bokken* again, just the same as before. And he said, matter-of-factly, 'What do you think about that?' I said, 'Sensei, that was tremendous!' But he smiled and said, 'Look at it.' And he let go of the *kama* and it was stuck into the *bokken,* the blade was buried almost a half-inch into the *bokken.* 'Look at it closely,' he said. And I looked at it, and the blade was stuck in the exact same spot where he'd stopped the *bokken* the first time, directly into the groove the *kama* had made in the *bokken.* The first time, he'd made the groove; the second time, he'd buried the *kama* into the groove. Now that impressed me. And then he said, 'I can do it a third time!' And I said, 'You don't have to prove anything to me. I know you can do it a hundred times!' And that's when I truly decided, 'I must learn from this man.' He was one of the greatest martial artists I ever knew. What O'Sensei was to me with aikido, Soken Sensei was [to me] with karate."

Even though Soken and Ueshiba were great masters, Suenaka cannot recall ever hearing either of these two great men refer to themselves as such:

"Soken Sensei never called himself a master. He would always refer to himself as *'tanmei,'* which in Okinawa *hogen* (dialect) literally means 'old man.' O'Sensei was the same way. He would call himself *'ojii-san,'* which is Japanese for 'old man.' O'Sensei would always say, even towards the end of his life, "This old man is still learning.'"

Despite his uneasiness with *kama,* Suenaka did learn a few *kata.* He spent more time, though, learning the *tonfa, sai,* and the *bo.* 'The *kama* was his forte,' Suenaka says of Soken, 'and the *bo.* We studied a lot with the *bo.*"

A few words of clarification are needed concerning the difference between Matsumura Seito Shorin-ryu kobudo and Hakutsuru Shorin-ryu karate styles. Although Suenaka studied both under Soken, the master concentrated their study in the Hakutsuru Shorin-ryu forms. Exactly what techniques and *kata* comprise the Hakutsuru system is a subject deserving of another book, and though he is familiar with them, Suenaka generally does not teach them all, as he explains:

"Soken Sensei told me, 'Don't teach them all to anyone unless you're certain they'll never use them against you.' I think he taught them all to me, although he might have had even more that he didn't. For him, the Hakutsuru were the *hiden,* the secret techniques. Some styles have *kata* they call Hakutsuru, like in Goju-ryu or Shito-ryu, and some of them are similar to Soken Sensei's *kata,* perhaps in the basic striking or parrying moves. But they're not the same."

"Matsumura Seito is what was taught to the general public. But the Hakutsuru forms were not. Although they were technically a part of the Matsumura Seito system, they were held separately from that system. Soken Sensei is the one who dubbed them Hakutsuru. They were the family *kata* only, a more pure form of Matsumura Seito taught just to the family which is why Soken Sensei knew them and nobody else did. Hohan Soken was the first person, and the last, to teach the Hakutsuru forms to those outside of the family."

It was also about this time that Suenaka met the woman who was to become his wife. In the coastal town of Itoman, on the southeastern tip of Okinawa, there is a place known as Kenji-no-To, or "suicide cliff." The origin of this rather doleful name stems from World War II, when many Japanese soldiers leaped off the cliff to their deaths rather than face the disgrace of capture by American forces. While on his way with a few friends to visit a shrine erected there, Suenaka stopped in town to enjoy the local festival of Haryusen, in honor of the god of the sea (Itoman was primarily a fishing village). While walking amongst the vendors, he spied a woman carrying a three-foot-wide basket on her head, filled to overflowing with fish as she wandered the festival, selling the catch of the day. Ever the gentleman ("She was a cute little thing!"), Suenaka offered to help her carry the heavy basket. "She laughed at me," Suenaka recalls. "'Oh, you couldn't carry this!', she said. But she put it down and I carried it . . . it was heavy. It must have been pretty close to seventy pounds!" The two walked together for a while, with Suenaka carrying the basket for his petite but surprisingly strong companion. When it was finally time for him to move on, Suenaka purchased a snapper for dinner that night and made a mental note to return. One meeting led to another, and on December 16, 1963, after more than two years of courtship, Roy Suenaka and Kanako Oshiro were married.

Even with his full schedule—including air force duties, studying and teaching aikido, studying karate under Soken, and his budding romance—Suenaka found time to meet and briefly study with other Okinawan karate elite. During his time on the island (briefly interrupted by assignment to Hawaii, discussed later), Suenaka sought out as many masters as he was able. The list includes Uechi-ryu successor Kanei Uechi, in his principal *dojo* in the town of Futenma; Kobayashi-ryu founder Chibana Chosin, as noted earlier; and many of Okinawa's most noted Goju-ryu practicioners, among them Shinjo Masanobu, Kinjo Masanobu (not related—Masanobu is a common Okinawan family name), Metoku Yagi (the current grandmaster of Goju-ryu), and Eiichi

Miyazato (founder of the All-Okinawan Karatedo Association), all of whom were senior students of Goju-ryu founder Chojun Miyagi. Miyazato at the time was a sectional chief in the Ryukyu Prefecture police department, headquartered in Naha (Ryukyu is the southernmost Japanese island chain of which Okinawa is the largest, and is a prefecture, or territory, of Japan itself). Miyazato was head of the riot police force as well as being charged with overseeing departmental self-defense instruction, and it was with Miyazato that Suenaka eventually developed the closest association and friendship, though not until his second stay in Okinawa.

It's not surprising that Suenaka's electrical skills would again get him noticed by Uncle Sam. In the fall of 1961, Suenaka found himself embarking on his first of three TDY assignments to Vietnam. The first trip was as part of MAAG, the Military Assistance and Advisory Group, departing in October and returning to Okinawa in December. During his stay, Suenaka acted purely as a technical advisor to the South Vietnamese military, based out of the joint U.S.-Vietnamese air base at Tan Son Nhut, just outside of Saigon. His second trip was longer, beginning in June of 1962 and ending six months later, again in December. Unlike his first stay, this time Suenaka traveled as the primary electrical engineer for what was euphemistically known as "Prime Beef." Consisting of a select group of soldiers, technicians, and engineers, Prime Beef was on constant stand-by, and had to be ready to depart for Vietnam or elsewhere with twenty-four hours notice or less.

For this second trip, Prime Beef was temporarily assigned as part of the 555th Red Horse combat engineering squadron. Working out of Tan Son Nhut, plus the huge U.S. coastal complex at Cam Ranh Bay, and other bases (Da Nang, Phuket, Pleiku, Chu Lai, Thuy Hoa), the 555th were loaded onboard C-130 cargo planes (or occasionally transported overland by truck) and parachute-dropped into the jungle, whereupon they would quickly bulldoze the area and build a temporary airstrip so heavier planes could land with the troops and materiel necessary to construct a more permanent field support base, as Suenaka recalls:

"It was a fast, fast operation. We did low static line drops . . . we'd jump and go hide in the trees, and then the other planes would come and drop the equipment, the bulldozers. We worked like wild men! We'd bulldoze out a field, knock all the trees down, then they would have the graders come in and level out the fields, and we would put down the steel grids . . . for the makeshift airfield. Then we had to run all the runway lights, put up buildings. . . . After the airfield was built, the planes would land and load up the heavy equipment and take it back. . . . Usually it took us two days—sometimes three or four. We *had usually a sixty-man team."*

Although already a seasoned hand-to-hand fighter, Suenaka's time in Vietnam introduced him to combat of a very different kind:

"We were attacked many times, with rockets, regular ground fire, lots of mortars, and RPG's (rocket-propelled grenades). We held our own; we didn't have any other support from anybody, except for air support and sometimes artillery, if they weren't too far away. . . . Sometimes there were times when some of the other teams got hit by our own air fire, but we were lucky. They would strafe the area around us and that would chase the enemy away. It was scary at times, but exciting. Good experience—maybe not too good, but it made men out of boys."

Suenaka's third trip passed a bit more uneventfully than his second, lasting from mid-summer of 1964 to December, the first two months of which were spent primarily at Da Nang or Cam Ranh Bay ("It had the best beach in the world . . . we used to go surfing and have luaus there."), and the last four at the Royal Thai air base at Don Muang, Thailand, not far from Bangkok, helping to build support bases against possible Communist expansion from Vietnam or China. "The day after we left Da Nang for Thailand, I got a call in Don Muang from a radio buddy of mine," Suenaka recalls. "He said, 'You're damn lucky you left yesterday. The barracks you stayed in is gone.'" It had been hit by a rocket less than a day after Suenaka left, leaving no survivors.

Busy as he was, Suenaka found time to engage in some informal aikido instruction wherever and whenever he could, beginning at Tan Son Nhut during his second Vietnam trip and continuing during his third, both in Vietnam and in Thailand. Of the type of *waza* he taught, Suenaka notes, "It was more combat-oriented, more brutal, because of the war. It was about fifteen guys, mostly people on the base including some special forces personnel, the base doctor, even the base Catholic chaplain. We had classes about twice a week maybe, fairly regularly."

His time in Vietnam aside, Suenaka's stay in Okinawa was not continuous. Military personnel were only allowed to remain at an overseas assignment for a limited period of time before mandatory rotation stateside, and Suenaka's number was called in the summer of 1965, when he received orders to return to Hawaii for assignment at Hickam Air Base in Honolulu. The timing could not have been more inconvenient. Not only was Suenaka's aikido *dojo* flourishing and his studies with Soken equally successful, but also his new bride was pregnant with their first child; not the best time to pull up stakes and move, even if it was back home to Honolulu. Before they departed, Suenaka resolved to request transfer back to Okinawa as soon as regulations allowed. As for the Okinawa Aikikai, since Suenaka was the only government-certified aikido instructor there—indeed, the only instructor—he was forced to sell off his mats and close it down. Although the class continued on the base for a short time, taught by Suenaka's senior students, soon after they transferred, the classes ended entirely.

As soon as Suenaka learned of his assignment back to Hawaii, he traveled to Japan to inform O'Sensei and take his leave. "I told him I had to go back to Hawaii, and he said, 'Oh, well, that's good for you!', because he knew it was my home. He said, 'You keep it up, keep practicing!' But I told him, 'I will be back!' And I had a final dinner with him before I left."

After settling down in Honolulu, Suenaka lost little time establishing a class on the air base ("I called it Hickam Air Base Aikido. Pretty simple.") and renewing contacts with his former teachers and friends. Even though just twelve years had passed since Koichi Tohei's initial visit, and seven since Suenaka departed (recall that he was assigned to California in 1958, then Japan in 1961), aikido in Hawaii—at least in Honolulu—was showing signs of the personal, political, and philosophical rifts that were just surfacing at the Aikikai Hombu. The first indication of trouble was evident in the *waza* Suenaka witnessed in Honolulu, as he recalls:

"My aikido was different from theirs. Even though it was Tohei Sensei who taught us all, and who taught me in Japan, when I got back to Hawaii I could see many changes. I tried to contact the others, the people I studied with before I left for Japan, but I didn't get along with a lot of them. They had their own, I suppose, ideas and philosophy of what they thought aikido was. The only reason they wanted to reestablish ties with me at all was because I had studied with O'Sensei. They said, 'Show us what he taught you,' and I said, 'Well, come to my dojo and I'll show you.' Not many of them did.

"By that time, the aikido in Hawaii had become very physical. Of course, it had been twelve years since Tohei Sensei's visit, and many of the *aikidoka* had become very established and very high-ranking instructors, and had their own ideas about what they wanted to do with aikido, their own agendas, and they weren't going to see eye to eye with anyone else there because they thought, 'Hey, I've got just as much experience as you, you can't tell me what to do. I'm going to do my thing and you do your thing.'"

It bears reminding that all of the aikido instructors appointed by Tohei at the end of his first stay in Hawaii were already high-ranking instructors in other arts, such as judo and karate, arts relying more (though not exclusively) on physical strength, rather than subtlety, for their effectiveness. As any *aikidoka* knows, one's first impulse when experiencing difficulty in making a technique work is to "muscle through it," to force it to work using physical strength exclusively, rather than relaxing into the technique and letting one's *ki* flow to perform it correctly. In a standard *dojo* situation, the instructor would step in and correct the problem. However, although Tohei made regular visits to Hawaii, the instructors he left behind were largely on their own and, despite their considerable experience in other arts, new to aikido. As such, it's not surprising that when they encountered difficulty in making a technique work, they would either force it with physical strength, modify it into what they felt was a more "effective" form, or both. This, Suenaka feels, was much of what was at the heart of the changes in aikido technique he saw upon returning to Hawaii. There were also other, more political reasons for the contrast in Hawaiian aikido *waza:*

"By the time I returned, about half of the instructors were going the other way, they were allying themselves with the Hombu. Tohei Sensei taught a lot of *ki,* and I think around that time Doshu had already paid at least one visit to Hawaii, or had sent instructors over from the Hombu, who taught differently from Tohei Sensei, and Tohei himself continued to visit, and sent instructors. There was already some friction between Doshu and Tohei Sensei at the Hombu, and some of it was spilling over into Hawaii. Since Tohei really stressed *ki,* and Doshu didn't, it was causing some problems. So some instructors were gravitating towards Doshu, and others towards Tohei."

As much as Japan had been foreign to Suenaka when he first arrived there, Hawaii now seemed almost as unfamiliar, more so because of the aikido politics and changes in *waza.* Suenaka pretty much kept to himself, avoiding contact with the other *aikidoka* and attending to his new duties as husband and father; his first child, Valerie, was born Thanksgiving Day. He also continued to study the karate he had learned under Hohan Soken, though again, he did so on his own, avoiding any real contact with area practitioners: "Karate was getting like aikido, really politicized. I wasn't interested in politics. I just wanted to train." The one exception to this self-imposed isolation was his renewed friendship with "Koa" Kimura (see chapter two). "We called him 'Koa' after the koa tree," remembers Suenaka, "because it was one of the hardest trees on the island, and that's what he was like. He was hard as nails. He owned a chain of auto body shops and had a dojo in Pearl City, next to Pearl Harbor—the Pearl City Aikikai."

Kimura's techique was as hard as he was, in the sense that he'd rattle your brains when he threw you, yet he still stressed *ki,* just as Tohei did. "Nobody stood a chance against him, even as old as he was," states Suenaka. "He was a tough guy. He'd begin every day with a thousand punches, hitting this big tractor tire he kept by the door to his office, and he wouldn't go into the office to start his day until he'd done his punches." Kimura and Suenaka got along splendidly, and

Kimura's *dojo* was the only one in the area that Suenaka allowed his students to visit for additional study. Likewise, many of Kimura's students often studied with Suenaka. Ultimately, when he finally returned to Okinawa in August of 1967, Suenaka left his students in Kimura Sensei's care.

Suenaka was thrilled to return to Okinawa, as was his wife. He actually had requested assignment to Japan over Okinawa, but by that time Japanese assignments were scarce, as it had become a popular station. But Okinawa was just fine. For Kanako Suenaka, it was a return to her home, and for her husband, a return to Soken Sensei, and much closer to O'Sensei than Hawaii. However, he wasn't returned to Kadena. His initial station was on the island of Miyako (part of the Ryukyu chain and just under two-hundred miles southwest of Okinawa) as part of detachment one, 437th AC&W (aircraft control and warning) squadron, in charge of the electrical section. Small as the base was, it had a recreation hall, and shortly after arrival Suenaka was again teaching aikido and karate to all comers.

Suenaka's fondness for brawling has already been noted. He never went out looking for a fight, but he certainly didn't retreat from the opportunity when it presented itself. Although one can look at this dispassionately and accurately conclude his many fights provided an opportunity for him to test his technique in an actual combat situation, much like the way he handled challenges at the Okinawa Aikikai, Suenaka readily admits his basic reasons for fighting were no more complex than his simple love of a good knock-down drag-out brawl. Even though his time in Miyako was short, he was there long enough to enjoy the biggest single street fight of his life. Suenaka describes it thusly:

"These two coast guard guys—one was a big Samoan, Ro Faleafine, and the other was a coast guard chief named George, about six foot or so—they and I were out drinking at a local bar one night, sitting and having a good time, minding our own business, and there were some local women sitting with my friends. So this man comes in with about a dozen or so guys with him, and he said to us, 'You guys get out.' And we said, 'Who are you?' He said, 'I own this place.' 'You own nothing,' we said, 'You get out. We're having a good time. Don't bother us.' By now the women are scared, so we say 'Who the hell do you think you are?' It turned out it was his bar, and the women were his employees, you know, in the bar to 'entertain' people. Evidently he didn't like it when they hung out with American servicemen. Well, we didn't want to leave, so we said, 'Make us!' All the guys with the bar owner started tensing up and moving in, and the owner pulls a knife. So when Ro sees the knife, his eyes light up, he says, 'Oh! You want to fight with knives? Wait! Wait!' So he leaves, and the owner sits down and waits! I swear, he waits! So we had another beer while we waited for Ro, and about half-an-hour later he comes back with this five-foot-long staff with machete-looking blades on the ends . . . turns out he was a Samoan knife dancer! He'd gone all the way back to his base to get it! So he comes in there and starts whipping this thing around, spinning it, and says, 'Okay, now I'm ready to fight!' Well, everybody in the place backed up and went, 'Whoa! Big knife!' And the owner says, 'No, maybe we won't fight with knives.' I mean, Ro was awesome. So they decided to just jump us, and we started fighting hand-to-hand, right there in the bar. Ro was so strong, he'd just pick up two guys and bang them together, bear hug them, toss them around, just knocking these guys silly, and when he hit them, they were out. Meanwhile, George and I were mixing it up, having a great time! There was stuff flying everywhere—chairs, tables, beer bottles, it looked like a scene from a Western movie.

"About that time two or three of the owner's guys ran out, and the owner had disappeared. So Ro and George and I went outside, too, and there must have been fifty guys out there! At least it looked like that many, and the owner standing with them, and he yells something like 'Charge!' So we waded in and started fighting. We fought from where the bar was, almost at the end of town, all the way to the other end of town. It wasn't very far, about two or three-hundred feet, and the street was really narrow, about twelve feet wide, maybe, just wide enough for two cars, with buildings on both sides. I was using a lot of *irimi* techniques, moving straight in *irimi-nage, ago-tsuki-age,* and a few *tenkan* techniques; when I'd see a guy coming out of the corner of my eye, I'd turn *tenkan* and throw him, or go *irimi-nage* again. Ro was still doing his thing, throwing guys around, and George was just beating people with his fists. He didn't have any training, but he had guts. He was a scrapper. By the time we got to the other end of town, we'd beaten anybody who'd attacked us. There were a lot of guys just standing and watching, but they didn't want any more of it, and there were a lot of guys just knocked out in the street, bleeding. Of course, we got hit several times, too. You can't get in a fight like that without being hit. But none of us went down. I think I had a cut on the back of my head, maybe somebody had hit me with a bottle. George was hurt the most, but he was still standing. We were looking for the owner, but he was gone, and when he left, everybody else went away. There was just the townspeople standing there watching us. So we went back to the bar and had another drink and then we left.

"Of course, the Coast Guard and Air Force commander both got letters from the mayor, and we all got called into a big meeting with the mayor and the commanders and a colonel who was the civil affairs team leader, sort of the head of the local American embassy. We didn't get a permanent reprimand in our personnel records, but they scolded us. 'We've got to have good rapport with these people,' they said. 'You can't go around beating up the locals!' 'But they attacked us first," we said, 'They wanted to kill us!' 'Well,' they said, 'then next time, run.'"

Even with his experience in jujutsu, judo, karate and boxing, aikido is what Suenaka found himself using the most in brawls of this kind. Rather than being the ineffective method of practical self-defense detractors say it is, aikido technique, properly executed, proved an ideal ally:

"In an encounter like that you have to constantly keep moving, because there's always somebody coming up behind you, trying to grab you and take you down. It's like in a *randori* (defense against multiple attackers) situation, where you try to stay out of the circle so you can see all of your attackers. There's no time to stand there and slug it out with one guy, other than a quick *atemi* to the face before executing a throw, because there's always another guy coming in at the same time. You always have to move, to make sure your back is covered. I didn't use too much hand stuff, because you didn't always have the room or time for *kote-gaeshi, shiho-nage,* or *nikyo.* Rather there was a lot of *ago-tsuki-age, irimi-nage, kata-otoshi, sumi-otoshi,* or *koshi-nage* whenever somebody tried to grab me. About the only real grappling techniques I used was a lot of *ude-osai,* a lot of arm drag take-downs, sometimes arm and joint breaking. The minute you feel someone grab you, boom! You take whatever you can get, and if you have to break a bone, you break it. People may think, 'That's so violent!' But it was either that, or get injured badly or die. You have to put yourself mentally into a situation like that and think, 'What would I really do?'"

Of course, not all bar confrontations ended in brawls. Suenaka recalls another incident during his first stay in Okinawa, during a visit to Futenma, which started much as the incident on Miyako, but which ended in friendship, and serves to further illustrate Suenaka's philosophy when it came to being challenged:

"I was sitting there drinking my beer, as normal, and there were several other Americans in there as well, we were all drinking together. So in walks this guy with a crowd of other guys with him, maybe a dozen or so, all packing guns. And he says, 'Everybody out! Out!' And everybody in the bar, including a lot of the GIs, they immediately split. But me and my friends, we didn't move. So the guy walks up to me and says, 'You Okinawan? What are you?' So I tell him, 'I'm from Hawaii. I'm an American soldier.' "Get out,' he says, and I said 'No! Why are you kicking me out? I'm just having a beer, and I'm going to have another after this one!' So he looks at me like I'm crazy and he says, 'Do you know who I am?', and I say, 'No, and I don't care. I don't care if you own this bar, I'm not leaving!' He says, 'Well, I do own this bar!' So I say, 'Then what are you doing kicking a customer out? Are you stupid or something?' Well, that's when the bartender's eyes got big and he goes like, 'Oh no!,' he starts getting real nervous, and he says to me, 'You must respect him! You can't talk to him like that! He's a big *oyabun* (crime lord) here!' I said, 'So what? He still can't kick me out!' "Well, by this time the *oyabun* is getting more curious than mad. He says, 'Aren't you scared of me?' I said, 'Why should I be scared of you? I haven't done anything wrong! If you want to fight, let's go! We'll go outside, just you and me, leave your boys behind, and we'll fight!' So he says to me, 'You're either cocky or stupid or both, but you've definitely got balls!' But I told him, 'No, it's not that. If I'm not doing anything wrong and you pick on me, I'll fight you, anytime, if you force me.' 'You're not afraid to die?,' he said. I said, 'No, not if I'm fighting for my rights. Now, if I've done something wrong, I might run instead!' And that's when he laughed and he came over and put his arm over my shoulder and said, 'I like you. My name's Kuba. I'm the *oyabun* here in Futenma.'

Left to right: Mrs. Soken, Mrs. Kanako Suenaka, Valerie and John Suenaka, Hohan Soken, at Soken's home; Summer, 1970.

And I said, 'Oh, well, it's very nice to meet you! You're a good man to know!' He said, 'From now on, any time you come here, you don't pay for anything; the drinks are on me!'"

Back to Miyako. By this time Kanako was pregnant with their second child, due in March, and Miyako was no place to have a baby, nor raise the one they already had. As with his initial assignment to Okinawa, Suenaka called in a few favors. "I had some Hawaiian friends in assignments in Naha, in Okinawa, and one of them was a major. I went there and asked them to help me get an assignment to the main island, to Okinawa." Three months after arriving on Miyako, Suenaka, wife, and daughter packed up and headed for their new station in Naha.

Suenaka's second stay in Okinawa was even busier than his first, especially since he now had a wife and family to provide for, a family which shortly grew by one with the birth of son John in March of 1968. Kanako Suenaka was unfailingly supportive of her husband's martial pursuits, understanding that the man she married was who he was. In return, Suenaka realized his partying days, with the exception of his visits to Tohei in Japan, were at an end, and so too his brawling days. It was just as well, as he had little time for it anymore, busy as he became with not only his family and job but his martial studies, which quickly surpassed the intensity seen

Grandmaster hohan Soken with Valerie and John Suenaka in Suenaka Sensei's home at Naha Air Force Base, Okinawa; 1971.

during his first Okinawan stay, with Kanako allowing her husband time to continue both his frequent trips to the Hombu and his studies with Soken Sensei. Indeed, the aged karate master became a close family friend and something of a surrogate grandfather to Valerie and John, who called him *ojii-chan*. As most photographs of Soken show a stern and unsmiling man, it is quite something to see photographs of the celebrated master bouncing Suenaka's children on his knees, his face creased by a rare, gentle smile. Soken himself had two sons, both of whom were born in Argentina during the twenty-one years he spent there and both of whom elected to remain upon their father's return to Okinawa in 1945 (though one later returned).

Suenaka reunited himself with Soken Sensei less than a week after his arrival in Naha ("I didn't write him to let him know I was coming, or call him. . . . I don't even remember if he had a telephone."). Lessons resumed as if they'd never stopped, with Suenaka studying with the master about two days during the week, a few hours at a time, plus Saturday and Sunday ("Usually on Saturday and Sunday, I lived there! I would sometimes stay at his house.").

Although from day one Soken insisted Suenaka wear a black belt when studying ("You've practiced enough martial arts to wear a black belt," Soken said), he never tested Suenaka, nor assigned him any rank. Suenaka, thankful to be studying under Soken—and by this time well familiar with the master's rather eccentric ways—paid no mind to rank. To this day, he prefers not to mention rank at all. "Belts are just something to hold your *gi* closed," he says. "If you're studying something just to get a rank, you're studying for the wrong reason."

When the day of Suenaka's first karate promotion under Soken arrived in 1968, not only was the honor unexpected, but the method even more so, as Suenaka recalls:

"One day were were practicing, and he gave me his certificate. I said, 'Oh, what's this for?' I thought he was just showing me the certificate. He said, 'This is yours.' And I said, 'My certificate? But I didn't even test!' He said, 'You are always being tested, whenever you practice with me. . . . I don't do formal tests.'

"I said, 'Well, you know, there's nothing on this.' He had the wording, but not the date, or name, or rank. And he said, 'Well, you fill in the blanks.' I said 'Fill in the blanks?! You mean, the date and name?' And he said, 'Yes, and the rank.' So I said, 'Well, what rank do you want me to put down?' And he said, 'What rank do you think? What rank do you want?' I said, 'Well, this is my first rank—*shodan* (first degree black belt), right?' By then it had been over seven years that I had been studying with him. He said, *'Shodan?* No, no, no, you're above a *shodan.'* So I said, 'Well, okay, *nidan* (second degree black belt).' And he said, 'No, no, no, that's still too low.' So I said, 'Well . . .'"—I thought I'd play a joke on him!—'Well, *hachidan* (eighth degree black belt) is okay.' And he said, 'Well, that's a little too high.' I said, 'Well, I really don't know, Sensei,' and then he said, 'You can put yourself down as a *godan* (fifth degree black belt).' I was really touched by this. I said, *'Godan, Sensei?* I never even tested once! I've been a no-rank!' He was very special to me, and I guess I was special to him, because he said, 'You worked for this—you devoted a long time and its been a long time coming. I want to promote you to *godan.'"*

Suenaka continued to study with Soken for the remainder of his stay in Okinawa. Before his departure back to the U.S. in June of 1972, Soken promoted Suenaka once again, this time a more modest jump to *rokudan* (sixth degree black belt). It was to be his last promotion under the Master: Soken retired from active teaching in 1978 and died in 1982, at the age of ninety-three.

As always, Suenaka had begun teaching aikido and karate at the Naha air base gym not long after his arrival there, only this time he also taught judo. It had been a while since he had been truly active in judo, busy as he was with aikido and karate. Although he'd enjoyed limited study at the Kodokan as time allowed during his visits to Tokyo, he felt it was time to become more involved again. Another reason for his return to active judo study was the arrival in Naha of his brother Greg, who studied aikido, Kyokushin-kai karate, and judo. Greg had enlisted in the air force four years earlier and, as fortune would have it, had been assigned to Suenaka's station. Greg urged his brother to begin a class (not that Suenaka needed urging), and include judo instruction.

Suenaka's judo class wasn't the only one on Naha air base. There was another, taught by an Okinawan, though he primarily taught children. In addition, Suenaka one day noticed a group of airmen studying tournament judo on their own, obviously training for competition. Among them was James Hatch, at the time a *sandan* (third degree black belt), whom Suenaka happened to know as both were assigned to the same squadron, though they'd been unaware of their shared interest. Suenaka and Hatch began talking and a few minutes later found themselves on the mat together. "I dumped Jimmy a couple of times, and he said, 'You're only a *nidan?*' I said, 'Yes, but I've been a *nidan* for almost ten years.' Jimmy said, 'Oh, man! That's when I started judo!' He said there were some tournaments on the islands they wanted to compete in, and he asked me if I would coach them, so I said yes. I became the coach of the Naha air base judo team."

As noted earlier, during this second assignment in Okinawa Suenaka also developed a friendship with Goju-ryu stylist Eiichi Miyazato, then forty-five years old, and founder of the All-Okinawan Karatedo Association. In addition to karate, like Suenaka, Miyazato was a *judoka,* and it was through this shared study that Suenaka first made Miyazato's acquaintance, since both men were members of the All-Okinawa Judo Association (AOJA). Suenaka had joined the AOJA not long after he began coaching the Naha air base judo team, since one had to be a member to compete in area tournaments. Local AOJA members met and trained at the Naha Budokan, which was where Miyazato taught both judo and karate (in addition to teaching at his own *dojo*), and it was there that the two men first met.

As both Suenaka and Miyazato were busy with their own *dojo*s, they didn't have much time to study together, other than shared study at the Budokan and the occasional tournament. Suenaka would sometimes visit Miyazato's *dojo*, and Miyazato, Suenaka's, though not very often. Suenaka occasionally gave aikido demonstrations at the Budokan at the request of the judo *renmei* (organization). "Everyone was very diplomatic with their comments about aikido. They would say, 'Oh, it's very nice,' but most of them only cared about judo and karate." Miyazato was the same. Although a *rokudan* in judo at the time and a former all-Okinawa judo champion, his heart belonged to karate, as Suenaka notes:

"I think at the time he was an eighth or ninth dan in Goju-ryu, and, of course, a senior student of Chojun Miyagi Sensei. All the others studied for a while and then left to open their own schools, but Miyazato was really the only student who studied continuously with Miyagi Sensei until he died. In recognition of his loyalty, just before he died Miyagi gave Miyazato many of his family treasures, including his belt."

Suenaka, Hatch, and the rest competed in many of the island's judo tournaments, as well as some international tournaments held in Japan:

"We did pretty well, recalls Suenaka. We didn't take very many first [places], because those Okinawans and Japanese were tough. Jimmy was good; he took several firsts in his weight class, but almost every tournament in which we competed we'd go home with one or two firsts, one second, and several thirds. Of course, this was all in randori; there was no kata competition then. And that was pretty good, because we were fighting some internationally-known names in judo, and we were nobodys! Yet we would place second against these guys. And we fought people like Paul Maruyama, who was at least four-time national grand champion, Dean Tower, Willie Peavey, and Ben Nighthorse Campbell, who of course now is the senator from Colorado. Our guys competed against these guys and more, some of the biggest names in judo, and we did really well. And of course through judo is also how I was able to meet Miyazato Sensei and Tamaki Sensei, who was the chief instructor of all Okinawan judo—he was a huge man, real tough, but really nice—all these big guns on Okinawa. All through the Budokan."

Even though Suenaka was heavily involved in judo and karate, his heart remained true to aikido. He made his first trip back to the Hombu a few months after he arrived in Naha, and continued making regular visits thereafter, about half-a-dozen in all in the two years from his assignment to Naha up to O'Sensei's death in April of 1969. "I used to take off every three months and stay there for several weeks at a time. A lot of it was accumulated leave time, and a lot of it was permissive TDY, which I was able to get because of the nature of my duties." Suenaka also used his time in Japan to study at the Kodokan with Mifune and Ito Senseis (as mentioned earlier), and also to compete in judo tournaments with the Naha air base team. Suenaka was a happy man when he made the journey back to the Hombu that first return visit, as he recalls:

"I entered the front office and I asked if O'Sensei was in. Of course, you didn't just walk in and demand to see O'Sensei, so I just politely inquired if he was around. I guess somehow word got back to him that I was there, because a few minutes later he came walking in and said, 'Where have you been?' And we embraced, just like the first time I ever visited there. I was so happy to see him; I was always happy to see him!"

Notwithstanding that he'd just turned eighty-five years old, O'Sensei was still a robust and active presence in the Hombu. By then, however, it was known that the Founder was ill, and that the malady was serious. Though it is common knowledge today that O'Sensei died of liver cancer, none but a select few knew then the true nature of O'Sensei's illness:

"All I ever heard was that he had a serious liver problem. The family had taken him to doctors by then—he never went to the doctor—and he had been diagnosed, but the doctors didn't really tell anybody what it was. Maybe some people knew, but it wasn't common knowledge. It wasn't until after he died that it was revealed he'd died of liver cancer. And that's very typically Japanese. They believe if they tell you, say, that you have a fatal illness, the diagnosis will become a self-fulfilling prophecy. So they'll maybe tell a close associate or family member, and leave it up to them to tell the patient. I don't know if O'Sensei knew it was cancer, or if he was told. He might have known anyway because of how well he knew his own body, and how in tune he was with his own *ki*. But he never showed any weakness when I saw him. He never seemed feeble. I saw him for the last time about two months prior to his death, and he was out on the mat, even more dynamic than I had ever before seen him! In fact, he gave a final demonstration just a few weeks before he died, ill as he was. Some people say that on the very day he died, he got up from his death bed and grabbed a *deshi* and conducted a final practice, and then he went back to his bed and lay back down and passed on.

"I know he was in Iwama while he was sick, and his family coaxed him back to Tokyo, because the doctors were better there. But he knew his death was imminent, and he wanted to die in Iwama, because that was his most favorite place on Earth, his spiritual center was there. His farm was there, and the mountain with the waterfall where he did *misogi;* there's pictures of him standing under that waterfall, even one with him and Doshu practicing together beneath it. He was very connected to that place; for him, that was where the *Aiki O'Kami* resided, the Great Spirit of Aiki, where he went to renew his own spirit. But the family prevailed and brought him back to Tokyo, and I know he wasn't very pleased about that. Morihiro Saito Sensei wanted to accompany him, but O'Sensei told him to remain in Iwama and take care of the *jinja,* rather than watch him die, which I know was extremely hard on Saito Sensei, because of his tremendous loyalty to O'Sensei.

"Even though he died in Tokyo and his ashes were buried in Tanabe, where he was born, you can still feel O'Sensei's spirit in Iwama when you go there today. When you approach the *jinja,* it's electric; you can feel his presence. The last time I was there, the hair on my arms and the back of my neck stood up, just like it used to when I was standing close to him, and I thought, 'He's here!' The feeling is uncanny."

Suenaka was also thrilled to be reunited with Koichi Tohei, and as during his first stay in Japan and Okinawa, Suenaka traveled extensively with him. "O'Sensei was really semi-retired by then," Suenaka says," and he didn't travel all that much anymore, so I traveled even more with Tohei Sensei." Indeed, with the gradual retirement of O'Sensei from active practice, it fell to Tohei Sensei as chief instructor to assume an even greater role in supervising and structuring classes at the Hombu and in defining the *waza* that was taught. Kisshomaru Ueshiba Doshu continued to oversee the administrative details of the Hombu and Aikikai's daily operation but, like Tohei, O'Sensei's retreat from the day-to-day operation of the Hombu increased his duties as well. It was now Doshu, rather than O'Sensei, in his role as his father's successor, who approved rank promotions and signed the certificates, although it was usually Tohei Sensei who recommended students for promotion. (Note: Suenaka's last Aikikai promotion was to *godan,* although O'Sensei awarded him his *menkyo kaiden* when he was a *nidan.* Koichi Tohei later promoted him to *godan,* awarded him an *okuden* and made him a *shihan* in his organization, which will be discussed later. The Dai Nippon Butoku-kai [Japanese Association for Martial Virtues] has since recognized Suenaka as *hachidan,* as did the International Black Belt Federation in 1980.) Ultimately, Doshu's word was the final one in all Hombu affairs. Given the natures of these two proud men, it was sadly inevitable that the situation would give rise to the personal and political conflicts that ultimately caused the irreparable split between Tohei Sensei and the Aikikai. This, Suenaka recalls with sadness:

"It all boiled down to politics and egos. I'm pretty certain that O'Sensei was aware that there was trouble brewing, but his philosophy was, 'We must all stick together and learn together in the true spirit of aikido.' But it didn't turn out that way. By then, there were students at the Hombu who preferred one or the other, Doshu or Tohei; some would attend only Doshu's classes, and some only Tohei's. I attended both. Of course, there were very many other teachers who had broken away from Hombu well before this to establish their own styles, including Kenji Tomiki, Gozo Shioda, Rinjiro Shirata, Minoru Mochizuki. And there were other students, instructors still affiliated with the Hombu, who were aware of the political strife at the Hombu and who elected not to take sides and instead completely separated at that time, like Andre Nocquet and Mutsuro Nakazono. But this was a conflict beyond that, because it was occurring at the Hombu, right under O'Sensei's nose.

"Tohei Sensei was a very powerful figure in aikido at the time, politically as well as technically, his *waza,* so a lot of the students sided with him, because his technique was the strongest of all the instructors there. Because he was my first teacher in Hawaii, I felt I had no choice but to remain loyal to him, and because I knew his was the best technique. But there were also those who sided with Doshu, because they felt since he was the son of O'Sensei, they were showing their allegiance to him. For me, it wasn't a question of disliking Doshu, because I liked him very much and still do, or of siding with or against O'Sensei. My ultimate loyalty was to him, regardless of whom I sided with politically. Even then, O'Sensei told me, 'When you teach aikido, teach the principles that I have taught you. Don't go astray. Stay on the path of *aiki*.' He told me that more than once. Again, he knew what was going on, but I really think he was above such pettiness, he didn't care about politics. But the conflict concerned him. Like he said, no matter what happened, 'Just stay on the path of *aiki*.' But politically, you could see then that it was the beginning of the end."

Sometimes Suenaka saw O'Sensei in Tokyo. Other times, the Founder could be found in Iwama. In the latter case, Suenaka traveled there with either Tohei or Doshu, to pray and meditate. But as one of his chief *deshi*, Suenaka spent a great deal of time with Tohei, furthering their relationship:

"Whenever I visited Japan, Tohei Sensei took me under his wing, so I went everywhere he went. If I was in Tokyo for two weeks, just about the whole two weeks I would spend with him. Of course, he was still teaching at the Hombu, usually the second class, since Doshu or O'Sensei taught the first. After his class was over, sometimes he would say to me, 'You stay here.' So I would stay at the Hombu and practice there for the rest of the day, until he returned and said, 'Okay, let's go.' But most of the time after the morning workout, he would say, 'Come on, let's go,' and I would accompany him to his teaching assignments; universities, some of the other dojos. Most of the time I served as his *uke*, though occasionally he allowed me to instruct. I can't remember anyone else accompanying us. Usually it was just he and I, although there were times where people would meet us at an assignment, and then we would go out to dinner afterwards or back to his apartment to party. Sometimes I wound up staying there. Since he was the chief Hombu instructor, Tohei Sensei chose most of his assignments himself. O'Sensei wasn't really involved in that aspect anymore, even though Tohei always had a lot of autonomy. And Tohei didn't let Doshu tell him where to go."

During his first stays in Japan and Okinawa, Suenaka would always stay at the Hombu whenever he visited there. By this time, though, there were many more *uchi deshi*, and the Hombu was more crowded. Plus, Suenaka was older now, more mature, and so didn't feel as comfortable staying with the younger *deshi*. "There was a favorite place of mine, right across the street from the Hombu. It was the Kikyo-Kaku, a *ryokan*, or family-run Japanese inn, where I stayed most of the time when I was in Japan."

While O'Sensei and Doshu were reticent about their feelings concerning the political factionalism dividing the Aikikai, Suenaka recalls that Tohei was more vocal:

"He didn't go in-depth about his feelings at that time. He just said that he felt that there was a lot of animosity within the organization, and that something was about to happen. He didn't specify what, but I knew that he and Doshu weren't getting along. He was making plans then, but he didn't really make those plans clear until after O'Sensei's death. Everybody then knew that O'Sensei didn't have much longer, and I think they were just waiting for him to die to make whatever move they wanted to make."

Suenaka Sensei saw O'Sensei for the last time in late January of 1969, just under three months before the Founder's death. By this time, O'Sensei was in Tokyo, and was spending his days in rest, meditation, and prayer. As such, the two men found more time to talk privately than in past visits. Suenaka fondly remembers these visits:

"We had a few times at the Hombu where we just sat and talked. We didn't talk too much about the general state of aikido; he seemed more interested in what I was doing with aikido, especially in Okinawa. He always asked me to tell him all about that; it always seemed very important to him, and up to the end he encouraged me to keep promoting and teaching aikido there. I told him, 'It looks like aikido is going to flourish in Okinawa,' and he said 'Great! Keep doing what you're doing.' He was very pleased that of all the places in the world, aikido was establishing itself in Okinawa, and that made him very happy. There's several schools there today, Tomiki schools and Aikikai schools, but the Okinawa Aikikai was the first, and I'm very glad that I could give that to O'Sensei, to give back just a little of what he gave me.

"But more than anything, O'Sensei would tell me, 'Don't go astray.' He was seeing what was happening around him, and again, he was concerned, but not because of the politics. He saw that people were already going astray, straying from the path of *aiki,* doing their own thing, teaching their own style. I never asked him what he thought about what was happening around him; I doubt he would have wanted to talk about it. Plus I didn't think it was my place; I was a little fish in a big pond, you know? And although he knew I was allied with Tohei Sensei, he knew why, and that I didn't want to make waves as far as completely separating from the Aikikai or his son.

"Our very last conversation, we were sitting in the front office. It was brief, but I remember it very well. 'Always stay with the same principles I have taught you,' he said. 'Make aikido better, but don't change the principles. Whatever you do, don't stray from the path of *aiki.'* That was the last thing O'Sensei ever told me. 'Don't stray from the path of *aiki.*'"

Morihei Ueshiba O'Sensei died in Tokyo of liver cancer on April 26, 1969. Suenaka was in Okinawa when he learned of the Founder's death, two months after it happened, in June. "Someone mentioned to me that they'd heard O'Sensei had passed away, so I immediately sent a letter to the Aikikai, and Masatake Fujita Sensei sent me a letter back confirming that O'Sensei had died." Not knowing the state of the Aikikai now that O'Sensei was gone, Suenaka wrote a letter to Tohei Sensei, asking what to do. A few weeks later Suenaka received a reply from Tohei, requesting that Suenaka join him and others in Japan for a meeting in September at his apartment in Tokyo. The gathering turned out to be the first organizational meeting for Tohei's new organization, the Ki no Kenkyukai:

'There were a lot of guys there. There was Fumio Toyoda, Shizuo Imaizumi, Mitsugi Saotome, about a dozen people. It was an informal party, but the purpose was to discuss the fate of the organization and apparently to entice us to side with him in the event that he was to split from the Aikikai. It was pretty obvious by then that that's exactly what he was intending to do. He said, 'Are you coming with me or not? What are your plans?' And we all said, 'You're our teacher. We're with you.' We were all his *deshi,* you know? O'Sensei's death was still having a big impact, not so much on the whole aikido community as it was on those of us that were closest to him, as all of us at the party had been at one time his *uchi deshi.* Some of us had mixed emotions about the decision, that splitting away from the Aikikai was in some ways, not a betrayal, but a very hard decision to make. And some who sided with Tohei eventually re-affiliated themselves with the Aikikai. But a handful of us remained with Tohei Sensei, because again, he was our teacher. It wasn't that I felt I was betraying O'Sensei or his memory, because I remained loyal to his teachings and his spirit. But now that he was gone, Tohei was my teacher, and I felt now I had to give him my love."

It was easy to love Koichi Tohei. While possessed of considerable ego, he could definitely walk his talk. His *waza* was as powerful as the best *aikidoka* of the time, and his command of *ki* surpassed all but that of O'Sensei himself. He was handsome, urbane, and charismatic, naturally outgoing and social. "He loved to sing, just ham it up, and to dance," recalls Suenaka. "He was a very good dancer, and just naturally gregarious. He was one of the greatest partiers of all time! He knew all kinds of people, and everybody loved to see him. I loved him a lot; it was hard not to."

Having taken a side, Suenaka found himself practicing less at the Aikikai and more with Tohei at the Ki no Kenkyukai, first established

Suenaka Sensei with Koichi Tohei at the Ki Society Headquarters in Tokyo; Summer, 1971.

in 1971 and where Tohei taught his newly-created style of Shin-Shin Toitsu aikido. As the name suggests, Shin-Shin Toitsu aikido was very much influenced by Tempu Nakamura's Shin-Shin Toitsu Do. It is very indicative of the increasing bitterness that Tohei was feeling towards Doshu that he brazenly situated his new *dojo* just a few blocks away from the Hombu; an unmistakable affront, whether intentional or not. All this, despite the fact that Tohei was still technically chief instructor at the Aikikai, and hadn't yet officially separated from the organization. However, as Suenaka said, it was evident to all who cared to notice that the split was both inevitable and close at hand. By this time, Tohei was adamant about concentrating his instruction at the Aikikai on *ki* and *ki* principles, teaching Shin-Shin Toitsu technique, despite Doshu's repeated warnings to concentrate less on *ki* and more on the technical aspects of *waza*. Yet Tohei continued to ignore Doshu's edicts, just as Doshu made it increasingly clear that he would not tolerate Tohei's disregard for his authority much longer.

Even allied as he was with Tohei, Suenaka could not in good conscience completely divorce himself from the Aikikai. He did not share Tohei's bitterness towards Doshu, and Doshu was still O'Sensei's son, his designated heir. Suenaka made a point of practicing regularly at the Aikikai Hombu, and continued to accompany Doshu on trips to Iwama, to pray at the *aiki jinja*. It speaks to Doshu's high character that he did not seem to resent Suenaka's alliance with Tohei, although the two never discussed the current political situation. Perhaps Doshu knew that, regardless of politics, Suenaka's heart remained true to O'Sensei.

Although he had declared his allegiance to Tohei, Suenaka kept recent events to himself when he returned to Okinawa and continued to teach as if nothing unfavorable had happened. Officially, nothing had; again, Tohei was still chief Hombu instructor, and wouldn't completely sever ties with the Aikikai until several years later. But tensions between Doshu and Tohei continued to build. As always, at the heart of the dispute was Tohei's continued insistence on emphasizing *ki* and *ki* methods over straight *waza*, as Suenaka states:

"He concentrated a lot more on the four basic principles to unify mind and body, *ki* exercises, *ki* training methods—*kiatsu-ho, ki-no-kempo, ki-no-seiza-ho*, what he called the six *ki* training methods, and much of what he'd learned from studying with Tempu Nakamura, rather than O'Sensei. And Tohei's command of *ki* was really

Suenaka Sensei with Koichi Tohei at the Ki-no-Sato in Tochigi, Japan; December, 1993.

incredible. When we would do *ibuki* breathing, he could make one breath cycle last three or four minutes, sometimes more. There was no doubting he knew what he was talking about.

"Tohei's technique definitely changed at the same time he began to emphasize *ki* more. He became a lot more fluid, and although it was still physical, it was not quite as physical as it had been in the beginning, like in the fifties and early sixties. Back then he was almost totally physical, you could feel his sheer physical power. But during the time O'Sensei was dying, Tohei began to change, he knew he was going through a transition, from aikido technique to just *ki*. I think he always patterned his technique after O'Sensei's, but he was more of a technician, whereas O'Sensei's technique was obviously much more intuitive. But their *waza* was very similar. Also, by the time of the change, Tohei was pushing fifty [years of age], and that affected his *waza*, too. I think he was forced to become less physical and concentrate more on *ki*."

Suenaka noticed that despite Tohei's growing control of *ki*, his control was markedly different from that of O'Sensei:

"O'Sensei's *ki* was a palpable force, you could feel it emanating from him just standing next to him. It was almost like a vibration that filled the air around him. It probably had a lot to do with psychology, too, knowing that he was such a powerful man definitely had a psychological effect on you. And then when you touched him, you could immediately feel the energy flowing. Tohei Sensei's *ki*, though, was a lot more physical. You didn't really feel his *ki* until he touched you or you touched him. Only when he began to move did you really feel it, a lot of power, a lot of force there. He was a strong man physically, and so was O'Sensei, but with O'Sensei it was more subtle, whereas Tohei Sensei, when he threw you, you knew you were being thrown by someone! There was a high degree of physical command, and his *ki* was manifested in it."

The difference between O'Sensei and Tohei Sensei's grasp and command of *ki* was also readily evident in their *kiai* (spirit shout):

"[O'Sensei's *kiai*] was a high, ear-piercing shout that you could hear almost half-a-mile away, and it would just stop you dead in your tracks. It was deafening, it hurt your eardrums. It permeated your whole body, your entire being, you could feel it spiritually, mentally, and physically. It made you weak, made you sometimes want to just collapse. Tohei Sensei's *kiai* was much lower, very guttural. When he directed a *kiai* at you, it was like a blast of wind, like something physical had hit you, like the sound of a steamship's horn. It scared the hell out of you! You'd jump when you got hit with it. With O'Sensei, you didn't jump. You just collapsed, you felt instantly sapped. I suppose you could sum it up by saying Tohei Sensei's *kiai* was more physical, external, while O'Sensei's was more spiritual, and affected you on a more visceral level, internally."

Suenaka's visits to Tokyo dropped off after O'Sensei's death. Between then and the time Suenaka made his final departure from Okinawa two-and-a-half years later, he visited perhaps two or three times, though he continued to stay for several weeks at a time. Things at the Hombu obviously weren't the same anymore, and for Suenaka, the escalating tension between Doshu and Tohei definitely detracted from the pleasure of the visits:

"Tohei was continuing to teach Shin-Shin Toitsu aikido at his school, and he was teaching much of the same at Hombu, and Doshu didn't like it. But Tohei's attitude was, 'Well, I'm chief instructor, so I'll teach what I want.' By this time (1970) Tohei was spending more time teaching *ki* than he was teaching *waza,* much more than ever before O'Sensei's death. The change was quite obvious; at least half of every class, Tohei would spend on *ki* exclusively, and it was getting to be even more than that. Sometimes, he taught entire classes on nothing but *ki.* Doshu obviously saw this as a direct challenge to his authority, which it was. I think perhaps had Tohei Sensei not been chief instructor, Doshu would have been able to overlook their differences and said, 'Fine, do what you want to do,' because different Aikikai instructors always taught differently, in many ways. None of the *shihan* taught the same way. It was wrong, but that's the way it was. To challenge each and every *shihan* I think would have destroyed the entire power structure at Hombu. But because of Tohei Sensei's position within the Aikikai, second only to Doshu, Tohei really left Doshu with no choice but to confront him."

The strained relations between Doshu and Tohei came to a head about eighteen months after the first meeting in Tohei's apartment.

Suenaka himself witnessed what became one of the final nails in the coffin during a visit to the Hombu in 1971:

"It was my second-to-last trip or so to Japan, in June or July. I was staying at the Kikyo-Kaku across from the Hombu. I'd been there about two weeks by then, and nothing really remarkable had happened, the visit was going along pretty much like any other. I was studying both at the Aikikai Hombu and at Tohei Sensei's dojo. I was at the Hombu that day, and Tohei came by to get me, like he usually did, we were going out on a teaching assignment. Before we left, he told me, 'Wait a minute, I have to go take care of some business.' And then he walked into Doshu's office, which was at the end of the hall as you entered the Hombu, to the left. So I waited out in the hall.

"It wasn't long after Tohei went in there that I heard them arguing; it was a rather loud argument, and I could hear it easily from where I was, just outside the door. Basically, it was things coming to a head; that they didn't see eye-to-eye, and that the split between them was imminent at that point. I was becoming concerned as I listened, because they were obviously so angry, I thought maybe something was going to happen, you know? So I knocked on the door and peeked in, and they immediately said to me, 'Get out! You have no business in here.' It was very intense in there, so of course I immediately backed out and closed the door. They each issued an ultimatum. Tohei said, 'Fine, if you don't want me to teach *ki* here, I won't,' and Doshu said, 'I don't. If you want to teach ki, you'll have to go do it somewhere else, but not here.' And then Tohei came out of the office, very angry. He didn't say anything; he just said, 'Let's go,' and we went out. Of course, I didn't ask him about what had just happened, because I never questioned him. It wasn't the final split, but I think that was the first time that they'd confronted each other directly about what was going on, and they recognized that the split was by then inevitable. I really believe that argument was the beginning of the end."

In late 1971, Suenaka received word from his command that his time in Okinawa was again at an end, and he was asked to submit his list of preferred assignments stateside. Knowing that his next station change was imminent, Suenaka had been giving some thought to the matter, and had decided a Western U.S. assignment would be best. When he submitted his dream sheet, high on the list was California, Hawaii, and Colorado. Naturally, the air force sent him to Charleston, South Carolina. Suenaka wrote Tohei about his impending departure, and Tohei asked Suenaka to join him in Tokyo for one last visit. The two met at the Ki no Kenkyukai Hombu. By then, Tohei's blueprint for what would soon become the International Ki Society was almost completed, and included establishing several bases in the U.S. After again affirming that Suenaka remained loyal to him, Tohei designated him *shihan,* and Ki no Kenkyukai representative for the Southeastern United States.

This last trip to Japan was the first Suenaka made where he did not visit the Aikikai Hombu. The reason was Tohei Sensei. "He said, 'You have to pledge all of your allegiance to either me or the Hombu. And if you're with me, I don't want you going to the Hombu at all.' So I spent all of my time that last trip with Tohei Sensei." Nor did Suenaka submit a formal letter of resignation to the Aikikai:

"Tohei said, 'You're either with me, or you're not. It's just that simple.' So that was that. I don't know if I offended Doshu by not officially resigning. I didn't mean to, but perhaps I did. But given the circumstances, I had to do what I had to do, and I can't go back and change it. I ceased being a paying member, I stopped paying dues, so I suppose they (the Aikikai) eventually realized I had split, too. And of course they knew I was allied with Tohei Sensei. But there was no formal good-bye. Nothing. It was just over."

Suenaka Sensei and family departed Okinawa for Charleston, North Carolina, on June 25, 1972—his thirty-second birthday. He had thirty days leave to kill, plus a week's alloted travel time, some of which he spent in Hawaii with his family, before reporting to his new assignment. When it came time to leave, he flew to San Francisco, then took a bus to Reno, Nevada, where he had a car waiting. ("We didn't need a car in Okinawa, so I bought one there before I left and arranged to pick it up in Reno.") From Reno, Suenaka and his family drove east to Connecticut to spend a little time with the ever-gracious Yoko Bartlett and her family (a longtime friend of Kanako Suenaka and whose son, Masaharu, hosts several golf tournaments every year which are attended by many of the East Coast's prominent Japanese *budoka* and businessmen) and do some sight-seeing in New England before heading south to Charleston, where he arrived August first.

More than any other previous assignment, Suenaka made the move to Charleston with significant reservations. His reasons for requesting a Western U.S. assignment extended beyond the familiarity of the locale and the close proximity to his family home. Japanese-Americans were more common there than perhaps any other region in the U.S. His wife, though learning, still spoke very little English. For her, the United States might as well have been another planet, so Suenaka was more conscious than ever of finding a place to live where she might at least discover a few friends who spoke her native tongue, and so feel less a stranger. Understandably, his Charleston assignment came as a total surprise: "I said, 'Charleston? Where is that?' And they said, 'South Carolina.' I said, 'South Carolina? Where is that?'"

Suenaka's friends only increased his growing doubts about his new assignment. Discrimination and racism seemed to be the words on everyone's lips: after all, they said, it *was* the South. Finally, he became concerned enough to bring his worries to the attention of his command. Paradoxically, he was told his mixed ancestry was the very reason he was being assigned to Charleston. Besides Charleston Air Force Base, the Lowcountry, as it is known to natives, at the time boasted Charleston Naval Base, one of the largest on the East Coast, and it was not uncommon to find sailors with Philippine, Okinawan, or Japanese brides. As such, he was told, the locals tended to be more tolerant of these "mixed marriages," and so Suenaka, with his Okinawan bride, would no doubt feel more welcome. To this day, Suenaka has yet to comprehend how a Japanese-Hawaiian marrying an Okinawan could be considered a "mixed marriage," but one does not question the wisdom of Uncle Sam—at least not while you still work for him.

Upon arrival in Charleston, Suenaka and his family immediately set to work settling into their base housing. To his great relief, as time passed Suenaka realized the stories of Southern discrimination were largely exaggerated. Indeed, he encountered no more racial intolerance in Charleston than he had anywhere else he'd lived. If anything, Charleston's role in the Civil War and the inevitable changes that followed served to make Charlestonians perhaps more tolerant than most, for what their ancestors, regardless of race or politics, had survived. This, combined with the local economy's heavy reliance on tourism and the area's famed "Southern hospitality," resulted in a populace more likely to welcome strangers than exclude them. While he occasionally encountered instances of intolerance, they were few, and always the exception rather than the rule. The final proof: Suenaka is still there. "This has been my home for the past twenty-five years now, so that says a lot for Charleston," he says. "If it was as bad as everyone said it was, I wouldn't have stayed."

Just as with his other assignments, Suenaka wasted no time in finding a place to teach aikido, an effort lent even more importance this time because of Suenaka's affiliation with the fledgling International Ki Society. It was important to both Suenaka and Tohei to set up shop as quickly as possible. Other than a few cursory excursions, Suenaka didn't spend much time checking out the local martial arts scene, being more concerned with starting his own *dojo*. Surprisingly, considering the great number of current and former military personnel living in the area, there was only one martial arts school in Charleston at the time, headed by Albert Church and offering Kamishin-ryu karate and a smattering of other martial arts. Not only was there no aikido, few people Suenaka questioned had even heard of it.

As always, Suenaka first investigated teaching in the base gymnasium. Unlike before, his request was denied because of lack of space. As he was assigned once again to the base civil engineering squadron, he asked his squadron chief if there were any empty buildings on base where he might teach. One month after his arrival in Charleston, he found himself martial lord and master of a tin-sided qounset hut:

The Charleston Air Force Base quonset hut which housed the head-quarters of the Southeast U.S. Ki Society; Summer, 1973.

Left to right: Ricardo Sosa, Suenaka Sensei, Charles Lewis, at the Southeast U.S. Ki Society headquarters; Summer, 1973. The pieces of paper affixed to the wall in the upper right corner list Tohei Sensei's Four Basic Principles and six basic ki training methods. The ki kanji below them is by Tohei Sensei.

"It was about a thousand square feet. It had about ten windows, a door at each end, a wooden floor, no bathroom and no air conditioning, so it got hot, even with the windows and doors open. It had two small rooms at one end, and we used one for a changing room and the other was my office. It was actually a pretty good-sized building, but sometimes we had up to twenty-five people working out in there, so it got crowded fast. I didn't have any mats, but I met a guy named Wylie Howell who taught taekwondo on base and he had three mats that he wasn't using, so he let me have them. I called it the Charleston Air Force Base Aikido Dojo."

Unlike previous assignments, this time Suenaka advertised for students. Part of the reason was because he could do it for free in the base daily bulletin, and also because Tohei was actively seeking students for his new organization. As such, Suenaka's first Charleston students consisted entirely of base personnel and their families. Also, as word got out that he was teaching, he encountered others on base who'd had training in other disciplines, and many of these people began study as well (his first student was a former *judoka,* his second the *judoka's* friend.) Ultimately, his students brought civilian friends to study. While this method of building a student body was nothing new to Suenaka, the general level of his students' inexperience certainly was. In Okinawa and Hawaii, it seemed you couldn't turn around without bumping into someone who had trained for years in this style or that. Consequently, the majority of his students came to aikido already familiar with what it was like to step onto the mat, even if it wasn't an aikido mat. Not so in Charleston. Suenaka's students were, more than ever before, complete beginners. It was from this base that Suenaka was faced with building the charter membership of the Southeastern U.S. Ki Society.

Suenaka charged his first Charleston students dues of fifteen dollars a month, almost all of which he sent straight to Tohei Sensei, keeping only what he needed to purchase supplies for the *dojo*. Suenaka was of course keeping Tohei apprised of his progress with regular letters to Japan. Likewise, Tohei wrote personal letters back to Suenaka, encouraging him and relating the latest organizational news, augmented by occasional printed bulletins from the Ki no Kenkyukai Hombu.

Despite its humbleness, Suenaka's Charleston *dojo* was the first known aikido school in South Carolina, and one of the few on the East Coast at the time. Although aikido was flourishing on the West Coast, given its close proximity to Hawaii, by the early 1970's it was still relatively unknown in the rest of the United States, with but a few major East Coast schools. Perhaps the most notable at the time was Yoshimitsu Yamada's *dojo* in New York City, opened under the auspices of the Aikikai upon his arrival there in 1964. Mitsunari Kanai also had a *dojo* in Boston, Massachusetts, established in 1966, about the same time that Shuji Maruyama began teaching aikido in Philadelphia, Pennsylvania. Although there were other *aikidoka* who taught in the Eastern United States. at about the same time, Yamada, Kanai, and Maruyama seem to have been the major players.

Koichi Tohei visited the United States the following year, in the spring of 1973, to conduct a major seminar at the University of California, Fullerton campus, and at which he requested all his *shihan* be present for an organizational meeting. Roderick Kobayashi was teaching there at the time, and he, like Suenaka, had declared his allegiance to Tohei. Besides Suenaka and Kobayashi, others who attended this first U.S. Ki Society meeting included Shizuo Imaizumi and Fumio Toyoda, who accompanied Tohei from Japan; Yoshihiko Hirata, based in Seattle; San Francisco's Hideki Shirohira, Hawaii's Calvin Tabata and Ben Sekishiro; plus Shuji Maruyama, Harry Ishisaka, and several other senior instructors, most of whom had already allied themselves with Tohei or were considering doing so. (All of the *shihan* just listed have since broken away from the Ki Society and have either re-affiliated with the Aikikai, or formed their own independent organizations. Also, as an interesting side note, Suenaka recalls using one of Ishisaka Sensei's students, a *kyu*-grade *aikidoka* named Steven Seagal, as *uke* while demonstrating a technique at the seminar.)

Those attending the Fullerton meeting were told to prepare for major changes, as Tohei was now making no secret of his definite plans to split from the Aikikai. By this time, Tohei and Doshu had struck a draconian agreement: Tohei was free to teach what he wished, as he wished, but he would have to do so completely separate from the Aikikai— in effect, Tohei was forced to formulate a new style of aikido, without the benefit of Aikikai resources or drawing on the Aikikai student body. (Tohei's description of circumstances leading up to this agreement, as well as the particulars of the agreement itself, can be found in his *Book of Ki: Co-ordinating Mind and Body in Daily Life.*) Shortly after this agreement was struck, Tohei mailed a letter to all his *shihan* describing the new arrangement, and in effect saying, 'It's finally time to go public.' The creation of the Ki no Kenkyukai was well and truly under way.

Indeed, the chief purpose of the Fullerton meeting was to further lay the foundation of the Ki Society itself. Tohei gave to all attending a copy of *Ki Sayings,* a small black book he wrote which contained the fundamental philosophies of Shin-Shin Toitsu aikido, as well as Ki no Kenkyukai membership certificates, and even Ki Society lapel pins. It is important to note that although Tohei would not officially announce his separation from the Aikikai until May 1st of the following year, it was at this meeting that he first declared to all who would follow him that the split was, in his mind, already a reality.

Even though Tohei had all but officially divorced himself from the Aikikai, no longer teaching at the Aikikai Hombu, he continued even then to teach Hombu-style aikido *waza* in addition to his exclusively *ki* techniques. However, he was actively creating a new teaching syllabus for his *shihan,* with the express intent of gradually shifting instructional emphasis from conventional *waza* to *ki* alone. Central to this new teaching philosophy was that the primary purpose of aikido, specifically Shin-Shin Toitsu aikido, was as a vehicle for demonstrating the power and potential of *ki*. In order for this to occur, Tohei felt the *waza* itself had to undergo a fundamental change. Consequently, he introduced a body of new techniques, some modified from existing techniques, which he dubbed the *taigi* (body exercises). These *taigi* were not *waza* in the general accepted sense, nor are they to be confused with *aiki taiso,* which are basic exercises that embody actual aikido technique, similar to *kata. Taigi,* rather, contained what Tohei felt were the essential techniques of his new system of *ki* training, as well as such pre-existing *ki*-training methods (at least, among his *shihan)* such as the "Four Basic Principles" (keep one point; relax completely; keep weight underside; extend *ki),* and Tohei's six basic *ki* training methods (Four Basic Principles, *ki-no-taiso, ki-no-seiza-ho, ibuki-no-ho, ki-no-kempo, and kiatsu-ho).*

Like his organizational peers, Suenaka Sensei received Tohei's updated teaching syllabus, including the *taigi,* which were similar to existing aikido technique but which bore different names (discussed in more detail shortly). While the changes Tohei proposed were not immediately implemented (nor would they be for several years), Tohei made it clear they would ultimately form the foundation of Shin-Shin Toitsu aikido.

The significance of Tohei's introduction of the *taigi* cannot be underestimated. Remember, at the time Tohei first asked his *deshi* to declare allegiance to him, he was still essentially teaching O'Sensei's *waza.* Political repercussions aside, *deshi* who sided with Tohei were ensured of continued instruction in "conventional" aikido *waza,* albeit more *"ki-*centric," so to speak. Now, Tohei was presenting his *shihan* with an entirely new body of techniques which, though still recognizable as "conventional" aikido, were clearly meant to deemphasize the practical self-defense aspects of the *waza* and ultimately supplant conventional aikido *waza* altogether (again, discussed shortly).

Remember, too, that conventional aikido versus exclusively *ki* aikido was at the heart of Doshu and Tohei's disagreement, and Doshu had made it clear that if Tohei was to teach his *ki* aikido, he would not only have to do it outside of the Aikikai, but he could also not call it aikido, or use conventional aikido names *(e.g., shiho-nage, kaiten-nage, etc.)* to describe his techniques. Perhaps Tohei could have satisfied these conditions by merely assigning new names to conventional techniques, then modifying them as he chose, but the point is academic. The changes Tohei proposed during this California meeting, regardless of their practical validity, were a direct, physical embodiment of the philosophical and political differences that soured his relationship with Doshu and the Aikikai. For his *shihan,* however, the changes were a totally unexpected and, though none would openly admit it at the time, not entirely welcome new development. Among those who suddenly began to doubt their decision to affiliate with Tohei was Suenaka:

"When I returned to Charleston, I began to reflect on what aikido was really all about, and what was about to happen with Tohei Sensei. I remembered what O'Sensei had told me before he died, not to stray from the path of *aiki.* I felt that what Tohei was proposing was doing that, it was abandoning what O'Sensei had taught, and that if I continued to stay with Tohei Sensei, even though I still loved and respected him very much, I would be abandoning O'Sensei's teachings, and I didn't feel that was right. Aikido belongs to all of us, but what

Tohei Sensei was proposing wasn't aikido, at least I didn't feel it was. The only other choices I had, though, was to re-affiliate with the Aikikai, or break off and teach on my own. Because I had already severed my relationship with the Aikikai, and because of the politics there, I didn't really care to involve myself with them again. By this time I was sick of politics; I never cared about politics before, but now I was even more fed up. I didn't devote my life to aikido because of politics, I didn't side with Tohei Sensei because of politics. I studied aikido out of love, love for the art and for O'Sensei, and like I said, that's also why I went with Tohei Sensei. All I wanted to do was to study and to teach the aikido that O'Sensei taught me, and that he taught Tohei Sensei. And I wasn't sure anymore that I could do that and remain with Tohei Sensei."

Despite his doubts, Suenaka continued his affiliation with the Ki Society, remaining the Southeastern U.S. respresentative, continuing to promote his students under the auspices of the Ki Society and send dues to Tohei. Although the Four Basic Principles and six *ki* training methods were an integral part of his teaching, being as they were already established years before, the *waza* Suenaka taught remained completely unchanged, unaffected by Tohei's evolution:

"I taught the exact same way I always had, the same techniques performed the same way, just like O'Sensei taught Tohei Sensei, and the way they both taught me before all the politics. The original aikido, but combined with Tohei's *ki* principles, which were essentially, at least at first, a distillation of what O'Sensei taught. What Tohei did was take O'Sensei's *ki* lectures and demonstrations, and even many of his techniques, and codify them, give them names, or put them in a form so they could be more easily taught. I never saw anything wrong with that. He was doing that years before O'Sensei's death. After all, he was O'Sensei's chief instructor. That was part of his job."

On May 1st, 1974, Koichi Tohei officially resigned from the Aikikai, and two weeks later mailed a letter to noted *aikidoka* worldwide explaining his reasons for separating from the Aikikai. As before, Tohei called his *deshi* together for another meeting in California, another rallying of the troops around their general. Although Suenaka's military duties didn't allow him to attend this meeting, he received a copy of a letter mailed to all of Tohei's *shihan,* formally declaring their independence from the Aikikai. It was essentially a written statement of what had already been proposed and discussed at the earlier meetings over the years. Although the announcement certainly was no surprise, the timing was actually precipitated by prior events in Hawaii. As Suenaka recalls:

"Tohei Sensei had sent a letter to all of us, saying that he had been invited to Hawaii, but Doshu was already there when he arrived. I think they had both been invited to the same demonstration or whatever it was. But because Doshu was there, Tohei had been, I guess you could say, overlooked. He was still officially chief instructor at the Aikikai, although by this time he was more of a figurehead—I don't think he was really involving himself at all in the Aikikai, not even to teach. When he arrived in Hawaii, more attention was paid to Doshu than to him, and he was left in the shadows. I don't know the details on who invited whom, but whoever it was had to know about the problems between Tohei and Doshu. Of course, Doshu and Tohei both had their supporters in Hawaii, and this snub enraged Tohei's supporters. They let those loyal to Doshu and the Aikikai know how they felt, and evidently they were told, 'If you don't like it, get out.' And so Tohei left. I think that's when Tohei Sensei said, 'That's it.' And it wasn't long after that that he called us all together in California again to announce his separation from the Aikikai."

As *aikidoka* reaffirmed their allegiance to Tohei, so did their schools become central in the expansion of the Ki no Kenkyukai. It was during this time that a series of five booklets written by Tohei began to appear, detailing the first of his new *taigi ki* training methods, which he distributed to his affiliated *dojos*. These slim volumes deal entirely with *ki,* with no real mention of *waza* or technique, and show not only Tohei's personal evolution, but also the rapid growth and expansion of his organization. The initial publication, titled *Ki no Shuren Ho* (How to Develop Ki) was published in early 1974. Successive booklets quickly followed: *Ki no Toitsu Ho* (How to Unify Ki), in March of 1974; *Ki no Seiza Ho* (Ki Meditations), printed just five months after the first, in August of 1974, three months after Tohei's formal declaration of independence from the Aikikai (and the first to feature Tohei Sensei's photo on the inside); *Ki no Kokyu Ho* (Ki Breathing Methods) in April of 1975 (the first to note the Southeast Ki Society, c/o Mr. Roy Suenaka, Charleston A.F.B., South Carolina, as an affiliated *dojo*); and the last, *Ki Hygiene.* Suenaka is also listed as the Southeastern U.S. Ki Society director in the 1975 edition of Tohei's seminal instructional book, *This Is Aikido.* Little did readers know that the headquarters of the Southeastern U.S. Ki Society was a modest, sun-baked quonset hut.

It was also around this time, during the rapid expansion of the Ki Society and just prior to the publication of *Ki no Kokyu Ho,* that Tohei awarded Suenaka his *okuden,* or certificate of advanced proficiency, in Shin-Shin Toitsu aikido. Tohei also designated Suenaka a chief Ki Society lecturer, and awarded him a certificate proclaiming same. Even though Suenaka was having strong feelings about the *taigi,* he was still loyal to Tohei, and supported the organization as a whole. However, this would soon change.

With his final split from the Aikikai, Suenaka recalls Tohei telling his students to begin incorprating the next, physical phase of the *taigi* into their general instruction:

"The first *taigi* I think were seven sets of five techniques, basic techniques, that were similar to existing techniques. The main difference was that *uke* and *nage* were to cooperate completely with each other, there would be no resistance at all from either party. In other words, if the nage moved, the *uke* was to move with him, the *uke* would literally throw himself for the *nage*. The purpose was purely *ki* development, and not self-defense at all. The nage never really knew if he was performing correct technique, because the *uke* was taking the fall for him, rather than being thrown with correct technique. There was no *atemi,* even. It wasn't a martial art at all, and it certainly wasn't aikido."

Although Suenaka received the same instructional materials sent to all of Tohei's member *dojo*s, he never incorporated the physical *taigi* into his teaching, consciously keeping them separate from his aikido. His reasons for doing so have already been discussed, and in reality it would still be a year before Tohei began insisting on exclusive *taigi* instruction. However, there were plenty of others who did begin incorporating the *taigi* into their teaching, replacing earlier technique, and those students who began their study of aikido at Ki Society *dojo*s in the years after this change never knew what they were missing. And here, we come to the origin of the wide disparity of aikido perceptions that exist today. In Suenaka's words:

"There are people out there who insist that aikido was never intended to be a martial art, that it was never meant to be a method of self-defense, and that's just baloney. There's a lot of people in California who think that way, and that's where Tohei Sensei had the majority of his dojos in the early days of the Ki Society, so it makes sense that that perception would develop. If you only studied the *taigi,* of course you would think that way. On the other hand, those people who didn't associate with Tohei Sensei, who aligned with Doshu, all they really learned was *waza,* with no real emphasis on *ki.* People who didn't associate with either one, they teach whatever they teach; some of it is good, and some of it isn't so good. But you can't have one without the other! You can't have just *waza* or just *ki* and expect it to be aikido.

"Aikido is a method of self-defense, it always has been, that's what O'Sensei intended it to be. But he also intended it to be a path of love; like he said, the way to spiritual harmony, and that's the path of *aiki.* But O'Sensei managed to do both, to make it a martial art and a way to spiritual perfection, a way to develop your *ki.* But *ki* without real, practical technique isn't aikido, and neither is aikido technique without *ki.* You can't grasp the essence of aikido without the hard, physical technique, and you can't perfect your technique without *ki.* At least I don't think you can, and neither did O'Sensei, because he told me so. O'Sensei taught *ki* and *waza* together, as a whole, because that's what aikido is. So you see people in some dojos today throwing each other without technique, *uke* just taking the fall, and others being really brutal, really physical, no *ki,* and that's where this comes from, the split between Doshu and Tohei. This is what is giving aikido a very bad name. It all boils down to politics. But at the time, I had a very big problem with the *taigi.* I wasn't interested in it at all, and so I didn't teach it. It wasn't aikido."

Suenaka's problems with the Ki Society extended beyond the *taigi,* as he recounts:

"Tohei was pushing for a lot of new memberships, telling us to promote more people to raise more funds for his new Ki-no-Sato, which means the birthplace of *ki,* his *ki* college, which he finally built. He was becoming more and more involved with raising funds for the college, not just from his dojos, but soliciting private donations. He eventually was able to raise about eighty million dollars to build it, and some of that was the money I had been sending him; it was going to build this college, not the organization. But because of this, he became more inaccessible. Instead of being able to deal with him directly, you had to go through others, like Sumiko Ito, whom I had known—she was the administrative head of the Ki no Kenkyukai in Tokyo—and Shinichi Suzuki, from Hawaii, who lived in Japan at that time. When I would send a letter addressed to Tohei Sensei, the reply would come back signed by them. They would read the letter and reply, not Tohei. I had the authority to make contact with Tohei, and yet I wasn't allowed that privilege anymore. I'm not talking about strictly business matters, that's one thing. I'm talking about personal letters to him. I wasn't some Johnny-come-lately. I had been with him from the beginning, in Hawaii, for over twenty years by that time. Our relationship was more than just teacher to student. And yet suddenly I couldn't even talk to him anymore. So I was becoming more and more disillusioned."

Things finally came to a head for Suenaka Sensei in the summer of 1975, during yet another Ki Society organizational meeting, this time in Chicago, during the United States leg of a major Ki Society promotional tour. He met Tohei at Shuji Maruyama's Philadelphia *dojo,* along with Shizuo Imaizumi and Fumio Toyoda, and a seminar was held at Temple University. Strangely, considering the increasing emphasis he was placing on it, Tohei didn't demonstrate the physical *taigi* during the seminar, concentrating instead on conventional *waza,* supplemented by *ki* demonstrations. Tohei also gave a demonstration during a program on a local television station, notable in that actor David McCallum, at the time best-known as one of the stars of the television program *The Man from U.N.C.L.E.*, was also in the studio for a TV interview scheduled for immediately after Tohei's demonstration. McCallum was so intrigued by that brief exposure to aikido that he became a part of the televised demonstration: "Tohei didn't want to throw him around, of course, so he threw us around instead, although he demonstrated a few *nikyo* and things on McCallum, and let him try a few things on us. Nice guy."

After about three days in Philadelphia, Tohei, Suenaka, and the rest headed north to New York City for a demonstration at St. John's University. Shizuo Imaizumi had not yet been installed as the Ki Society representative there, and this demonstration was intended to introduce both him and aikido to New York; Imaizumi remained there upon Tohei's return to Japan. Likewise, the stop in Chicago was to officially install Fumio Toyoda as the Ki Society representative there; he, too, remained behind when Tohei returned to Japan. Other of Tohei's pivotal *deshi* joined the group in Chicago, including Roderick Kobayashi, Calvin Tabata, and more. The days were devoted to giving demonstrations, after which Tohei and his *deshi* would gather for dinner at a local restaurant. The night before their scheduled organizational meeting, dinner was held at a Japanese restaurant on North Broadway, near what was to be the Midwest Ki Society headquarters *dojo*. Suenaka sat at the main table, with the rest of Tohei's senior *shihan:*

"Midway through the meal, Tohei made several organizational announcements, and asked several questions of us. One of them was if we all had his photo displayed in our dojos, and we said yes. He also wanted us all to give him an eight-by-ten photo of us, to put up at the headquarters in Japan. I hadn't gotten mine made yet, and of course he reprimanded me, gently, 'I told you to make it, you have to send it to me,' and I said, *'Hai, hai Sensei.'* . . . And I fully intended to, at that time. And then he said to me, 'And by the way, O'Sensei's picture is down from your wall?' You see, he had asked us all after the official split to remove O'Sensei's picture from our dojos, and I hadn't done it yet. I couldn't. I just couldn't. But I didn't lie to him, I said, 'No, Sensei, not yet.' 'I told you to take it down, didn't I?,' he said. It's not that I was insubordinate or anything. I told him, 'But Sensei, I studied under O'Sensei also. I feel that because he was the founder of aikido and I'm teaching aikido, I revere him as my *sensei* just as you do.' That's when Tohei said, 'But now, I'm your *sensei.* He is no longer your *sensei.* He is dead.' That's what he told me. I don't know if his attitude was influenced by his bad blood with Doshu, but what he said, it stunned me. I didn't tell him no right then, but I said, 'I'm not sure if I can. I love you, I respect you, I'm devoted to you, but that's a hard thing to make me do, Sensei.' But he said, 'You must.' So I said, 'I'll have to think about it.' I began to lose respect for him then, at that moment."

Tohei's demand that Suenaka remove O'Sensei's photo from his *dojo* immediately (no doubt influenced by Doshu's earlier directive to Aikikai-affiliated *dojo*s to remove Tohei's protrait) brought to the surface the misgivings with which he'd been wrestling. "[His request] stirred up all kinds of emotions in me, all kinds of confusion," recalls Suenaka. "I was thinking, 'What do I do?' You know?" As much as he loved the man who first introduced him to aikido, Suenaka began to seriously consider resigning from Tohei's organization. But still, he held out some small hope that maybe a reconciliation could be had, that perhaps he would discover during the meeting the next day some way to remain loyal to both Tohei Sensei and O'Sensei, to remain in the Ki Society without compromising his beliefs or his conscience. It was not to be, as Suenaka explains:

"We were all gathered together in a hotel room, and there was a big argument with Tohei Sensei present. Several people there didn't see eye-to-eye amongst themselves, they differed in their interpretations of Tohei's policies, and weren't following the standards he set. It was blatant insubordination. This wasn't about the *taigi,* mind you, this concerned other things. The quality of instruction was deteriorating, and some instructors were going to seminars and openly propositioning women students, personal misconduct. I witnessed it personally. These were high-ranking instructors in the organization, and they were behaving like this. I would tell them, 'Stop that!,'" and they would say, 'You have no right to talk to me like that!' But I did; I was one of Tohei's *shihan,* and I felt they were conducting themselves unethically and bringing shame to the organization. I brought this to the attention of Tohei Sensei during the meeting, with all the others there, and said, 'Sensei, something has got to be done. I've tried talking to these people, but they don't want to listen. Do you want me to do something about it?' But Tohei said, 'Oh, no, we must all live together in harmony.' I said, 'I'm trying, Sensei, but they're laughing in my face and in your face! Either they're punished, or we have to take it, and I'm not going to put up with it!' But Tohei refused to take any action. He wouldn't deal with what was happening."

It was more than Suenaka could take. In addition to his grave misgivings about the changes in *waza,* Tohei's increasing disassociation from the realities of building the organization and Tohei's denial of O'Sensei's legacy, now Suenaka was seeing the standards of the Ki Society collapsing around him, even before they had a chance to cement. For him, it was the final blow. For the first time in their twenty-two-year-long relationship, Suenaka openly disobeyed Tohei Sensei's wishes:

"I was flabbergasted by Tohei's reaction, and then I became

furious. I turned to these others and said, 'Look, if I have to, I'm ready to take you out right now! We'll do it here in this room, or we'll go outside and do it there, wherever you want, but don't give me this crap anymore, I will not take this anymore!' I said, 'I'm one of the senior *shihan* in this organization, and if I have to enforce Tohei Sensei's policies, I will, I'll do it myself.' And the people I was addressing said, 'We don't have to take this!,' and they walked out of the meeting. Without a word to Tohei Sensei, no explanation, no apology, nothing! They just turned their back on us and left."

It was at that moment that Suenaka made up his mind about what he had to do:

"Sure, I was mad, but it's those kinds of attitudes, not just in the room but the things that I had observed, that can completely destroy any organization, that kind of immaturity. Insubordination, direct disregard for Tohei Sensei, and the reputation of his organization. There was no discipline! I had always lived with discipline; by my father, in the military, in my studies and in my teaching, and I never acted like that at all! These guys had no respect at all for anybody, including Tohei! So after those guys left, I turned to the rest and I said, 'That's it. I want it to be known that this is the last time any of you are going to see me.' The others in the room were dumbfounded. I know a lot of them agreed with me, but they didn't say anything, they didn't support me. I was up there all by myself. I said, 'Look at you! I can't belong to an organization like this! We can't survive like this! I can't be a part of this anymore.' And the entire time, Tohei Sensei just sat there, not even looking at me, not really looking at anyone. He never said anything. If he had shown me some support, just a little, I would still be with him. But after that, I couldn't remain and keep face.

"The meeting broke up then; what more was there to say? I didn't even speak to Tohei Sensei, I was too angry to talk. I left the next day and went home. A lot of the people at the meeting later told me they agreed with me, but a lot of them called me a turncoat, too, you know, 'How could you do that?' But I told them, 'You'll find out one day.' And that's what happened. Today, all of the people who were at that meeting, except for maybe one or two, are no longer members of the organization. After the meeting, after I saw what happened there, I wasn't confused anymore. I knew what I had to do. I don't know what anybody else in that situation could have done, really."

Tohei Sensei remained in the United States for several weeks after the Chicago meeting, still touring the country, giving demonstrations and placing his designated instructors in their new homes. About a month after he returned to Charleston from Chicago, Suenaka telephoned Tohei, who was then in Boston:

"The first thing I did was apologize to him for what had happened in Chicago. I told him I was sorry for becoming so upset, but not for why it had happened, or for what I did. I told him I felt something had to be done, and that he hadn't supported me one iota. He said, 'Well, I know there were problems, but that was not the time for arguing.' I said, 'Yes it was! What other time is there? When are you ever going to get everybody together in one place again like that? Now we can't anymore, nobody is going to want to talk now. That was the time for it, when we were all there.' But Tohei didn't agree, he said, 'No, this is something we must bring up again later, at another time.' He simply did not want to discuss it, or to deal with it.

"'I'm very sorry,' I said. 'I'm very sad, because I've been with you all these years, for almost twenty-three years I have followed you. I revered you, I loved you, you have made such an impact on my life. But now I'm very disappointed in the way things are turning out.' I didn't tell him off or anything. I was just telling him how I was feeling. I said, 'You've taught me more than almost anybody else I have ever known, and given me just as much. But after all I've given you, all the support I have shown you, sending you every bit of the money I have made, doing as you have asked without any compensation or question, now you're not supporting me anymore. You don't have to respect me,' I said, 'I'm the one who has to respect you. But support is what I needed, and you didn't give me any support. And if I can't get any support from you, if this is what I can expect from you from now on, then I don't want to stay around, I don't feel I can be of any use to you anymore. So at this moment, I'm tendering my verbal resignation from your organization. If you want an official one, a written one, I'll send it to you.' And all Tohei said was, 'I am very sorry you feel that way.' And that was the last time I ever spoke with him, the last time I spoke to him for over twenty years.

"After that call, I went to my *dojo*, and I took his photograph down from the wall, next to the *kamidana* (Shinto altar), and I took down the framed calligraphy of *ki* that he'd painted. I gathered together all of my students, including Ron Granville, who was a student of mine from Okinawa who was now teaching in Riverside, California and was part of the organization under me. And I told them what had happened, and why, and that we were no longer part of the Ki Society, and we were not a part of the Aikikai. We were on our own. I have never denied the role Tohei Sensei played in my life. All of my students know the story of my involvement with him, and I still teach everything he taught me, before the problems started. He gave to me more than I can ever really repay. But O'Sensei's photograph is the one hanging in my *dojo* now. It always has, and it always will."

Following his resignation from the Ki Society, Suenaka immediately began work establishing his own organization. He had been pondering the particulars ever since his first doubts about the Ki Society surfaced. It wasn't that he actively desired to set up his own independent shop— he didn't. But seeing the increasingly visible writing on the wall, he realized that it was becoming more inevitable that he would soon find himself on his own, and he wanted to be ready. Still, at the time of his split from Tohei, Suenaka had nothing firm established, only ideas. One of them was to call his new organization the American International Ki Development and Philosophical Society (AIKDPS).

It is readily apparent that the AIKDPS, at least in name, echoed the International Ki Society. It was a conscious decision. "The only words that are really different are 'American' and 'Philosophical,' " says Suenaka. "I still believed in much of what Tohei had taught me, including the importance of *ki* development, and the more philosophical aspects of aikido, so that's where the name came from."

A more thorny issue was what Suenaka would call the *waza* he taught. Yes, it was aikido, but it wasn't strictly Aikikai-style *waza,* nor was it Shin-Shin Toitsu aikido. It was a synthesis of the two. The *waza* was identical to the *waza* Suenaka had learned under O'Sensei, and under Tohei Sensei as the Founder's chief instructor. Yet it actively incorporated the basic *ki* development techniques that bore Tohei's stamp—again, not the physical *taigi,* but the more meditative aspects, personified by the six methods of *ki* development. For obvious reasons, Suenaka needed some way to differentiate in name the *waza* he taught from Shin-Shin Toitsu aikido and what was taught at the Aikikai, as well as other styles:

"I had always tried to avoid the politics whenever I could, yet all of a sudden, there I was, split off from everybody, just like I'd seen so many other people do before. I had tried to avoid it, but I hadn't been able to. Yet not just because of the split, but because of all of the splits that I knew were going to come, all of the others that I suspected would also leave Tohei Sensei, I felt it was proper to give our aikido a name, to set us aside from all of the existing and future aikido schools and organizations.

"I gave it a lot of thought, about what to call it. I talked to several friends, friends outside and inside the martial arts, and they gave me a lot of different ideas. I had some communication with Toyoda and Maruyama and some other people, because they were starting to have feelings as I had, so we kept in touch with some regularity. They and some others were suggesting that maybe we should all join together and form our own organization, apart from the other organizations, but I didn't feel that it would work. It wasn't a selfish thing on my part, nor do I think it was on their parts, either. We all just saw what was happening around us, and we were looking for some solidarity. I said no, if we do that, we'll just end up the way Tohei Sensei did, no matter how hard we try not to. I was so tired of the situation by then, I just didn't want to take the chance of finding myself in that boat again. I said, 'You do your thing and I'll do mine.' And of course, that's what happened. Maruyama now has his Kokikai, and Toyoda formed the Aikido Association of America, although he recently re-established ties with the Aikikai. And I have my organization."

The name Suenaka ultimately chose for the *waza* he teaches was Suenaka-ha Tetsugaku-ho aikido:

"The term *ha* means an offshoot of a style or system. It means other things as well, but in this context, it means a system. I chose Suenaka-ha rather than Suenaka-ryu, because *ryu* means style, and aikido isn't my style, it's O'Sensei's. It would have been too egotistical to call it Suenaka-ryu, whereas the term Suenaka-ha means just that; it's my system of aikido, the system I teach. Of course, the term *tetsugaku-ho* literally means 'the philosophical way.' I suppose I could have just called it Suenaka-ha aikido, but I wanted to stress the philosophical aspects of aikido, which a lot of people at that time weren't doing, and many still are not. That's Tohei Sensei's influence on me, in a lot of ways, although he never used that term. Again, a lot of people were teaching aikido as being exclusively physical, or completely spiritual, like Tohei's methods. Instead of separating the physical and the mental, the spiritual, the aikido I teach is both, and I wanted the name to reflect that."

The AIKDPS was formally chartered in the summer of 1976, the organizational umbrella under which Suenaka taught Suenaka-ha Tetsugaku-ho aikido and, not long after, Hakutsuru Shorin-ryu karatedo. Suenaka called his senior students together at his home and announced his decision. Of course, his most senior students at that time had studied maybe a year at the most (Ron Granville excepted), making the AIKDPS in every sense an infant organization. Rather than being a detriment, the inexperience of his students proved to be a bonus to the organization's growth and development. Suenaka wasn't interested in establishing branch *dojos,* rapid promotions, or feathering his nest with dues and testing fees:

"All I ever wanted to do was teach the aikido that O'Sensei taught me, and Tohei Sensei, too. I was tired of aikido taking a back seat to politics and egos, of having to promote so many students in a certain period of time, whether they were ready or not, just to collect testing fees or so I could say, 'I have this many *shodan* in my organization,' you know? The decision to split off on my own was a very hard one, but it was nice to finally just teach aikido. I have sometimes regretted the bad feelings the decision caused, but I have never regretted the decision itself."

CHAPTER EIGHT

AIKIDO IN CHARLESTON

On October 1, 1978, TSgt. Roy Yukio Suenaka retired from the United States Air Force after twenty years of service. While the occasion was understandably bittersweet, it was also exciting, as he now had the opportunity to do what he'd never before been able: teach aikido full-time. The first order of business was to find an off-base *dojo*, as obviously he could no longer use the quonset hut.

Over the years Suenaka had developed a friendship with Albert Church. As noted earlier, Church taught Kamashin-ryu karate in Charleston, and at the time of Suenaka's arrival there Church's was one of the only martial arts schools in the area, if not the only one. Suenaka initially contacted Church to ask his help in finding a place to teach. Church was kind enough to invite Suenaka to share space in his *dojo* until a more permanent arrangement could be had, and the two split the rent of $100 a month. It wasn't long, though, before it became apparent the arrangement wouldn't work out, mainly because of scheduling conflicts. Suenaka began looking in earnest for a place of his own.

Church's school was located at the south end of Savannah Highway, sandwiched between two bars, Gene's Hafbraü and Clay's Lounge. Suenaka had noticed an empty room next door to Clay's, and he visited the bar one night to enquire about it. As it happened, Clay Dockins owned not just the bar, but the entire building. Dockins readily agreed to rent the space to Suenaka for $250 a month. Okay, $175. How about $150? They shook hands on $140 a month. Suenaka paid him the first month's rent in cash on the spot, Dockins handed him the key, and Suenaka had his *dojo*.

The new *dojo* was basically a big empty space. There were lights, peeling paint, a few windows and no air conditioning (in Charleston, people value air conditioning almost as much as iced tea), and a poured cement floor which reminded you of its presence with each and every *sutemi* (sacrifice fall), regardless of the thickness of the mat. With the exception that it had a restroom, it very much resembled the Okinawa Aikikai. And like the Okinawa Aikikai, there were challenges almost immediately, although the intent was somewhat different, as Suenaka recalls:

"Because we were right next door to a bar, guys would stumble in almost every night, saying, 'Hey! Where the hell's the lounge?' Some of them were drunk, and some were just troublemakers who thought they were tough. They had no idea what we were doing, all they saw were these people dancing around in white jackets and skirts. Sometimes we'd just walk them out of the door, and sometimes we had to put a *sankyo* on them and convince them to leave. I told Clay, 'You've got to set your customers straight, tell them not to bother us.' But Clay just said, 'If they bother you, kick their butts and then kick them out! I don't care what you do to them. Call me over when you do, because I want to watch (laughs)!' So that's what we did."

Occasionally, a more interesting challenge would come through the door:

"We didn't have as many martial artists challenging us, like we did in Okinawa. We had a few. But compared to Okinawa, these guys were nothing. We had these two guys come over once, they said they wanted to 'comp.' They were pretty big, they looked solid, like they'd had some training. They were talking to one of my seniors, and he didn't know what the heck 'comp' meant. 'Fight, man! We came to fight!' That's what they called competition, you know, 'comp.' We told them, 'We don't fight here.' 'Then what the hell good is it?' they said. 'Aikido is for self-defense,' we said, but they just wanted to fight, and they weren't going to leave until they did. My students were pretty nervous, because they'd never run into a situation like this, they'd never had to fight for real before.

"So by that time I saw what was going on and I walked over and asked what the problem was. I said, 'You guys looking for trouble?' 'No, we just want to fight.' I said, 'Oh, then you came for trouble. Okay.' So I started taking off my *hakama* and walked outside, I said, 'Come on, then. We're not going to fight in my *dojo*. We'll do it outside. I'll fight you one at a time, or you can both jump me at once, if you like. But one thing is for certain: Somebody's going to die tonight (laughs). Are you prepared to die? Because you don't fight for fun; you fight for keeps.' Well, they immediately backed off, 'We didn't mean it!' they said. 'Then get out,' I said, and they left. It was pretty funny, actually.

"If you want to fight competitively, you find a school that does that. But you don't just go barging into a school you're not familiar with and say you want to fight, whether you're interested in straight competition or just showing off. I don't have time for that, and I've never put up with it. It's disrespectful, and where I come from, it's a good way to get yourself hurt."

Although there's no doubt Suenaka would have, in Southern parlance, "put a hurtin'" on anyone foolish enough to ignore his warnings to leave, his threats to kill troublemakers were more a statement for effect than a promise. However, there was one time when he found himself closer than ever before, or since, to making good on his threat. Suenaka was loading his bags into his car after class when he saw a drunk threatening his son John, at the time just twelve years old. Suenaka told the man to stop. The drunk reached for him, and in seconds the bully, though a foot taller than Suenaka, found himself bent backwards, held in place by a fistful of hair, with Suenaka's face inches from his and his other fist in the man's spine. "I told him, 'All I have to to is jerk your head backwards and your back will break. Do you understand that you are about to die?' I was so mad I was shaking." With a warning never to come back, Suenaka let the drunk go. However . . .

"I saw him one more time after that. He came out of Clay's Lounge, saw me outside, and ran back inside. I went in after him, I said, 'I told you never to come back!' He said he was drunk the last time we met, that his friends had to tell him what had happened. And he

Suenaka Sensei and wife Kanako, at ceremonies commemorating the opening of the new Wadokai Hombu in Charleston, S.C.; 1994.

gave me some hamburgers! He said, 'Would you give these to your kids? I don't want any trouble!' He'd bought some hamburgers inside, and he was giving them to me as a peace offering—only after he saw me there, of course. The kids really enjoyed the hamburgers, and I never saw him again."

The next seven years passed uneventfully, with Suenaka continuing to teach at the AIKDPS Hombu next to Clay's Lounge. As the student body grew, Suenaka began looking for a better space to house his *dojo*. In 1985, he transferred shop to the Expressway Center, a low row of brick office buildings a few miles up the highway. It wasn't much larger, but it had several other advantages. The location was better, for one thing; by that time Suenaka and his students had derived about all the pleasure that could be had from tossing drunks. While it had no windows, the new space had an office, changing room, bathroom and, most importantly, central air conditioning. Charleston's sub-tropical climate meant regular evenings of one-hundred-degrees, ninety-percent humidity, and no breeze. Half-an-hour of hard *waza* in those conditions is enough to sap the strength of even the most hardy *aikidoka. Gi* would become literally wringing wet with perspiration; *nage* would go home with friction burns on their wrists from the force needed for them to keep their grip on sweat-slick limbs; and class would regularly pause long enough to towel sweat from the mat, to keep students from slipping and twisting an ankle. Even with the air conditioner going at full blast, temperatures in the *dojo* often touched ninety degrees. Even so, compared to the old *dojo,* the new locale was a palace. Suenaka's wife, Kanako, performed traditional Shinto purification rites, and the new *dojo* was in business. In 1994, the AIKDPS Hombu moved into a larger space next door, where it remains today. Two years later, Suenaka changed the name of his organization from the American International Ki Development and Philosophical Society to the more manageable Wadokai Aikido. *Wadokai,* roughly translated, means "The Way of Peace" – a direct expression of the fundamental philosophy of aikido, as expressed by O'Sensei himself.

Also in 1994, Suenaka listed his school in the local *Yellow Pages™,* the ad nothing more than a single line. It was the first time, other than the Charleston Air Base bulletin, that he had ever advertised his *dojo.* It was a conscious decision, based not on cost but personal philosophy, as he states:

"When you advertise, you get all these crazy nuts that are attracted to the martial arts; you can call them martial arts junkies, who hop from one school to the next, studying a little of this or a little of that, and never really learning anything. They hang around for maybe a few months, and then they leave. Then you get word that so-and-so went to such-and-such school and said they had studied under you and were demonstrating technique. Of course, it's usually bad technique, and the end result is that your school gets a reputation for teaching bad technique. My philosophy has always been that the best advertising is word of mouth. If people are meant to find my school, they'll find it."

Over the years, hundreds of people have found what eventually became known as the Suenaka School of Martial Arts. Students studying other styles at other schools (Charleston now has many more martial arts schools than when Suenaka first arrived) naturally heard of Suenaka through the local grapevine, and would drop by to get what was usually their first glimpse of aikido. More often than not, a student saw the sign on Savannah Highway, or heard about the school from a friend of a friend of a friend who had themselves paid the *dojo* a visit or perhaps studied there. Until the move to the Expressway Center, the *dojo* did not even have a telephone; anyone who wanted more information looked up Suenaka's number in the phone book and called him at home. It still happens that way today:

"Working by word of mouth, I knew that was what had to happen. A lot of people are surprised when they call to find they're not only talking to the head of the *dojo,* but talking to him at home. So I spend a few minutes talking to them, tell them where the *dojo* is, and then they come. And that's the way I want it. I don't want a big rush of people coming in, two hundred students to handle, then half of them leave and another hundred come in. That's how it is with a lot of schools. I want a loyal, quality group of people. I don't care to exploit aikido and make a lot of money. Aikido is how I make my living, but I'm not growing wealthy from it. I make just enough to get along. But again, that's the way I wanted it.

"My goals have never been to get rich from aikido, to make a big name for myself. If I had wanted to do that, I would have stayed with Tohei Sensei. My goals are to reach out to as many people as I can, to get more students, sure, but in a subtle way, not commercially. To teach aikido to as many people as I can, having more affiliated schools open up as time goes by, like we have now. Word is getting out now. Not word about me; I'm not looking for self-aggrandizement. Word about aikido, that aikido does work, that it is a valid martial art."

Unlike many organizations, Suenaka does not actively seek to open affiliated schools. If a student moves away from Charleston, and if Suenaka deems the student ready, he or she opens a branch *dojo* at their new home, with Suenaka's blessing:

"I don't sell franchises, like a lot of people do. I don't have contracts, either. That's not how it should be. I don't wish to ever do that. I don't want to sell franchise rights to some instructor I don't really know, and just have them send me my share of the dues and testing fees, without having any real involvement in the schools. There's some schools like that I know, the instructors are fourth-rate teachers. A lot of them are the equivalent of rank beginners in any good organization. And yet they're out there running a school, many of them claiming to be third, fourth, fifth-degree black belts, advertising like crazy, running hundreds of students through their schools. The turnover is incredibly high, sometimes almost a complete turnover. People come in, study for a while, then decide they don't like it and leave. But, the instructor has their money, you know? That's what it's about in so many schools today: money.

"I can't believe some schools will say, 'You sign this contract and pay us this much money, and in a year I guarantee you'll be a black belt!' It happens! And it's unfair to the students, because most of them don't know any better, they really think they're learning something. A lot of these people have come into my *dojo,* saying, 'Well, I'm a black belt in so-and-so's school,' and they know nothing.

"I had a woman student come to one of my karate classes one time. She said she was a black belt at another school, and that she didn't understand the way I was teaching the class. So I asked her why, and she said, 'You teach all of the different striking techniques? All of the kicking techniques, all of the blocking techniques? All of the *katas,* all of that fancy stuff? My God, that must cost a lot of money!' I didn't know what she was talking about, you know? It turned out when she first started studying at her school, they only taught her one technique, the straight punch. Her instructor had her do that for several weeks, and then showed her another strike, which she would practice for another two or three weeks. After four years she knew a dozen different strikes, a dozen kicks, blocks, and so on. She said she didn't even remember a lot of them, and the ones she showed me, she couldn't even do correctly. It was as if her instructor made her pay for each technique. She said we were doing more in one night than she'd ever seen, and we were just having a basic class. She was supposedly a black belt with four years experience, and yet our beginning students were doing more in one night than she'd seen in four years. That's the kind of situation you have out there today. Not at every school, of course, but at too many. That's what happens very often when you start aggressively expanding, selling franchises, offering contracts.

"If you want to study with me, you don't need a contract. You pay your dues and come to class. If you study hard and sincerely, you will advance. If you don't, you are not welcome to stay. And of course, if you want to leave, you are welcome to at any time. But those who are not meant to stay always leave. Those who are meant to stay, always do."

CHAPTER NINE

MARTIAL OBSERVATIONS

Suenaka Sensei has never been impressed by rank, only by the quality of the experience behind the rank. Indeed, the reader may have noticed few references to Suenaka's rank in this text, other than late in his study, and then only for illustrative purposes. The reason is simple:

"I don't care for people to know what rank I received from whom and when. To me, that isn't important. My rank is really insignificant because, in my opinion, it's what I am able to do—my ability to perform—that counts. One of my favorite sayings is: 'It's not what you know, but what you can do, and how well you can do it, that counts.' That's been said by everyone from Confucious to Bruce Lee, and it's true. The certificates I received from O'Sensei, and Tohei Sensei, and Soken Sensei, they mean something to me, but because of who they came from, not what they are. A colored belt is nothing more than something to hold your *gi* closed."

A perfect illustration of what Suenaka values in a martial artist is found in an incident that occurred during his first visit to his affiliate school in Buffalo, New York, located in the Kin-Tora Martial Arts Center. Kin-Tora is primarly a judo school, and its walls are lined with scores of trophies the school has earned in competition, including numerous national and international first places. Kin-Tora's chief instructors are Tony and Marty Grisanti, brothers and noted *judoka* who have won many personal firsts against world-class *judoka* in national competition. Tony Grisanti is the elder brother, a *godan,* and primary instructor. After welcoming Suenaka to his school, Grisanti left him alone to teach his seminar.

All who visit a Wadokai school or attend Suenaka's seminars who are not members of his organization, even if they study aikido, are requested to wear a white belt on the mat unless Suenaka himself allows them to do otherwise. Although they may be skilled in other styles and disciplines, they are newcomers to his style of *waza*. Plus, it is one of the ways he tests the attitude of potential students. In Grisanti's case, since Suenaka was a guest and his credentials were well-established, this admonition did not apply. Nevertheless:

"Toward the end of the seminar, we were doing *jo kata*. I was busy watching one of my senior instructors demonstrating a *kata*, and out of the corner of my eye I saw this big guy in a *gi* walking to the back of the dojo with a *jo* in his hand. It took me a minute to realize it was Grisanti Sensei, and he was wearing a white belt. Even though it was his *dojo*, and he had the right to wear his black belt. And he sat at the back of the class, with the rest of the white belts. That sort of attitude impresses me more than anything in the world, more than if you were a twentieth degree black belt. For that is the mark of a true martial artist."

"There was another time, back at the Charleston Hombu, when a man came in who said he was a *nidan* from an Aikikai-affiliated school. He was a very nice guy, and he wanted to study. I mentioned to him that we don't recognize ranks from other schools, so for now, he wouldn't be allowed to wear his *hakama* and black belt. So he said, 'Sure, no problem. I just want to practice.' I could see right away that he had a very good attitude. So I told him, 'In that case, go ahead and put on your belt and *hakama*. If you have that kind of attitude, then you must be a true *nidan*.' It's people like that that really make me feel good."

For Suenaka Sensei, proper attitude has always been his primary criterion in choosing which students to accept, and rank is a consistently accurate barometer:

"You can tell if someone has the right attitude by the way they deal with rank. Usually the ones with the best attitude, you have to drag their rank out of them, you know, 'Be straight with me. What have you studied? How long?' Sometimes you need to know. There's phony ranks, and there's true ranks. It's the people who come in and say, 'I'm a master! I'm a *godan*, I'm a *rokudan!*' those are the ones who usually wind up knowing nothing, or are flat-out lying. And even if they were awarded that rank, their attitude shows they're not ready for it. And sometimes you'll ask someone, 'How long have you studied?' and their answer is, 'I'm a *shodan*, I'm a *nidan*.' Well, you can study for ten years and still be a *kyu*, or you can study for five and be a *sandan*. What does the rank mean? What was the quality of instruction? I had someone call me once who said they had 'extensive' experience in Shotokan karate. Turned out it was four years! I told him, 'That's not extensive, young man! I've studied for fifty, and that's not extensive! Maybe when I'm ninety, and I've been studying for eighty-five years; now that's extensive!'

You know? People who come in and try to impress me with all the different styles they've studied and all that, their rank, that doesn't impress me at all. It's the people who are humble and show humility, they're the ones who impress me, regardless of the quality of their technique. Attitude is what really matters. That's what distinguishes a true student."

Just as he has strong opinions concerning rank and what constitutes a true student, so too does Suenaka Sensei have equally firm beliefs concerning what aikido is and is not:

"Firstly, if it's competitive, it's not aikido. It's some other martial art, because the essence of aikido as expressed by O'Sensei is non-competitive, non-resistant. It is strictly an art of self-defense. Although it is very spiritual, it can also be a very deadly art, and if you have competition, you can get very badly hurt. But that doesn't mean you cannot resist at all. When you are learning to perform a technique, the *uke* offers very little resistance, so that the *nage* can feel what it is like to perform the technique. But as *nage* progresses, *uke* begins to offer more resistance, so that the *nage* can feel what it like to defend against a realistic attack, because when you are on the street, believe me, your attacker will resist! You can't say, 'Hey, you're not supposed to resist! You're supposed to let me throw you!' So there must be some resistance. But in the *dojo,* this resistance isn't competition. It is harmony, because in resisting, you are helping your partner learn and grow, to perfect his technique, just as he does the same for you. Do not interpret this kind of resistance as competition or disharmony. It is not *uke* against *nage.* Rather, they are one. But competition for competition's sake? That is not aikido."

Although aikido is first and foremost a method of self-defense, that does not mean one immediately resorts to physical violence when faced with the threat of attack. That is not true aikido, just as remaining passive or employing what is sometimes called "verbal aikido" is often not enough to diffuse a potentially dangerous situation. Aikido is not one or the other. Suenaka asserts it is both:

"In aikido, we learn to first resolve any kind of conflict verbally, without violence. But if it can't be resolved verbally, you have to be prepared to immediately incapacitate your attacker, to the point where you are in complete control of the situation. There's no room for fooling around. You must be totally prepared, physically, mentally, and spiritually, to deal with a given situation on any number of levels at any moment. That for me is what aikido is all about. That's what O'Sensei taught me, that's what he hoped aikido would be forever. But apparently, people today have different ideas of what aikido should be.

"Some people say aikido should be a soft art, some say it should be a hard art. It's true that aikido is an art that should enable you to be able to put down an attacker, for good if you have to. But that's not the aim of aikido. You have to resolve the situation, but in a way that will not harm the attacker. That's part of what O'Sensei meant by 'the loving protection of all things.' It doesn't mean you don't hurt your attacker at all, because aikido is a method of self-defense. It means that you do only what is necessary to gain control of a situation, causing as little harm to the attacker as you can in the process.

"Some people go to the opposite extreme, and say aikido should be only love, and not meant to hurt anyone. But if you practice a philosophy such as that, and you are attacked, then you have no means to protect yourself. And 'the loving protection of all things' includes yourself and your loved ones. You must be able to make aikido work

A monument to Morihei Ueshiba O'Sensei in Tanabe, Japan.

for yourself before you can make it work in any other situation."

So what place, then, does the *ki* that is at the heart of aikido really have in physical *waza?* Is *ki,* as some assert, simply universal love for all things? Is it some mystical force which all but a rare few can command, and which few *aikidoka* can ever hope to use or understand? Suenaka makes a specific distinction between *ki* in the broader sense and *ki* as it pertains to the execution of proper aikido technique:

"Many people misunderstand what *ki* is, and how it relates to the martial arts, and

The Marker placed next to the Morihei Ueshiba O'Sensei monument in Tanabe, commemorating his life and the creation of aikido.

aikido in particular. Some know *ki* as the vital life force, the energy of the universe that connects us to the universe. But it goes beyond that. In terms of aikido, *ki* refers the latent energy within a person. For instance, if someone is excited, or if someone is afraid of something, his body automatically produces adrenaline to make him stronger, to make him faster. That's what *ki* is all about in aikido—the ability to call upon this energy, to utilize it and control it without having to be excited or scared and, in so doing, to perform a technique with the proper amount of energy necessary for that technique to work against a certain size person or in a certain situation. Of course, at the same time you have to utilize proper technique, to use the attacker's force also. I do not mean to say that *ki* is adrenaline, but it is like adrenaline. For aikido purposes, you can define *ki* as spiritual adrenaline. It is a very real energy, energy of purpose and of intent, of focus, of uniting body, mind, and spirit together in one moment, to allow *ki* to flow through you and through your technique.

"Just because aikido is a method of self-defense, doesn't mean there can be no *ki*. I have met some people who have studied purely physical aikido for a number of years, who say, 'Aikido does not need *ki* to work.' These same people have no real power in their technique. They have no knowledge of the true mechanics of aikido, the subtlety. They move physically, and that's it. They use all muscle. If they're extremely strong, they might get it to work, but not likely. Even a weaker person will be able to resist against a stronger person who does not use *ki* in his technique, and of course, a stronger person won't be affected at all, and no matter how strong you are, there is always someone out there who is stronger. So strength alone is insufficient. But, if you know the mechanics of proper technique, and proper flow of *ki*, you can throw someone very easily, no matter how strong they are. Even if you have good technique, but no *ki*, it isn't aikido, and it won't be as effective."

O'Sensei's birthplace in Tanabe, Japan. The building in the background is the house in which O'Sensei was born.

O'Sensei's command of *ki* was preternatural. All who studied with him relate tales of seeing the Founder perform seemingly impossible feats, or being a part of such a demonstration, unexplainable by physical strength or body mechanics alone. For example, some readers may have seen a film of O'Sensei holding the end of a *jo* in his right hand, extended parallel to the floor, with four or five *uke* pushing against it with all their strength, unable to move it more than an inch or two. Finally, with a dip and a shrug of the shoulders, the Founder sends his *ukes* stumbling forward onto the mat. Again, the uninitiated may say it is all show. It is physically impossible, and therefore impossible, period. And yet, O'Sensei made it work. How, then, does one explain this apparently inexplicable act?

"With O'Sensei, *ki* was more than just spiritual adrenaline. There was an enormous amount of pure spirituality in his technique, and of course in his life. The only proper term I can think of to explain O'Sensei's power is *seigyo,* meaning to have complete control of a situation, being able to completely control the strength and the force being extended by your attacker. Being able to absorb this force, and use it as you will, against the attacker.

"*Seigyo* is so important. It is what enables you to utilize *ki* correctly. It goes beyond the physical. People mistakenly use the word *ki* as just being natural flow of energy. That's true, but you can control that flow at will. And that's what proper use of *ki* is."

One of O'Sensei's better-known sayings is: "I am the universe." It's a brief yet eloquent summation of the connection of all people, all things, to the *"universal ki,"* the energy of life; that we all, at any given moment, stand at the center of the universe, a philosophy common not only to metaphysics but increasingly more accepted in quantum physics. While we all arguably tap into this universal *ki* unconsciously, through the very act of living, O'Sensei was able to do so consciously, at will. Perhaps it is this ability that enabled O'Sensei to perform his miraculous feats, such as with the *jo;* the ability to channel the universal *ki* through his being, standing as he did at the center of the universe:

"It was times like that that O'Sensei would say it was the *Aiki O'Kami,* the Great Spirit of Aiki, that enabled him to do what he did. It was him, coupled with the force of the Divine Spirit moving through him. There were several times I was with O'Sensei when I actually felt it happen, in different ways.

"There was one time when I was asleep in the *uchi deshi* room at the Hombu, the old Hombu, what they called the 'Hell-Hole of Ushigome.' It was early in the morning, about two o'clock, and I felt a vibration. It woke me up. I thought it was an earthquake, because in Japan there are earthqukes almost all of the time. It was a very fine, low-level vibration. So I got up to see what was happening and walked outside onto the veranda, which wrapped around the entire building, like a porch or walkway. I rounded the corner and I saw O'Sensei standing at the other end of the building, about fifty feet or so away, maybe more, doing his *kotodama* meditations. He was holding a *bokken,* holding it in front of him, raising the point into the air and emitting what he called these pure sounds, like tones, and that was what was causing the vibrations I felt. I could still feel them, in the wood beneath my feet and in the air around me. I felt very much enlightened, standing there. It was exhilarating, it made me tingle all over. I felt like I was getting a glimpse, a feeling of something I certainly had never experienced before and maybe never would again. O'Sensei never showed off. He would never do something like that just for effect.

"I watched for a few moments. I didn't want to bother him, so I returned to my room. I didn't think he'd seen me, because I was just peeking around the corner, but the next morning at breakfast, he said, 'Why didn't you come and join me?' So he obviously was aware of my presence. It was that command of *ki* that made him so amazing, that sense of being so centered that his perception expanded all around him, that sense of knowing and being aware of everything around him. Every time I got close to O'Sensei, I could feel that same energy, even at a distance. Whether you saw him or not, you had the feeling that he was there, somewhere.

"You could especially feel O'Sensei's *ki* when you meditated with him. We were at a temple once, outside of Tokyo, though I don't remember exactly where. He never told me where we were going—we just went. We were on our way somewhere else, and he wanted to stop at this temple to meditate. There were times when several other people went with him, but this time it was just the two of us. So we sat in *seiza* on this wooden platform with a thin *zabuton* (pillow) under us and meditated for a long period of time! Minutes stretched into hours—it felt like we sat there forever. I was young, and impatient, and was wondering the entire time, 'When is this going to end?' So we sat there, and my feet started hurting, then my legs, then the pain crept up my back, my shoulders . . . pretty soon my entire body was in pain. But eventually the pain went away, and I started to feel cold, and then just numbness. Of course, the entire time, O'Sensei didn't move a muscle. I finally stopped fighting, and thought, 'Well, I just have to do this, no matter what happens.' And then, suddenly, I felt complete serenity. And it was then that O'Sensei said, 'Well, we're finished. Let's go.' I have no doubt he knew exactly what I was going through, and when he felt me reach that state, he got up and said it was time to go. I tried to get up and fell over. I was so numb, I couldn't move my legs, I could actually hear the blood rushing into my legs. But O'Sensei got up without any difficulty at all, and he reached down with one arm and stood me up and helped me stumble away. It took me about an hour before I felt right again. But that was another time when I experienced the power of his *ki,* sitting there with him, on a more subtle level, his awareness. It was a singular experience, one that's pretty hard to forget."

Use of *ki* in the martial arts is not the exclusive province of aikido. All true martial artists ultimately develop an awareness of *ki,* whether the awareness is nurtured consciously or arises as a natural result of devoted study. As Suenaka explains:

"Hohan Soken understood *seigyo,* he used *ki* too, but in a slightly different way. It was the same *ki,* but not used in the same manner that O'Sensei used or defined it, where he would use *ki* to control your entire being. Hohen Soken Sensei used *ki* more physically, to resist against your force. He was able to control your physical being at a given point. The term we used in this context is *shuchu-ryoku,* which O'Sensei also used. That is, energy of intent, being able to concentrate and utilize a given amount of force at a given time to a certain effect. It's energy in addition to physical force.

"Neither O'Sensei nor Soken Sensei were very large men. O'Sensei was muscular, even in his later years when I knew him, but Soken Sensei was not muscular at all. He was very slight, very wiry. But yet, he was very powerful for his size, because he was able to utilize *ki* in a certain way. I think in his case, his command of *ki* developed more naturally from his years of training. I don't think he consciously tried to develop his *ki,* like O'Sensei did, although he did a lot of *ibuki* breathing exercises and *meiso* meditation. He had extensive knowledge of anatomy, body mechanics, how to direct force and control force, which naturally leads to control of *ki.*"

While it is obvious that *ki* is what was at the heart of O'Sensei's aikido, it should be equally obvious by now that the study and development of *ki* exclusive of *waza* is not true aikido, and vice-versa. Before he began devoting his entire attention to *ki* development, Koichi Tohei was first and foremost a superb aikido technician, with a natural flow of *ki* that manifested itself in his powerful technique. As noted, his increasing de-emphasis of physical *waza* was as much a function of personal growth and philosophy as it was politics. To a lesser degree, the same can be said of the stress the Aikikai Hombu placed on the perfection of physical *waza,* separate from discussion and active practice of *ki* on the mat. History also shows how these two competing philosophies affected the overall growth of aikido worldwide, resulting in the two primary schools of thought discussed earlier. Suenaka posits that O'Sensei's example stands at the center of the confusion: a calm, constant and immutable point of reference for all *aikidoka:*

"I think the reason there are so many different opinions and philosophies today concerning what aikido should or should not be is because people have lost sight of the founding principles. They have lost sight of what O'Sensei tried to teach. People say, for example, that you can't follow O'Sensei's philosophy of love and protection and cause pain to anyone, that the true nature of aikido is not to foster conflict or to cause pain of any kind, physical or mental, emotional, spiritual. So when they study, when they perform their technique, they do not cause any pain. Maybe a little, but not enough to make anyone really submit, no authority. But that's not what O'Sensei did. Sometimes when O'Sensei would throw you, it was as if a big hand had reached down out of the sky and grabbed you. There was no pain, only exhilaration as you flew through the air, came down and rolled, and then sprang to your feet and ran back for more. But let me tell you, there were other times that he performed *sankyo* or *nikyo* on us, and the pain was exquisite. It made your eyeballs vibrate, made your whole body twitch, to the point where you felt you were about to pass out from the pain. But you didn't want to, because it hurt so good!

"Just look at the films of O'Sensei. There are times where he's performing a technique on someone, or a submission, and it's quite obvious they are in extreme pain. There's an O'Sensei film featuring Tohei Sensei that was taken before his trip to Hawaii in 1953. There's a point in the film where O'Sensei throws Tohei Sensei (with a) *kote-gaeshi* and then pins him with a pressure point technique to his head. You can see Tohei Sensei's face pressed into the mat, and there's no doubting he's feeling real pain. How can you look at that and say O'Sensei didn't mean for anyone to cause pain?"

The misguided philosophy that aikido should not be painful or at all injurious is also at the heart of the mistaken notion that there is no *atemi* in aikido. One can look to O'Sensei for the answer to this argument as well, as Suenaka recounts:

"O'Sensei used *atemi* all the time. Not with every technique, but when necessary. He would strike you and then he would throw you. But the strike is only part of the technique, not the technique itself. It is used to disorient the attacker so you can apply your technique. And when you punch somebody, it hurts. But in order for certain aikido techniques to work, there must be some element of pain somewhere. So yes, there is the loving protection of all things, but part of that, again, is causing no more pain to the attacker than is necessary. It is not pain for pain's sake. That's part of why O'Sensei developed aikido, because people were getting seriously injured studying other arts. So he modified his technique so that the pain was kept to a minimum, so that you could control it. And that's very much where the spiritual aspect of aikido comes into play. Knowing when to cause pain, how much, and for how long, depending on the situation.

"O'Sensei believed in the old samurai adage that one must always try the utmost to avoid conflict. But if you cannot, then inflict pain before you injure, injure before you maim, and maim before you kill. And if you must kill, squeeze every bit of life out of the attacker to the last drop. Make it a clean kill. Because life is so precious, it cannot be wasted, even in death."

Ironically, it is by observing O'Sensei in action in the many films currently available that some have concluded that aikido as a whole is an ineffective art for self-defense. One of the more notorious examples is an American television show titled *Rendezvous With Adventure*, filmed in 1958 and available on video, which shows one middle-aged host attempting to attack Tohei as O'Sensei watches. Rather than immediately performing a technique on his ersatz antagonist, Tohei does his best to move out of the way; at one point, the host steps on Tohei's *hakama*, causing him to momentarily stumble. Some have taken this as proof that aikido doesn't work. 'If it did work, then why wasn't Tohei able to immediately overwhelm his obviously unskilled attacker?,' one might think. Suenaka dismisses such reasoning thusly:

"I know Tohei Sensei. He could have subdued that guy if he'd wanted to. But you have to remember, these men were guests, they were foreign guests, and they had no training. They weren't limber, they didn't know how to fall. You don't grab someone like that in that kind of situation and slam a technique on them. Tohei was making sure no one got hurt, even if it meant he looked foolish in the process. He was protecting his attacker. He finally did subdue the guy, but when he did, he didn't cause him any real pain. He didn't want to hurt him.

"There's another film of O'Sensei on a rooftop, executing *shiho-nage* on a civilian in street clothes, I think he was a police officer, and the guy almost spins out of it. It's not that O'Sensei couldn't make the technique work. He was being gentle. They were on the roof! There were no mats, and this guy didn't know how to fall. If O'Sensei had put a full *shiho-nage* on him, like he did us, the guy would have been wiped out. In both cases, what you're seeing isn't ineffective technique, but the loving protection of all things. You know? When somebody walks into your *dojo* for the first time, you don't slam a full-force technique on them. That's a sign of weakness on your part. That's being cruel. That's competition. They may ask you to show them something, to prove to them that what you are teaching really works, but there's not much you can do in a situation like that. If they challenge you, that's one thing, if they're obviously looking for trouble. But if they're watching the class, seeing people cooperating with one another, and they think, 'Hey, this stuff doesn't work . . . nobody's getting hurt! Nobody's mixing it up!,' well, that's just ignorance and incorrect attitude on their part. If they're not willing to look deeper, you show them the door.

"Aikido is so subtle, at first glance it can be hard to figure out what the heck is happening. You just see all of these people dancing around, and then all of a sudden somebody goes flying. Or you see a submission and you can tell the *uke* is in pain, but it might not be clear why. It's not like karate, where you can see a punch, a block, and a counter-punch, even though they can be very subtle as well. Aikido isn't so obvious. Even if you think you understand it intellectually, you must experience it to truly understand the forces involved.

"I think most students have a pivotal experience early in their study where they begin to realize just how effective aikido can be, where suddenly they are thrown and they can't figure out how, just suddenly, boom! They're on their back. Or maybe it's when somebody gets them with a really good *nikyo,* and you feel that sudden, intense pain. You were studying very slowly, being treated very gently as a beginner, and then, you get a real taste. It's like when you were first told fire can hurt you. You may accept that claim at face value, intellectually you may think you understand why, but it's not until you stick your finger in the flame that true understanding begins."

Nowhere do Suenaka Sensei's experiences, *waza,* and philosophy come together more than during the Wadokai annual *Gasshuku,* or summer camp. For the last twenty years, every June or July, before the weather gets *really* hot, students pack their *gi* and their sleeping bags and journey to a state park outside of the old railroad town of Cheraw, South Carolina, in the rolling hills and thick pine forests just south of the North Carolina state line. Gasshuku is an intense, week-long training session, featuring classes in all aspects of Suenaka-ha Tetsugaku-ho aikido, encompassing everything from *tachi waza* to *zazen, jodo* to *misogi.* A typical day begins at seven, when students rise and perhaps grab a bite of breakfast and a cup of coffee before the day's instruction begins. For anywhere from eight to ten hours, interrupted only by lunch, students train non-stop, sometimes for up to four or five hours at a stretch.

The *dojo* is as rustic as the camp; a large, non-air conditioned wooden building dominated by thick wooden rafters and a huge stone fireplace. Temperatures inside regularly exceed one hundred degrees Fahrenheit. Veteran campers are fond of describing one day at camp years ago when the National Weather Service declared Cheraw, South Carolina the hottest spot in the United States. It was so hot, Marines at North Carolina's Camp Lejune canceled the day's activities, yet Suenaka and his students were body-slamming each other on the mat. During breaks in practice sessions, students head to the nearby spring-fed lake to cool off, or to engage in *ibuki-no-ho* or *misogi* sessions led by Suenaka Sensei.

Meals are taken in the nearby dining hall and are prepared by the students themselves, under Suenaka's supervision (he once had his own restaurant, aptly named *Shinbashi,* opened not long after retirement from the air force). After the evening meal, students are encouraged to study on their own, though more often than not they wind up gathered on the mat around Suenaka, listening to his seemingly endless repertoire of stories. Most usually elect to retire at one or two in the morning, collapsing onto the metal cots in their plank-walled cabins before rising bright and early the next day to do it again. That is, assuming Suenaka doesn't decide to call an hour of *tokubetsu keiko,* or "special practice," usually around three in the morning, just when everyone is settling in to deep sleep, only to be unceremoniously roused by a *deshi* pounding on their cabin door: *"Tokubetsu keiko!* Ten minutes! *Gi* out!"

Gasshuku is very much the highlight of the year, for several reasons. As most students get perhaps five hours of practice a week at their respective *dojo,* by the time *Gasshuku* ends, students find they've logged the equivalent of eight week's practice in one, a fact to which their sore muscles will readily attest. It's also the time Suenaka conducts *dan* (black belt ranking) promotions. At the outset, both *kyu* (junior student) and *dan* promotions were conducted at *Gasshuku,* but as the organization grew, the time necessary for *dan* promotions made accompanying *kyu* promotions impractical. This might seem unlikely to some readers, as rank testing in many schools can take no more than ten or fifteen minutes. Not so for the Wadokai. Take, for example, the testing requirements for *gokyu,* the first rank—in the Wadokai, a blue belt.

A *gokyu* test begins with five to ten minutes of oral questioning concerning aikido terminology, philosophy, and history, including Suenaka's personal history. The inclusion of this last topic isn't the result of ego, but of Suenaka's desire for his students to know the lineage of the *waza* they're learning, if challenged. "So many students of different arts don't know what it is they're learning," Suenaka says. "Some don't even know the style, just 'Oh, I study karate,' or 'I study aikido.' But when you ask them who taught their instructor, they have no idea."

Following this oral test, students are asked to demonstrate their knowledge of *aiki taiso* and its purpose, after which comes *waza* testing. For *kyus,* they must perform fifteen basic techniques, left and right, beginning with basic *shomen-uchi kokyu-nage* and ending with *ushiro katate-tori kubi shime sankyo,* four variations. Students may also be asked to perform optional techniques; five *kokyu-nage* variations against different attacks, or five different defenses from a single attack. After the optionals comes demonstration of *kokyu-dosa,* or seated *ki*-centering techniques, followed by *suwari-waza* (defense in *seiza* against a like attacker) and *hanmi-handachi (nage* seated in *seiza, uke* attacking from a standing position). Then comes *tanto tori* (knife defense and disarming) and *jyu tori* (gun defense and disarming), from both front and back, plus *bokken-tori. Bokken-tori* is a good example of traditional techniques adapting themselves to modern times. While it is unlikely that one may find oneself confronted by a sword-wielding attacker, when one imagines the *bokken* as a baseball bat, pool cue or lead pipe, the practical efficacy of *bokken-tori* is easily seen.

Demonstration of the five, eight, twenty-one, and thirty-one move *jo kata* comes next, followed by *jo tori, jodo randori,* then general *randori* against a minimum six *uke.* The test culminates in *ryokata-tori randori,* where up to twenty *uke* rush the *nage* non-stop in an attempt to grab the *nage's* shoulders and knock him or her to the ground. The *nage* must remain in the center of the mat, throwing the attacking *uke kokyu-nage* until the *nage* literally drops from exhaustion, or is knocked down and unable to rise. This portion of the test alone often takes ten minutes or more, and is arguably the most important part. Suenaka consciously pushes the student to the point of physical exhaustion, then beyond, until all that sustains the candidate is *ki.* It is at this time, as the candidate struggles to remain standing and centered in the face of unceasing assault from all sides, that his or her true mettle is revealed.

In all, Suenaka's basic *kyu* test takes about an hour to complete. Tests for *nikyu* and above include all of the above, plus knowledge of fifty basic techniques, even more optionals, defenses from multiple grabs (up to four *uke*), demonstration of *kaeshi-waza* (technique reversals), *keri-waza* (defense against kicks), *henka-waza* (continual defense against continual attack by one *uke*), and *koshi-waza* (hip throwing techniques). There is also a teaching skit, where a student pretends to be a challenger walking into the *dojo* for the first time, and the candidate must explain and defend aikido, either verbally or, if necessary, physically. Although the teaching skits usually end up being improvisational comedy routines, one can see how they arose out of Suenaka's own experiences opening his many schools in different environments. As *dan* promotion brings with it the responsibility of teaching, the teaching skit serves as an early indication of how the candidate might acquit his or herself, and the school, in a delicate situation. Finally, following their test all candidates must submit a written thesis on an aikido-related subject of their own choosing. These theses range in length from a page or two for lower *kyus* to fifteen pages for *nikkyu* and above. After the rank is awarded, students are placed on probation for a year, to ensure they don't get "belt head," but rather continue to study humbly, with gratitude and respect; for O'Sensei, Suenaka Sensei, and their fellow students.

Finally, *Gasshuku* is an important event in that it brings together in one place Wadokai members from all over the country, often for the only time of the year. Suenaka considers these gatherings to be essential to the successful evolution of his organization, for it is during these seven days of non-stop training, completely isolated from the outside world—radios, televisions, newspapers, and magazines are prohibited—that students reaffirm their dedication to aikido, to Suenaka Sensei, to each other and, most importantly, to following the path of *aiki,* in keeping with O'Sensei's last request to Suenaka in the final months before the Founder's death.

Gasshuku is very much the living embodiment of what Suenaka believes aikido to be and to represent; hard study, self-perfection, fellowship, and love. And so, it seems proper to end this narrative here, with the image of Suenaka Sensei watching his students practicing in sweat-soaked *gi,* grunting and laughing, following the path of *aiki* in the hot Carolina sun as another hard day's practice draws to a close. Men and women of all ages, races, religions, and means, brought together in the spirit of love and harmony under the watchful eyes of O'Sensei, his portrait hung on the worn brick of a fireplace that for this week serves as the *kamiza.* For these men and women, there are no thoughts of job or current events, politics and division, loss or gain. Only the perfection of technique, the cleansing of the mind, the honing of the spirit. This is what it means to walk the path of *aiki.*

In the years before he died, O'Sensei was often heard to comment: *"Kono ojii-san mo mada naratemasu"*—"This old man is still learning." As we follow in his footsteps, we are reminded that the Path is one without beginning or end. Roy Suenaka Sensei has shown, through the example of his life, that our progress is measured not by the length of our stride and the weight of our possessions, but the firmness of our tread and the lightness of our hearts. As the founder said: "The true nature of *budo* lies in the loving protection of all things," so, too, does Suenaka Sensei express the same in the motto of the Wadokai:

> Let us have a universal spirit which loves and protects all creation and helps all things grow and develop. To unify mind and body and become one with the universe is the ultimate purpose of my study.

Throughout our lives, we have all at one time or another been told to "stick to our guns," or "do what we feel is right." It is overly simplistic to say it is not always easy to follow such advice, regardless of the truths contained therein. When such maxims are immersed in the reality of everyday life, they quite often become victims of the conflicts and politics inherent in survival. The immediate rewards for succumbing to the pressures and temptations of the moment may be alluring, and we may perhaps justifiably assert that such rewards are deserved, but too often the price for such compromise is an uneasy conscience that lasts long after the gleam has faded from the prize. The coin of character is patience; the rewards are not always immediate, but they do come.

In 1976, Roy Yukio Suenaka Sensei chose the latter course, standing on the firm foundation of his character in the face of what was one of the most difficult decisions of his life: to divorce himself from the company of his mentor and the notoriety and rewards to be reaped therein, in exchange for relative obscurity, all to honor his memory of Morihei Ueshiba O'Sensei. He did not know then whether he would ever again see Koichi Tohei Sensei, for whom he still had great respect and fondness, nor stand in the Hombu and visit once more with Kisshomaru Ueshiba Doshu, whom he held in equally high esteem. To embrace one would seem, in light of the events that transpired years earlier, to exclude the other, a tacit declaration of allegiance which might reopen old wounds perhaps better left alone.

February of 1993 marked Suenaka's fortieth year of aikido study. It is perhaps in contemplation of this milestone that he began entertaining thoughts of formal reconciliation. With the passing of years since his separation from the International Ki Society, Suenaka and Tohei's personal and political animus had begun to thaw. Though their contact was infrequent, they had occasionally spoken with one another by telephone. Similarly, Suenaka had maintained formal, yet cordial contact with the Aikikai Hombu. His own organization was well-established and growing. His students were familiar with his education and experiences, just as they were continually made aware by Suenaka that the aikido they learned was a synthesis of that which he had learned under both Tohei and O'Sensei, placing equal emphasis on *ki* development techniques and hard, physical *waza*—a consciously evident blending of those aspects of aikido that formed the political wedge that sundered the ties that bound Suenaka to Tohei, and Tohei to the Aikikai. Equally familiar were Suenaka's students with the story and circumstances of Suenaka Sensei's separation from the Ki Society. Not surprisingly, they often asked if their Sensei ever thought of returning to Japan. And so it was that, on the morning of December 18, 1993, almost twenty-three years after Airman Suenaka first stepped onto the tarmac at Tachikawa Air Base, Roy Suenaka arrived at Narita Airport in Tokyo.

Suenaka spent the next four days in Japan, accompanied by one of his senior students. A few hours after his arrival, he found himself again standing in the Aikikai Hombu outer office—a concrete structure now in place of the old wooden building—where O'Sensei had first embraced "Hawaii boy" in 1961. Kisshomaru Ueshiba Doshu, aware of Suenaka's impending visit, received him warmly in his home, and they spent about two hours talking of old times and the current state of aikido in the world. Before they parted, Doshu announced that he still recognized Suenaka's certification and his organization, and that his students were welcome to visit the Hombu and practice any time. Suenaka left the Hombu with a much lighter heart, yet realizing the hardest meeting was yet to come.

Two days later, on the afternoon of December 20, Suenaka arrived at the Ki no Sato in Tochigi. The night before, Suenaka had telephoned Tohei, requesting permission to visit. Uncertain how his former teacher would answer, he was gratified by Tohei's positive response. Though he arrived in the middle of a *kiatsu* seminar, Suenaka was greeted warmly by Tohei, and invited to remain for the seminar and dinner afterwards. The two men were able to spend only a few hours together before Suenaka had to depart, yet it was long enough to affirm that the ill will of years past was gone. Like Doshu, Tohei confirmed he still recognized Suenaka's certification and his organization, and welcomed future visits.

The next morning, Suenaka returned to Charleston, where he remains today.

末中派哲学法

合氣道

PART TWO

SUENAKA-HA TETSUGAKU-HO AIKIDO

This section is an overview of Suenaka-ha Tetsugaku-ho aikido. It is not, nor is it meant to be, an encyclopedic listing of every technique Suenaka teaches. There are literally thousands of aikido techniques possible simply by combining basic techniques. What you will find here are the basics, from etiquette to fundamental *waza* (the techniques themselves). You will not find detailed information on weapons defense. While Suenaka includes *keri-waza* (defense against kicking attacks) in his general instruction, all attacks illustrated here are hand blows. Likewise, *jo-kata* (wooden staff *kata*), and *jo-waza* (defenses and attacks using the *jo*) have not been included. The same goes for *koshi-waza* (hip-throwing techniques), *shime-waza* (choking techniques), *shinke-waza* (nerve pressure-point techniques), *kansetsu-waza* (techniques which go against a body joint), *suwari-waza* and *hanmi-handachi-waza* (defenses from *seiza*), *ne-waza* (ground grappling and submission techniques), and many others. Know as you read this section that the absence of these techniques is not an oversight.

Although you will find here illustrations of basic *ki-no-taiso* (*ki* development exercises), discussion of *ki* as a phenomenon is limited. To try and understand *ki* by reading a book would be like trying to understand the nature of water by reading a description of it. *Ki* development and understanding can come only with the experience born of diligent training. Suenaka discusses the nature of *ki* as it pertains to aikido technique in the later chapters of the biographical section. Likewise, we have not included descriptions of *zazen* (seated meditation), *misogi* (ritual purification), or other more esoteric practices which are a part of Suenaka-ha Tetsugaku-ho aikido.

Some may ask whether Suenaka-ha Tetsugaku-ho aikido is "combat" aikido. Suenaka addresses the "spiritual" versus "combat" aikido debate in the first section of this book. The stock answer is that any aikido, properly executed, is "combat" aikido: that is, it will work against a knowledgeable streetfighter. Because of Suenaka's street-fighting experience and his experience in other martial arts, karate in particular, the techniques comprising Suenaka-ha Tetsugaku-ho aikido are designed to be taught in the *dojo* for use on the street against an experienced and tenacious attacker.

While studying what is contained in this section, keep in mind that descriptions have been kept to a bare minimum, again in the interest of brevity. You may have questions about what you see and read here which are not addressed by the text. The only way to find further answers to your questions is to train as part of an ongoing aikido class taught by an experienced and competent instructor.

Japanese conventions and terminology are used throughout this section. While some may justifiably assert that it is not necessary to adhere to such conventions in order to study aikido, their use is customary even outside of Japan. The importance of conventions in etiquette is rather obvious, and goes beyond mere tradition. Concerning terminology, you are more likely to be understood, and sound less clumsy, if you call for *shomen-uchi ikkyo tenkan* than if you say you want to practice the overhead strike arm-cutting technique with the circular takedown. Of course, this is particularly true when visiting other *dojo*s. Also, some Japanese words simply do not have adequate English equivalents. While *seiza* is simply sitting on bended knees, *kokyu* is more than breath. Ultimately, you will find that knowledge of Japanese conventions will greatly enhance your study, and ignorance of them can very easily hinder it. Japanese words and terms are generally not defined in this section. Please refer to the Glossary at the end of the book for clarification.

Finally, do not allow yourself to be fooled into thinking you can learn aikido by reading this book, or any other. You cannot. Even if you memorize every word and technique contained herein, stepping onto the mat for the first time is an entirely different experience; attempting to defend yourself in the street, even more so. Trying to learn aikido from a book is inviting disaster, just as if you were attempt to learn how to fly an airplane solely by reading an instruction manual. As a manual, this book is a guide for the aikidoka, beginner and advanced alike. As such, we hope it is a clear guide, and wish you luck in your journey.

CHAPTER ELEVEN

ETIQUETTE
(REIGI)

Etiquette is an essential part of aikido study, as it is in all of the martial arts, for a number of reasons. Studying a martial art is an honorable pursuit, and honorable people behave politely and treat one another with respect. While it is not necessarily true that a person with good manners is honorable, lack of manners is usually an indication of lack of respect, for others and for oneself. Even the most unsophisticated person, if he or she is an earnest *budoka,* will exhibit good manners.

Just as etiquette provides structure to a society, so too does proper etiquette—called *reigi* or *reishiki* in Japanese—provide structure to one's aikido study. There is a certain way to begin a class, conduct a class, and conclude a class. Even when studying casually, one-on-one, an *aikidoka* observes proper etiquette. If etiquette is the grease that keeps social interaction from grinding to a halt, then *reigi* does the same for aikido study. It helps keep the class moving, and provides a common base of reference for all students. The structure it provides also helps to ensure class is conducted safely, with no "crossed signals." *Reigi* is especially important when visiting unfamiliar schools. Observance of proper etiquette in this instance reflects well on both you and your primary school and sensei, and—when visiting schools that teach other arts—reflects well on aikido, just as good manners in general reflect well on your family and your upbringing.

Finally, remember that the way you behave and treat your fellow students is as much a barometer of your martial and spiritual development as is competence in *waza.* It could be argued that a student whose *waza* is average, but who displays a sincere and courteous attitude towards fellow students and his or her study, would be promoted sooner than a student whose *waza* is outstanding, but whose attitude is lacking. The finest *budoka* are among the most courteous and humble people you will ever meet. Etiquette and aikido training go hand-in-hand.

Even outside of Japan, Japanese conventions of etiquette are usually observed during an aikido class. While it is not necessary to follow this tradition, it is generally customary.

BOWING

Proper bowing is called *ojigi*. While bowing is the customary greeting in Japanese society, it is more than just the Western equivalent of a handshake. The way in which one bows, the duration of the bow, and so on, can have deep, multi-layered meanings. In the *dojo*, however, things are a bit more simple.

Bowing is how an *aikidoka* shows humility and respect. Some misinterpret bowing as a show of worship or subservience, which it is not. Bowing to one's partner, instructor, or to the *shomen, kamidana,* or *kamiza* is more like a salute, an acknowledgement of gratitude and readiness for study. If you cannot grasp this difference, then you will have difficulty setting your ego aside while you train. There is an oft-repeated maxim in the martial arts: "The usefulness of a cup is in its emptiness, for a cup that is full can hold no more." In other words, if you resist the simple show of humility demonstrated by bowing, then you will inevitably find yourself resisting instruction and correction. Your cup will be full—of ego. Do not think of bowing as a sign of weakness. It is just the opposite—it is a sign of strength of character.

When you bow, give your full attention to the action. Do not let your eyes or your attention wander.

Stand with your feet together and your palms flat by your sides. (2) Bend at the waist, while keeping your eyes fixed on your partner. Note: Traditionally, Japanese women bow with their palms flat on the fronts of their thighs. This convention is not always observed in Western dojos.

BOWING WHEN SEATED IN SEIZA

Place your palms flat on the mat before you, left hand first. (2) Lower your forehead until it is about a foot above the mat. The deeper the bow, the more respect is conveyed. Touching one's forehead to the mat conveys the most respect, and is often done when bowing to the shomen *or one's sensei.*

SEIZA

Seiza, or sitting on bended knees, is the traditional way of sitting in Japan, and in the *dojo.* The Japanese consider it rude to sit with one's legs and limbs splayed or the soles of one's feet exposed. In the *dojo,* splayed limbs not only show disrespect, but create a hazard—they're easy to trip over, and one or both people could be injured. Unless otherwise instructed, when seated on the mat, you should always sit in *seiza.* Even when not sitting in *seiza,* you should always have your legs crossed and your feet tucked away.

GENERAL DOJO ETIQUETTE

The following rules should be observed at all times while in the *dojo:*

PERSONAL APPEARANCE AND HYGIENE

Your *gi* should be clean. Always wash it between classes, or have two *gi* so that you will always have a clean one to wear. Women should wear a tee-shirt and sports bra beneath their *gi* jacket. Men should wear an athletic supporter, for the obvious reasons.

Observe good personal hygiene. Keep your body clean, and use a deodorant. Brush your teeth and wash your hair. Keep your fingernails and toenails trimmed close, to avoid scratching or otherwise injuring your partner as you practice.

Remove all rings, bracelets, earrings, necklaces and other jewelry before beginning practice. This includes wedding rings and all body piercings, whether they are visible or not. If you must wear glasses, make sure they are secured to your head with a strap.

Bandage any minor cuts or abrasions and cover the bandage securely with medical or athletic adhesive tape, to prevent the bandage from coming off during practice or heavy perspiration.

If you have a communicable illness or condition (a cold, flu, fungal infection, etc.), bring it to the attention of the chief instructor before class. He or she may ask you to sit out a class or two until you are well, to avoid infecting other students. If you have a chronic communicable disease, tell your instructor before beginning your study in general.

GENERAL COURTESY

- Do not bring food or beverages into the dojo.
- Do not chew gum in the dojo.
- Do not gamble or make wagers in the dojo.
- Do not drink alcoholic beverages before class. Do not come to class while under the influence of alcohol or illegal drugs.
- Do not bring weapons of any kind into the dojo, where they may cause someone to be injured or killed. If you are a law enforcement officer or otherwise licensed to carry a firearm or other weapon, speak with the chief instructor and submit to his or her judgement.

Standing with your feet together, lower yourself to your knees.

Cross your right foot over your left. Sit back on your heels.

- Do not swear, curse, or tell dirty jokes in the dojo.
- Do not harass other students in any way in the dojo. This includes spoken, physical and sexual harassment, and intimidation.
- Do not act boisterously or engage in rough-housing or horseplay in the dojo.
- Treat others as you would like to be treated. Bring any questionable conduct you may observe to the attention of a senior student or your chief instructor.
- Unless otherwise instructed, always address any questions you may have to a senior student, rather than the chief instructor. If the senior cannot answer your question, he or she will ask the chief instructor on your behalf.
- Although rules and philosophies concerning rank often vary widely from school to school, it is generally considered very bad form to ask questions of your seniors concerning rank promotion, yours or anyone else's. If you study diligently, you will be promoted. The discretion lies entirely with your sensei. Questions concerning rank promotion requirements, however, are generally considered appropriate, but should be asked before or after class.

DOJO COURTESY

- Arrive at the dojo early enough to change into your gi and take your place on the mat before instruction begins. If you arrive at the dojo after class has begun, kneel in seiza at the edge of the mat and wait for the chief instructor to recognize you and invite you onto the mat. Unless otherwise instructed, ask the chief instructor for permission if you must leave the mat before class is over.
- Always bow to the shomen in respect before stepping onto the mat and before stepping off.
- Never step onto the mat wearing shoes. Depending on your dojo's rules, you may be asked to wear slippers when not on the mat. If so, always remove them before stepping onto the mat. Place them neatly side-by-side, with the toes facing away from the mat, in the designated place.
- Do not lean on the dojo walls when on the mat, either while standing or seated.

- Do not cross your arms or put your hands on your hips or in your pockets when on the mat or in the dojo. All are considered discourteous. In some very traditional dojos, it may also be taken as a challenge.
- Always sit on the mat when not standing. Do not lie down or slouch.
- Always cross your legs when seated on the mat, unless you are seated in seiza.
- Do not display the soles of your feet. Likewise, do not pick at your toes or toenails when seated.

GENERAL CLASS ETIQUETTE

The following rules may vary from school to school, but are fairly common. Before we begin, familiarize yourself with the following words and terms, which are defined here in the context of an aikido class:

ki-o-tsuke: "Attention!"

mokuso: A command to wait calmly and mentally prepare yourself.

yoi: Assume a ready position; prepare.

rei: Bow; to bow.

shomen-ni-rei: Bow to the *shomen.*

sensei-ni-rei: Bow to the *sensei* or chief instructor.

gomen-nasai: "Pardon me," or "Please excuse me."

onegai-shimasu: "May I practice with you?"

domo arigato gozaimasu: "Thank you very much" for allowing me to practice with you.

mina-sama: Everyone, as in *"Mina-sama domo arigato gozaimasu."*

otagai-ni: Similar to *mina-sama*, and more common, akin to saying "the feeling is mutual," as in *"Otagai-ni domo arigato gozaimasu."*

OPENING CLASS

Take your place on the mat when instructed to do so, seated in *seiza.* The chief instructor will kneel, facing the shomen. Traditionally, students line up facing the *shomen,* with the senior student seated behind and to the chief instructor's right, and the rest of the class lined up in descending rank order to his or her left. If more than one line is necessary, successive lines begin behind the senior student and proceed to the left in descending order, as before.

The senior student will shout *"ki-o-tsuke!"* This means he or she wants your full attention. After a few moments, this command will be followed by *"mokuso."*

Sit calmly and prepare yourself for class. After a few moments or minutes, the chief instructor will end the period of contemplation with *"yoi."*

The senior student will say *"shomen-ni-rei!"* Bow to the shomen, then rise. The chief instructor will turn and face the class. The senior student will say *"sensei-ni-rei!"* Bow to the chief instructor, and say *"onegai-shimasu."* Class has now begun. Remain where you are and await instruction.

DURING CLASS

Remain attentive to your surroundings. Aikido classes can be very dynamic, and it is easy to throw your partner into another person. Make sure you have the physical space necessary to execute a technique before you do so. Don't disrupt your fellow students' study by carelessly moving about the mat like a bulldozer, knocking away everything in your path as you practice. Nobody likes a "mat hog."

Be a good *uke,* or partner. This means being willing to work with any student, no matter how more- or less-experienced they are than you. It also means being sensitive to the skill level of the student with whom you are working. While a high-level black belt may want you to attack them with everything you've got, or set your weight and resist or counter their technique, such an approach would obviously be inappropriate for a beginner. Resistance is fine, but not for its own sake. It is foolish to expect a beginner to be able to throw you with any real skill. Therefore, don't be afraid to "give the technique" to a beginner; that is, to take a fall even if not truly thrown. Through this way will they learn, and you may correct them as you go. Otherwise, they will become frustrated and refuse to work with you, or stop coming to class altogether.

Be a good *nage.* This means respecting your *uke* and his or her body. Don't "slam on" techniques, or see how hard you can throw someone. Such behavior is the hallmark of a bully, and you will soon discover no one wants to practice with you. Even worse, you may find yourself on the receiving end of such behavior. Ultimately, tempers will flare and someone will be injured. Do not confuse bullish *nagemi* with strength, or consideration for your *uke* as weakness or "wimping out." Ideal aikido technique results in maximum control of your *uke* with minimal effort and pain. You can totally dominate your *uke* and still have them get up smiling. This is one of the hallmarks of a true *aikidoka.*

Should you bump into or collide with another student, turn, bow, and say *"gomen-nasai,"* then resume your training.

If you are injured in any way that interferes with your practice, bow to your partner and excuse yourself to the edge of the mat. If the injury is serious enough to warrant first aid or medical attention, consult your chief instructor. Any injury that draws blood, no matter how small, should be tended to at once before resuming your practice.

When the chief instructor calls for your attention, immediately stop what you are doing, bow to your partner, and seat yourself in *seiza*, unless otherwise instructed. When the chief instructor gives the word to resume your study, bow to him or her before rising from the mat.

Rules for asking questions vary from school to school. Some invite questions of their chief instructors and senior students, while others do not. Follow the rules of your school.

Do not argue when you are corrected by a senior student or the chief instructor. Correction is guidance and makes us all better, and willingness to accept criticism is another mark of a true *budoka*. Accept the criticism with thanks, and bow to the instructor when they are finished. If you do not understand the criticism—that is, if you are unclear about this point or that—follow the rules of your school concerning questions to seniors.

ENDING A CLASS

The conventions for ending a class are generally the same when beginning it. The one difference is, after the final bow, say *"domo arigato gozaimasu"* instead of *"onegai-shimasu."* Some schools also conclude class with a general *"mina-sama domo arigato gozaimasu"* or *"otagai-ni domo arigato gozaimasu."* Again, follow the rules of your school.

CHAPTER TWELVE

THE FOUR BASIC PRINCIPLES

(YON DAI GEN SOKU)

Practicing aikido successfully and correctly executing aikido technique requires a specific state of mind and body. You must be relaxed and centered, mentally calm, and conscious of *ki*. While this reality was an integral part of O'Sensei's teachings, it was Koichi Tohei Sensei who codified it and broke it down into four specific points, which he dubbed the Four Basic Principles to Unify Mind and Body. Generally, they are referred to simply as the Four Basic Principles.

Each of the Four Basic Principles is related to the other. If you don't have one, you really don't have the others, even if you think you do. This will become clear as you read the following definitions.

1. KEEP ONE-POINT

The one-point, in aikido parlance, is the spot about three fingers width below your navel. Physically, it is your center of gravity, of body mass. Spiritually, it is where your *ki* resides. The Japanese refer to it as the *hara*, the *seika-no-tanden*, the *seika-no-itten*, and other names. In Western parlance, we might call it our "gut"—not the stomach, but that place where our "gut feelings" are born. In aikido, all movement originates from the one-point, as does your *ki* extension. Think of your one-point as your *ki* generator. To keep one-point is to be actively aware of it as you move and practice.

Close your eyes and place your hand lightly over your one-point. Move your mind there. Focus, and feel yourself becoming more calm and centered. Now, remove your hand and open your eyes. Keep this connection with your one-point at all times. Don't be discouraged if you don't feel anything right away. The more you try, the more success you will have.

2. RELAX COMPLETELY

Any athlete will tell you that you must be relaxed to perform at optimum efficiency and skill. While this may seem a contradiction in terms, it is not. Stiffen your entire body, then try to move fluidly. You can't do it. The same goes for aikido. In order to successfully execute aikido technique, you must be as relaxed as possible. You must also be relaxed to truly connect with your one-point.

Stand in *shizentai,* with your feet shoulder width apart, arms hanging naturally by your sides. Flex your knees slightly. Beginning with your feet, consciously relax your muscles, until you are expending no more physical energy than is necessary to remain standing. Mind you, this doesn't mean you should be so relaxed that you would fall if lightly touched. Rather, you should feel grounded and solid, ready to move easily and instantly.

3. WEIGHT UNDERSIDE

Just as relaxing completely flows from keeping one-point, keeping your weight underside flows naturally from relaxing completely. You must keep your weight down to perform aikido technique. You cannot expect to capture someone's *ki* and physical momentum if your weight is up around your chest or your shoulders. Imagine trying to manipulate a heavy weight while standing on your toes. You would quickly lose your balance and topple to the ground. Keeping your weight underside makes it easier for you to move in a flowing, balanced, and centered manner, anchored firmly to the ground, and more difficult for you to be moved by another.

An excellent demonstration of the effectiveness of keeping your weight underside can be quickly performed with a partner. Stiffen every muscle in your body. Make your body like a board. Have your partner wrap his or her arms around you and lift you off of the mat. Providing you are of similar body sizes, it shouldn't be hard to do. Now, relax and move your weight underside. Have your partner attempt to lift you again. When they begin, drop your entire weight. Let your entire body go limp. It will be much more difficult for your partner to move you.

4. EXTEND KI

Once you are connected with your one-point, completely relaxed and with your weight underside, you are ready to extend *ki.* We are not talking about projecting energy in some mystical manner, like a laser beam. To extend *ki* means to allow your natural spiritual and mental energy to flow easily and steadily through your body as you execute aikido technique.

The difference between extending *ki* in your technique and not extending *ki* will become readily apparent as you practice. When *ki* is not flowing, you will feel as if you are using all muscle to execute aikido technique. You will clash with your partner, and you will both quickly become frustrated, and physically and mentally tired. When *ki* is flowing, your technique will flow. Your movements will seem like a dance. Your partner will enjoy being thrown, and chances are you both will wind up smiling.

Professional athletes constantly speak of practicing the Four Basic Principles—they just use a different terminology. When an athlete speaks of being "in the zone," they mean they are performing in accordance with the Four Basic Principles. When you are "in the zone," you feel as if you can do no wrong. You find you are "seeing the ball really well," or "reading the other guy" to perfection. It is as if the scoring lane or the path to the end zone or goal is crystal clear, waiting just for you. You know what the other guy is going to do before he does it. You don't know how you know—you just do.

Practice of the Four Basic Principles isn't limited to the martial arts and athletics. Artists, actors, musicians, business people, people who practice any craft or trade, whether it's figuring taxes, planting flowers, laying bricks, even just sitting outside and enjoying a beautiful day—when everything is going just right, and you are peaceful and quietly joyful, relaxed yet alert and at one with your work, you are in the zone. And when you are in the zone, you are practicing the Four Basic Principles.

CHAPTER THIRTEEN

PROPER BREATHING

(IBUKI-NO-HO)

The importance of breathing in daily life is obvious. If we don't breathe, we will die. Since breathing is automatic, most of us don't think about it at all, unless something happens that prevents us from breathing. Then, breathing suddenly becomes the most important thing in the world.

It may seem pointless to spend time discussing something as apparently simple and automatic as breathing. However, awareness of breathing is very important when studying aikido, just as it is in any physical pursuit.

THE MECHANICS OF BREATHING

With every breath we take, we provide our bodies with the oxygen necessary to think, to move, to focus. Fortunately, we don't have to consciously tell ourselves to breathe. Our autonomic nervous system takes care of that chore for us. Our blood flows into microscopic capillaries in our lungs, where it is charged with oxygen when we inhale. You can think of oxygen as the fuel that powers our bodies. Our blood then carries the oxygen to our brain and our muscles, where it is exchanged for carbon dioxide (CO_2), the chief by-product of respiration. If oxygen is to our bodies as gasoline is to an automobile, then think of CO_2 as the exhaust that results from burning oxygen, like carbon monoxide is the chief by-product of gasoline combustion. The CO_2 is carried by the blood back to our lungs, where it is exhaled out of our bodies, and the cycle begins anew.

Some people think that when we inhale, our abdomen should move inward, and outward when we exhale. Although this seems to make sense on the surface, it's actually the exact opposite of what should naturally happen when we breathe. Think of a balloon. When you blow up a balloon, does it get smaller? Of course not. When a balloon fills with air, it expands. When we let the air escape from the balloon, it collapses. Our lungs behave the same way. When you inhale, you should see and feel your stomach extend along with your chest, then shrink when you exhale. If you see the opposite, you are breathing improperly, and depriving yourself of as much as half of the oxygen you could be taking in. It's not uncommon, amazing as it may seem, to find people who have taught themselves to breathe incorrectly their entire lives, simply because it "made more sense." All that time, they have been fighting their own bodies.

The proper way to breathe is deep abdominal breathing, what voice and speech teachers would call diaphragmatic breathing; that is, breathing from your diaphragm muscle. This muscle sits at the base of your lungs, just above your stomach. When we inhale, the diaphragm contracts, creating a vacuum in our lungs that pulls the air in. When we exhale, the diaphragm relaxes, allowing air and CO_2 to escape. It is this contraction and relaxation of the diaphragm that causes our stomachs to move out and in when we breathe. The deeper we inhale, the more our stomach expands, and vice-versa.

It is just as important to exhale completely as it is to fully inhale. The deeper we inhale, the more oxygen/fuel we give our bodies to use. But remember, the chief by-product of respiration is CO_2. Although this gas is harmless to us in moderate doses, too much of it is actually poisonous. It makes us feel sluggish and sleepy. Our thoughts become clouded, and our attention wandering and desperate. In extreme cases, muscles can cramp from lack of oxygen, our brain becomes oxygen-starved, and we pass out. If we do not exhale completely, we allow carbon dioxide to build up in our lungs and bodies, which affects our performance even if we are not aware of it. Professional athletes, swimmers especially, know this. When you see them exhaling sharply several times before they perform, they're ridding their bodies of as much CO_2 as they can, and replacing it with oxygen.

BREATHING AWARENESS IN AIKIDO

As noted earlier, awareness of breathing becomes even more important when you study aikido. It is very easy to fight our bodies when we are in a stressful situation, such as *randori* (defense against multiple attackers), to make it harder for our autonomic system to do its job properly. We breathe shallowly, or pant, or sometimes even forget to breathe entirely by holding our breath. And then, we wonder why we stumble and are so exhausted and irritable. Our training and technique suffer dramatically. Proper breathing can make the difference between performing well and "losing it" completely. For these reasons and others, the importance of proper breathing in aikido cannot be overstated.

The importance of breath in aikido goes beyond mere physical efficiency. One of the Japanese words for breath and breathing is *kokyu*. *Kokyu* means more than simple inhalation and exhalation. It means to take your breath deep within your *hara,* your one-point, using it to gather and focus your *ki,* and then to exhale *ki* throughout every fiber of your being. Notice that many aikido techniques and movements begin with *kokyu-nage,* for example. The literal translation of *kokyu-nage* means "breath throw." In application, this refers to the technique of using your breath to gather and focus your *ki* and to capture your attacker's *ki,* and then to use that energy to execute the technique. This is done in every technique, however, not just those which include *kokyu* in their designation. In order to do this properly and consistently, you must purposefully train your breathing and practice breathing awareness.

IBUKI-NO-HO

There are many methods in aikido to train ourselves to breathe properly and to develop breathing awareness. One of them is *ibuki-no-ho*. Now that you are aware of what actually happens inside your body when you breathe, keep this in mind as you practice the following method.

Sit in seiza *with your hands lying one atop the other in your lap. Make sure that your back is straight, so that you do not put unnecessary pressure on your diaphragm, and so that your lungs can fill completely. While it is not necessary to close your eyes, it often makes it easier to focus if you do.*

Breathe in deeply through your nose for a count of six seconds. You can better control your inhalation by slightly constricting your throat, so that the air makes a hollow hissing sound in your head as it enters your body. As you inhale, raise your arms out and up before you, keeping them relaxed. This movement not only helps you to focus and visualize ki, *but further expands your chest so that your lungs can fill with air to their limit. Make sure you visualize bringing* ki *into your body with your breath, down into your one-point.*

When you reach the end of the six-count, your lungs should be completely filled with air to the point that you cannot inhale even a bit more. Your abdomen should be fully extended as well, and you should be able to feel the air all the way down into your one-point. Your arms should reach the apex of their motion. Hold your breath in this position for a count of three, but make sure that you keep your throat open as you do. You should have the sense of a balloon completely filled with air, but with the neck open, so that air can freely move in or out.

Now, exhale through your mouth on a final count of six, bringing your arms back to the starting position. As with the inhale, constrict your throat to better control your exhalation, so that the air hisses as it escapes. When you exhale, visualize expanding your ki all around you in a bubble. The bubble can merely surround you, or reach to the walls of the dojo, or past the walls to encompass the entire universe. Make sure you exhale completely, all the way down to your one-point. Tighten your abdomen until there is not a bit of air left in your lungs. Hold for a count of three, and repeat.

When you perform *ibuki-no-ho,* you should feel relaxed, clear-headed, and calm. If you find yourself gasping for breath, just alter the count to one that is more comfortable for you. Remember, the object of *ibuki-no-ho* is to train breath control and breathing awareness, and this process, like all aikido training, takes time. The more you practice *ibuki-no-ho,* the longer you can make the breath cycle, performing it on a count of twelve, thirty or more. You can also alter the length of time you hold your breath in-between inhalation and exhalation. At advanced levels, it is not unusual to practice *ibuki-no-ho* so that the entire cycle takes two minutes or longer.

If you find that *ibuki-no-ho* feels like meditation, you are correct. As noted earlier, it not only develops breathing awareness and control, but also *ki* awareness and projection. Remember, you must actively visualize your *ki* as you practice *ibuki-no-ho,* even if you feel silly doing so at first. When you complete a session of *ibuki-no-ho,* you should feel calm and relaxed, yet completely alert and charged with energy, ready to tackle whatever awaits you.

BREATHING AWARENESS WHILE TRAINING

Maintaining breathing awareness while training is as simple as it sounds, yet it takes a great deal of practice. No matter how dynamic your practice session becomes, always remain conscious of your breathing. If you make this breathing awareness and control a consistent part of your training, it will soon become as automatic as breathing itself.

Whenever possible, breathe in through your nose and out through your mouth, and breathe deeply. Inhaling through your nose will help you control your breathing and prevent you from panting or becoming winded, while exhaling through your mouth allows you to quickly rid your body of carbon dioxide.

Remember to take the air down into your one-point, rather than stopping it in your chest. The degree to which you may become winded or "out of breath" while training depends a great deal on your general physical conditioning, but no matter what your level of overall fitness, proper breathing and breathing awareness will give you more energy and stamina, and will greatly enhance your technique.

CHAPTER FOURTEEN

SPIRIT SHOUT

(KIAI)

The literal translation of *kiai* is "unification of spirit." In practice, it is demonstrated by giving a loud, piercing shout as you execute a technique. You may have seen someone *kiai* while practicing, and wondered what the heck they were doing by shouting at their partner. *Kiai* in fact has several very useful martial applications.

THE SCIENCE OF SOUND

The science of sonics tells us that sounds of various pitches vibrate at different frequencies. Depending on the frequency and application, sound can be soothing and healing, or can cause pain and disorientation. A familiar example of this is the reaction most people have to the sound of fingernails being raked down a blackboard. It is more than painful to the ears; it actually affects us on a psychic level. In extreme applications, sound can cause physical damage and actually disrupt the structure of matter at the molecular level. Thus, the ability to control and focus sound holds great power.

THE PURPOSE OF KIAI

As the translation suggests, *kiai* is first and foremost a way to focus your *ki* at a given moment. It is actually a very natural phenomenon. Whenever you perform a strenuous physical activity—say, lifting a heavy object—chances are you find yourself grunting or even shouting at the moment of greatest exertion. This spontaneous exclamation seems to give us that little extra boost we need to complete the task, to focus our energy and our attention. *Kiai* in aikido operates on the very same principle, only with more conscious control.

    Kiai in aikido also serves an offensive/defensive purpose. To have someone shout in your face as you attack them is very disorienting. To have them *kiai* while they deliver *atemi* is even more disorienting, and can cause you to momentarily lose your own focus just long enough for your opponent to gain control. Imagine how surprised you would be if someone just walked up to you and then suddenly shouted in your face. By the time you registered what had happened, a full second or more may have elapsed. In a real-life defensive situation, that mere second can make all the difference.

At highly advanced levels, *kiai* becomes a defense in itself. Practitioners of the ancient and esoteric art of *kiaijutsu* deeply studied the *kiai* and the nature of sound and tonal qualities to the degree that it is said they could debilitate an opponent with their *kiai* alone. O'Sensei actively studied *kotodama,* the ancient Shinto doctrine which holds that certain sounds and words are sacred and have divine properties. That his belief and study held merit is beyond question: those who studied with the Founder tell of being momentarily paralyzed by his *kiai,* and there is film footage of O'Sensei knocking a charging attacker to the mat by using *kiai* alone—twice! (Suenaka Sensei describes first-hand examples of the undeniable efficacy of O'Sensei's *kiai* in Chapter 9 of the biographical section.)

KIAI IN AIKIDO

You should always practice *kiai* during your aikido training. Do not expect to be able to control your attacker using *kiai* alone, since such ability takes a lifetime of study, and arguably is beyond the scope of all but the most dedicated and enlightened among us. As mentioned earlier, however, the simple act of shouting with focus and intent while executing a technique can make a dramatic difference in your ability to gain control of a situation.

Just as proper breathing originates in your one-point, so too does *kiai*. It is no coincidence that your one-point is where your breath and *ki* reside. *Kiai* should be very energetic and cleansing, and should not feel strained or forced. When you *kiai,* you should feel your abdomen tighten, and the air and sound should explode from your body. Do not shout solely from your chest. Keep your throat open when you *kiai,* so that the sound and energy can flow unobstructed.

It helps to visualize *kiai* as a physical thing, a ball of energy which leaves your body and strikes your attacker. This does not mean that you must always think of the ball of energy as coming from your mouth. If you *kiai* while delivering *atemi,* you can visualize the energy surrounding your fist, or being directed by it. When throwing someone, you can imagine the *kiai* exploding from your one-point and striking your attacker like an invisible hammer. What is important is that when you *kiai,* you do so with focus and intent, and make it an integral part of your training.

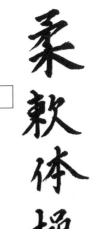

STRETCHING

(JU NAN TAISO)

Stretching is very important whenever you are about to engage in any physical activity. The more dynamic the activity, the more important stretching becomes. Even the most flexible *aikidoka* always take at least a few moments to stretch before practice: that's *why* they're so flexible. Like everything in aikido, however, it takes time and constant practice to achieve maximum flexibility, and there are specific ways to get there.

THE PHYSIOLOGY OF STRETCHING

Muscles are fibrous. That is, they are composed of thousands of microscopic strands of tough, yet elastic tissue. Just as muscles grow stronger and larger the more we exercise, they grow longer, stronger and more flexible the more we stretch. Stretching also gets the blood flowing in the muscles, helps keep body joints lubricated, and can help stave off many arthritic conditions, or better-manage existing ones. Once you attain maximum flexibility for your body type, continued stretching serves as maintenance to ensure you don't lose it.

THE BENEFITS OF STRETCHING

Aikido is a very dynamic activity. You must be able to move quickly and fluidly, to remain relaxed even in the most dynamic situations, and to tumble and receive wrist and joint locks without injury. The more flexible you are, the easier all of this becomes. Conversely, the less flexible you are, the more likely you are to be injured. It is as simple as the difference between a supple, green tree limb and a stiff, dry one. Where the dry limb is easily broken, the green one requires much more effort to break, simply because it's flexible. Even if it's smaller than the dry limb, its flexibility makes it much stronger.

Stretching has a mental and spiritual benefit as well. Flexibility

145

of the body helps cultivate flexibility of the mind and of the spirit. A person who is always tense and rigid is likely to behave in ways that reflect this state. The more flexible a person is, the more calm and centered they are likely to be, and the less likely they are to resist change and new ideas. Like the tree limb, they bend rather than break. This flexibility of mind and spirit is what all *aikidoka* seek.

You should always stretch thoroughly before every training session. Stretching thoroughly means stretching all the major muscle groups in your body, from your toes to your neck. Some schools stretch in unison as a class, while others expect students to stretch beforehand, on their own. Regardless of the rules of your school, always take time to stretch, even if it's only a minute or two. It's also not a bad idea to stretch after a training session, particularly if it's been very dynamic. Doing so will prevent your muscles from becoming overly stiff or cramped as they cool down.

STRETCHING SAFELY

It is deceptively easy to injure yourself while stretching. While you must stretch your muscles bit-by-bit past their comfortable limit to increase your flexibility, if you push your muscles too far too fast, you can easily tear or otherwise injure them. Such injuries are often quite painful, and can take weeks, even months, to fully heal. Not only will your study be hampered in the meantime, but the injured muscle will forever be slightly weaker than it was before, and more prone to future re-injury. You are the only person who can determine what your limit is. Don't let anyone cajole or force you to stretch past what you feel is comfortable. It's you who risks being injured, not they.

When you stretch, it is natural to feel a burning sensation in the muscle being stretched as it is pushed past its limit; "no pain, no gain," as the saying goes. However, if you feel a sudden, sharp pain in the muscle or joint, relax the stretch immediately. Work the muscle or joint to determine whether or not it has been injured. If you feel the pain again as you do so, give the affected area a day or so to rest before stretching it again. Remember, though, that it's natural to feel a burning sensation in the stretched muscle even after the stretch is relaxed, but it should quickly fade.

Don't lunge into a stretch. Rather, you should ease into it. When you reach your limit, hold the stretch for at least a count of ten, longer as you become more flexible. You may find yourself unconsciously resisting the stretch by tightening the muscle, especially when you near your limit. When this happens, relax the muscle being stretched as much as possible. Not only will this help deepen the stretch, but it will decrease the discomfort. Also, don't bounce into a stretch, in an attempt to force yourself to stretch further, a practice known as "ballistic stretching." Many people do this when stretching their hamstrings or other leg muscles, and it's a sure way to injure yourself if you're not careful, or if you're tight. There are many differing opinions on the pros and cons of ballistic stretching. For beginners, it's best to avoid it altogether. It's okay, however, to gently push yourself forward another fraction, then back, forward, back, and so on, in a controlled manner.

Remember to breathe while you stretch. Sometimes, you may find yourself holding or straining your breath. This is counterproductive, and will make stretching more difficult. Refer to the section on *ibuki-no-ho* for detailed information on breathing mechanics and proper breathing techniques.

Finally, you may have seen advertisements in magazines that offer "quick and easy" ways to achieve maximum flexibility. While there are certainly stretching techniques that are more efficient than others and may therefore help you become more flexible more quickly, there is no "trick" to becoming flexible. The only sure way to do it is to stretch every day, a little further each day. If you stretch several times each day, you will see faster progress, and your stretching sessions will become more efficient.

BASIC STRETCHES

All you need do is browse through a book on yoga to see that there are hundreds of stretches, each with its own unique benefits. Describing them all here is both impractical and unnecessary. The stretches illustrated should be all you need to achieve the flexibility necessary to safely and enjoyably study aikido.

The following stretches are presented in groups, each focusing on a different area or areas of the body (wrist stretches are covered in the next chapter). Likewise, the groups are arranged in a sequence designed to allow the stretching session to flow naturally from one group to another. While it's not necessary to follow the overall sequence, it's advisable. Certainly you should follow the steps in each group in order to get the full benefit of the stretch.

Don't be discouraged if you can't stretch as far as the people in the photographs. They all achieved their levels of flexibility through years of constant stretching. Do as much as you can, do it every day, and you will make sure and steady progress, guaranteed.

Begin by sitting in seiza. *Pound yourself firmly all over with your fists—chest, upper and lower back, arms and shoulders, abdomen, thighs, wherever you can reach (except your face and head, of course). While this may seem strange, it helps to stimulate blood flow to your body, and "wakes up" the muscles. It also stimulates many accupressure points and nerve meridians all over the body, further invigorating you and preparing you for your stretching session.*

Begin in seiza. *Close your eyes and rotate your head in large circles, taking it as far as you can in every direction. After several revolutions, reverse direction.*

Bow your head. Interlace your fingers and place them on the back of your head, as shown, allowing the weight of your arms to further stretch the muscles in the back of your neck and in your upper back. It's not necessary to pull downward.

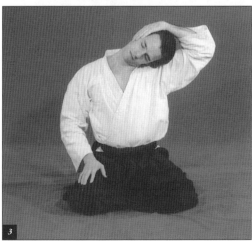

Tilt your head to the left. Place your left hand on your head, as shown, and allow the weight of your arm to stretch the muscles on the left side of your neck. Repeat on the right side.

149

Sitting in seiza, *let your arms hang naturally by your sides. Roll your shoulders forward in as big a circle as you can. After several revolutions, reverse direction. Lastly, alternate shoulders, with the left moving forward as the right moves backwards and vice-versa. (2) Raise your left arm in front of you, keeping it straight. Moving from the shoulder, cross it in front of you as far as it will go.*

Place your right forearm against the outside of your left arm, just above the elbow, as shown. Move your right arm to the right, pulling your left arm with it. You should feel the stretch in the top and rear of your left shoulder. Repeat with the other arm.

TRICEPS

Sitting in seïza, *touch your right shoulder with your right hand. Your elbow should be pointing away from your body at a forty-five degree angle. (2) Point your right elbow to the ceiling, as high as it will go. Grasp your right elbow with your left hand and pull it to the rear. You should feel the stretch in the back of your upper arm. Repeat with the other arm.*

KNEES

Sit on the mat with your back straight and your legs together and extended before you. Using both hands as shown, massage your knees briskly until they feel warm.

Sit on the mat and cross your left leg so that your left shin is resting on your right thigh. Take your left foot in both hands and rotate it so that your ankles pass through a full range of motion—point the toes, twist the instep, and so on. (2) Pound firmly on the sole of your foot with the knuckles of your right hand. The reason for this is the same as in the pre-stretch description, above.

Take your ankle in both hands and shake it vigorously, allowing your foot to move freely wherever it will. Return your leg to starting position and repeat steps one through four with your right leg. (4) Rotate your feet in a wide circle to the left. After several revolutions, reverse direction. Finish by pointing your toes forward, then backward, several times.

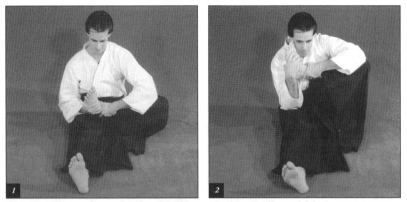

Sit as if performing step one of the feet and ankles stretch, above. Cradle your left leg in your arms as shown. (2) Pull your left knee up and into your body. Make sure you pull primarily on your knee and not your ankle. Pulling your ankle alone can cause your knee to be injured. You should feel this stretch deep in your hip joint. Repeat with your other leg.

HAMSTRINGS AND LOWER BACK

Sit on the mat and point your toes to the ceiling.

Reach forward and grasp your feet from above, with your hands above your toes. Do your best to keep your back straight. Don't let your legs bend, but neither should you lock your knees. It's okay to pull on your feet to help stretch forward. If you cannot reach your toes, stretch as far as you can, grabbing your ankles or shins. Make sure you keep your shoulders down and relaxed.

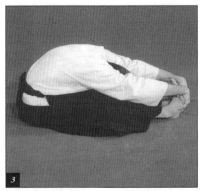

With continued practice, you should be able to stretch forward far enough to touch your chin to your knees or shin, as shown.

Sit with your legs spread as wide apart as possible. Keep your toes pointed to the ceiling. (2) Stretch to the right, grasping your foot as shown with your right hand. Keep your back straight and try to touch your head to your knee.

An alternate version of this stretch. Notice how the left arm is reaching for the right foot, and how the aikidoka is facing forward. This also helps stretch the outer side of the body and the upper shoulder. (3) With continued practice, you should be able to stretch far enough so that you can grab your foot with both hands and touch your chin to your shin, as shown. Now, repeat steps one and two on the other side.

Spread your legs a bit wider, if you can. Reach out to either side and grab your feet as shown. Try to touch your forehead to the mat. You should feel this stretch in your groin and the inside of your legs, all the way down to your knees. Be especially careful not to force this stretch, as groin muscle and inner thigh injuries are especially painful and take a long time to heal.

With continued practice, you should be able to lay your upper body flat on the mat, as shown, with your legs completely perpendicular to your torso. This, however, requires an extremely high degree of flexibility. If you never reach this level, you will have lots of company! (6) Bend your knees and bring your feet together with the soles flat against one another, as shown. Interlace your fingers and cradle your feet in them. Tuck your heels in as close to your body as you can, and then "butterfly" your legs up and down, like flapping wings.

Hang on to your feet with your left hand and press your right knee to the mat with your right hand, as shown. Repeat on the left. (8) Finally, cradle your feet once again with both hands and bend forward. Try to touch your forehead to your feet, or to the mat just in front of them.

UPPER THIGH STRETCH

For many people, this stretch is the most difficult. Take great care when practicing it, as it is very easy to injure your knees or lower back if you perform it carelessly.

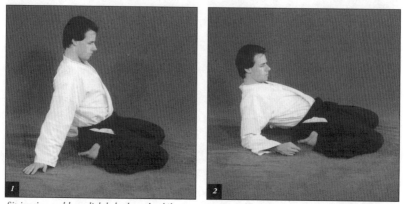

Sit in seiza and lean slightly backwards while supporting yourself on your arms and hands, as shown. For this stretch, your feet should not be crossed. (2) Slowly lower yourself backwards. You should feel the stretch in the tops of your thighs. When you have reached your limit, stop.

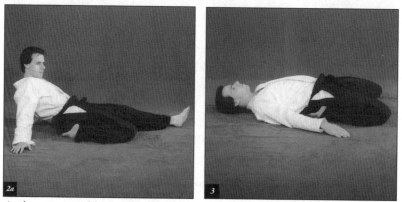

An alternate version of this stretch, stretching just one leg at a time. Perform this version if you are particularly stiff, or if you have physical problems such as bad knees. (3) With continued practice, you should be able to lay all the way back, as shown. If you take the stretch to this point, be very aware of any strain you may feel in your lower back in particular.

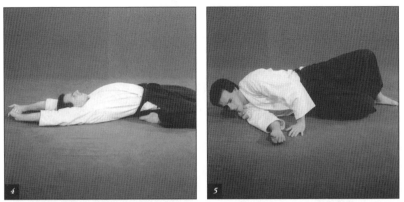

You can deepen the stretch by extending your arms as shown—left arm over your right shoulder, and vice-versa. Use your lower arm to help you fully extend the upper. (5) To recover from this stretch, you can simply roll to the side, or...

...extend your arms out to either side and use them to push yourself back into seiza.

Stand with your feet and knees together, as shown. Place your hands atop your knees. (2) Keeping your knees together, use your hands to help rotate them in a circle, first in one direction, then the other. You should also feel your ankles rotating, though not as much as your knees.

Stand with your feet shoulder width apart. Keeping your legs straight (but not locked), bend forward as far as you can. The goal is to place your palms flat on the mat. (2) Now rise, extend your arms above your head, and bend backwards as far as you can. Repeat steps two and three several times.

Place your left hand on your hip, extend your right over your head, and bend sideways to your left, as shown. Reach in the direction of the stretch with your upper hand. Alternate sides several times. (4) Finally, extend your arms over your head and rotate your body in a circle, bending at the waist. Think of tracing a circle that starts above and behind your head, moves forward to the mat before you, then back to the starting point. Perform several revolutions in one direction, then reverse and repeat.

CHAPTER SIXTEEN

FALLING AND TUMBLING
(UKEMI)

Although *ukemi* is most commonly defined as tumbling or proper falling, it is more than that. Just as *uke* means the person receiving a technique, *ukemi,* properly defined, means methods of receiving those techniques safely.

It could easily be argued that *ukemi* is the key to a complete understanding of aikido technique. It is certainly true that an aikido education will never be complete without a solid grasp of the fundamentals of *ukemi.* It's worth noting that, traditionally, novice students in jujutsu and other arts would spend months, sometimes a year or more, doing nothing but taking *ukemi* for their teacher and senior students before being allowed to try the first technique. This practice had several purposes: it built physical strength, flexibility and stamina in the student; it helped the student better understand the dynamics of a technique by feeling what it was like to receive the technique; and it tested the mettle and character of a student.

The value of this last purpose shouldn't be underestimated or taken for granted. On a base level, it can be viewed as "paying your dues." More importantly, however, a willingness to take *ukemi* is one of the signs of a true *aikidoka*. O'Sensei believed that *uke* and *nage* were one, for without an *uke,* there was no need for a *nage*. Therefore, in order to be a good *nage,* you must also be a good *uke*—you must be willing and able to take as good as you can give. It's selfish to view *ukemi* as a chore, something to be minimally tolerated until it's again your turn to be *nage*. Nobody wants to work with this type of student— it makes learning aikido a frustrating struggle. On the other hand, working with a sincere and skilled *uke* is a true pleasure, in the same way that taking *ukemi* for a skilled nage is a pleasure. Ultimately, in giving good *ukemi,* you not only better yourself, you become a teacher, helping your partner to better his or her technique. To be known as a good *uke* is one of the highest compliments an *aikidoka* can receive, and it is considered an honor to be asked to take *ukemi* for a student during rank promotion testing, for only the best *uke* are up to the task.

A final word on attitude towards *ukemi*. Some might argue that being a good *uke* doesn't matter, that a *nage* should be able to throw a person whether their *ukemi* is good or not. This is true, to a point. There is a story Suenaka Sensei tells of his early teaching days that perfectly illustrates the difference. He once had a well-built, rather dense young man visit his *dojo* and ask to be shown a technique. Suenaka obliged and gently applied *nikyo*, but the visitor resisted and refused to take *ukemi* (although obviously, he had no idea what *ukemi* was). Suenaka asked the man to relax, but he replied that he wanted to see if aikido "really worked." "What would you do if I did this outside?" he asked, meaning how would Suenaka respond if the encounter was taking place on the street. "I would punch you," Suenaka responded. "Well, then, punch me," said the visitor. So Suenaka further obliged his guest, punching the young man in the nose (much to his surprise), whereupon the *nikyo* worked like a charm.

The lesson of the preceding story is simple. While a skilled *aikidoka* can make his or her technique work against an unskilled *uke,* knowledge of *ukemi* is what prevents an *uke* from becoming injured during practice. Of course, *ukemi* doesn't mean knowing how to take a punch. As noted earlier, it means knowing how to receive a technique safely, without injuring yourself. This includes knowing how to tumble and fall safely in any direction, irregardless of the technique being applied. It is these aspects of *ukemi* which we will illustrate in the following section.

Sit with your left leg tucked beneath your right.

Round your back as you fall backwards, keeping your chin tucked into your chest to prevent it from hitting the mat. Rounding your back turns the backwards fall into more of a tumble, and lessens the impact.

As you complete the fall, extend your arms at roughly a forty-five degree angle from your body and slap the mat in concert with your impact. Don't bang your elbows into the mat or slap with your hands only. Your entire arm from the palm to just below your elbow (the fleshy part of your forearm) should strike the mat. This motion, called "slapping out," helps dissipate the force of the impact by spreading it over as wide a surface area of your body as possible.

Falling backwards from a standing position is really nothing more than sitting down:

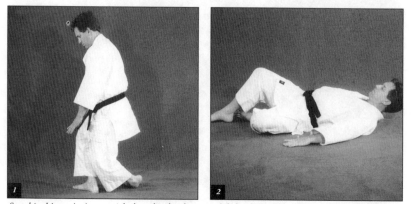

Stand in shizentai. *As your right knee bends, place your left foot behind your right, as shown and...*
(2)...sit down, moving smoothly into a seated rearward fall. Notice the foot position—the left leg is tucked beneath the right, and the right leg is raised and bent.

Usually when you take *koho-ukemi,* you will not fall directly backwards, but will instead find yourself falling at a backwards angle to the left or right, landing on one side or the other. The fundamental dynamics of this type of fall are the same as the basic example illustrated on the facing page, with only a few differences:

Begin in shizentai *and fall backwards, to your left. (2) When your left buttock touches the mat, continue tumbling backwards on the left side of your body until...*

...you are completely prone, slapping out with your left arm as you impact. Repeat on the right.

165

KOHO-TENTO-UNDO
(BACKWARD RISING AND FALLING EXERCISES)

Koho-tento undo is an exercise designed to help you become proficient in *koho-ukemi.* These "down-and-ups," as they're sometimes called, combine the seated and standing methods shown above, and can be repeated as many times as desired.

KOHO-TENTO-UNDO (A)

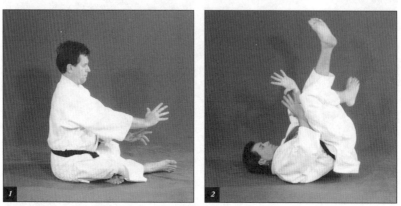

Begin in the seated koho-ukemi *position. (2) Fall backwards to the right, without slapping out, and...*

...immediately tumble back into seated position by extending your arms before you, as shown, switching your legs as you do so, so that they are in proper position as you come to rest. While rising, think of projecting your ki forward as you tug on an invisible rope. The more rounded your body is and the more your attention is focused forward, the easier it will be for you to return to the seated position. (It is even more important when performing the standing variation of this exercise, shown on the next page.) Take a moment to settle your weight and ki, *then repeat to the other side.*

KOHO-TENTO-UNDO (B)

Begin in shizentai. *(2) Fall backwards as before, without slapping out, and then...*

...rise to the seated position, switching your legs as you do so. (4) Once in seated position, keep rising until you are standing once again. Settle your weight and ki, *then repeat on the other side.*

ZENPO-UKEMI (FORWARD FALLING METHODS)

KNEELING

Begin on your knees. Raise your arms to your sides as shown, slightly forward of your torso, with your hands open and your palms facing forward.

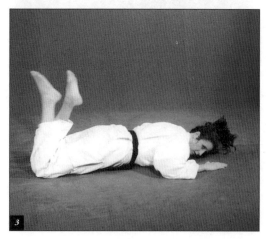

Turn your head to the side and fall forward to the mat. Your arms should hit first and absorb the brunt of the impact (just as when you slapped out in the previous ukemi *examples). Tighten your abdomen as you hit the mat, and exhale sharply through your teeth or* kiai *upon impact. Just like* koho-ukemi, *your head should never hit the mat.*

NOTE: IT IS VERY EASY TO LAND ON YOUR ELBOWS WHEN PRACTICING *ZENPO-UKEMI*. ALL IT TAKES IS ONE GOOD WHACK TO YOUR "FUNNY BONE" TO CURE YOU OF THIS HABIT! ALSO, MAKE SURE YOU KEEP YOUR MOUTH CLOSED, AND THAT YOUR TONGUE ISN'T BETWEEN YOUR TEETH AS YOU FALL.

Begin in shizentai.

As you fall forward, raise your arms into ready position and turn your head to the side.

Slap out and exhale or kiai *as before when you impact.*

ZENPO-TENTO-UNDO (FORWARD RISING AND FALLING EXERCISE)

Zenpo-tento-undo are exactly the same as *zenpo-ukemi,* only performed continuously. Fall, get up, and do it again. When performing *zenpo-tento-undo* from a standing position, it is often customary to take a step forward between each fall, working your way from one end of the mat to the other.

KOHO-KAITEN-UKEMI (BACKWARDS TUMBLING METHODS)

When you take a backwards fall, you don't have to slap out, dust yourself off, and get up. It's often much easier, depending on how you have been thrown, to simply turn the backwards fall into a backwards tumble, rising smoothly to your feet. It's also easier on your body. Tumbling is also tremendous fun, once you get the hang of it.

When performing *koho-kaiten-ukemi,* you do not tumble directly backwards, onto your head. Rather, you tumble over your shoulder. The shoulder over which you will tumble is determined by whichever leg is raised and bent. If it is your left leg, you will tumble over your left shoulder, and vice-versa.

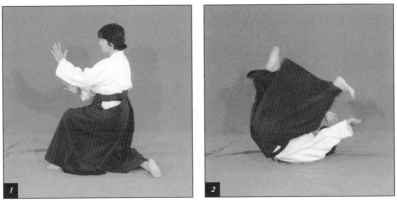

Begin in the usual seated koho-ukemi *position. Since* uke's *left leg is raised and bent, she will roll over her left shoulder, and so she has tilted her head to the right and tucked in her chin. (2) Keeping your body tightly tucked, roll backwards over your left shoulder. It is helpful at this point to think of tossing a bag of sand over your "active" shoulder. Not only does this help focus your* ki *in the proper direction, but it also places your hands in the proper position...*

(3)...for the mid-point of the tumble. Your inside arm (the left) will lay flat against the mat, while your right arm is bent, with the hand helping to support your weight and keep you from tipping over. Notice how uke *continues to keep her head tucked and to one side. (4) Continue rolling backwards until you return to the starting position. Switch legs and repeat on the other side.*

NOTE: GETTING THE HANG OF BACKWARDS TUMBLING IS HARDER FOR SOME PEOPLE THAN FORWARD TUMBLING. THE MOST COMMON REASON IS FAILURE TO KEEP THE BODY TIGHTLY TUCKED. THE MORE OPEN YOUR POSTURE, THE HARDER IT WILL BE TO GET EVEN HALFWAY THROUGH THE TUMBLE WITHOUT TIPPING OVER TO THE SIDE.

Begin in shizentai *and perform* koho-ukemi.

Instead of slapping out when you impact, tilt your head to the proper side and turn the fall into a tumble, and…

…rise to your feet when the tumble is complete.

KOHO-KAITEN-UNDO (BACKWARDS TUMBLING EXERCISES)

Koho-kaiten-undo are nothing more the continuous repetition of the backwards tumble. From the seated position, tumble backwards from one side of the mat to the other, then turn around, switch sides, and do it again. You can also try following the perimeter of the mat, but be forewarned—it's tricky! When performing *koho-kaiten-undo* from standing position, you usually switch sides every time you rise. Tumble to your left and rise, tumble to your right and rise, and so on.

ZENPO-KAITEN-UKEMI (FORWARD TUMBLING METHODS)

Zenpo-kaiten-ukemi are perhaps the most dynamic tumbles in aikido. It is quite something to watch someone sail over the mat after being thrown, and then tuck, tumble, and rise to their feet as if nothing had happened. With practice, a skilled *uke* can leap over a six-foot barrier from a standing start and tumble to his or her feet on the other side, or leap from a running start over half-a-dozen or more adults kneeling side-by-side on the mat. While such feats aren't the purpose of learning *zenpo-kaiten-ukemi*, they illustrate the flexibility a solid grasp of *zenpo-kaiten-ukemi* skills can give an *aikidoka,* and the value of *ukemi* in general. Imagine taking such falls if you didn't know how to tumble—the damage to your body would be tremendous, especially if you were thrown on the pavement.

Like *koho-kaiten-ukemi,* you don't tumble directly over your head and back, but over your shoulder and side. If your right arm and leg are forward, you tumble over your right shoulder, and vice-versa.

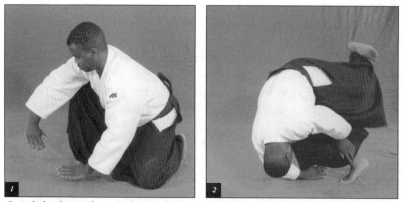

Begin by kneeling, as shown. In this case, the uke's *right leg is up, so he will tumble over his right shoulder, and tilts his head to the left and tucks in his chin. (2) Extend your right arm forward and down to the inside of your raised knee, as shown. Notice how the* uke's *arm is slightly curved, forming an arc which begins at his fingertips, curves over his right shoulder and down his back, and ends at his left buttock. The imaginary line inscribed by this arc indicates which parts of the* uke's *body will come in contact with the mat as he tumbles. Also, notice that the* uke's *left arm is extended before him in a mirror position to his right, so that both arms together form a circle.*

(3) Keeping your body tightly tucked, roll over your right shoulder, twisting your body slightly to your right as you do so. Make sure you keep your feet tucked in as you roll. (4) Complete the tumble and return to the starting position. Switch sides and repeat.

NOTE: AS IN *KOHO-KAITEN-UNDO,* IF YOU'RE HAVING TROUBLE MAKING IT THROUGH THE TUMBLE WITHOUT FALLING OVER, YOU'RE PROBABLY NOT TUCKING TIGHTLY ENOUGH. IF YOU CAN'T RETURN TO THE KNEELING POSITION, CHECK YOUR LEGS AND FEET—CHANCES ARE, YOU EXTENDED THEM AS YOU WERE ROLLING. MAKE SURE YOU KEEP THEM TUCKED AS WELL.

Practice *zenpo-kaiten-ukemi* from a kneeling position until you feel comfortable before trying it from a standing start. Taking a standing tumble for the first time can be a bit intimidating, and it's easy to get hurt if you don't know what you're doing. Although you can just as easily begin in *shizentai,* it's easier to learn *zenpo-kaiten-ukemi* from a standing position if you begin in *hanmi.*

Uke *is standing in* migi-hanmi, *since he is going to tumble to the right. Notice that his head and upper body position are exactly the same as* zenpo-kaiten-ukemi *from a kneeling start, and that he is slightly bent at the waist. (2) Slowly lean forward until gravity causes you to fall. Tumble over your right shoulder, tucking your legs and body into a tight ball as you do so. Since* uke *is tumbling to the right, he has tucked his left leg behind his right. It may help to push off on your right leg as you begin falling, you give you more impetus.*

Rise to your feet as you complete the tumble. Notice how uke *has extended his arms before him, ready to meet an attack.*

NOTE: WHEN TAKING DYNAMIC TUMBLES, YOU CAN HELP DISSIPATE YOUR MOMENTUM BY SLAPPING THE MAT WITH YOUR OUTSIDE HAND AS YOU TUMBLE. YOU CAN DO THIS FROM ANY FORWARD TUMBLE.

Zenpo-kaiten-ukemi from a leaping start should not be attempted until you're comfortable with taking a tumble from a standing start.

Step briskly forward on your right leg, and push off into a tumble.

Rise to your feet as you complete the tumble.

Zenpo-kaiten-ukemi from a running start is self-explanatory. Just remember to push off on your leading leg, and don't attempt the tumble until you are proficient in the first three.

ZENPO-KAITEN-UNDO (FORWARD TUMBLING EXERCISES)

Like *koho-kaiten-undo, zenpo-kaiten-undo* are merely continuous repetition of *zenpo-kaiten-ukemi* from a kneeling or standing start. When kneeling, you can tumble continuously from one end of the mat to the other. Unlike *koho-kaiten-undo,* however, you can also easily tumble around the mat, following the perimeter (it's usually easier to move clockwise when tumbling over your left shoulder, and vice-versa). *Zenpo-kaiten-undo* from a standing start can be performed in the same fashion, or one can alternate sides—standing, leaping or running.

For a complete *ukemi* workout, combine the different methods. For example, you can start at one end of the mat and perform a forward fall, rise, tumble forward and slap the mat, rise, turn 180-degrees and tumble backwards, rise, turn 180-degrees and take backwards fall while slapping out, rise, tumble forward again, rise, turn 180-degrees and take a leaping roll, and so on. Don't be afraid to mix it up!

SUTEMI (SACRIFICE FALL)

The only *ukemi* that rivals *zenpo-kaiten-ukemi* in sheer impressiveness is the *sutemi*. Common in judo, in aikido it technically falls under the umbrella of *zenpo-kaiten-ukemi,* but it is specialized enough to merit separate discussion. Its use is equally specialized.

As the definition implies, a *sutemi* sacrifices the body in order to save it. This sounds contradictory only until you see a *sutemi* performed. Study the following examples:

You can take a *sutemi* out of dozens of techniques—the list is much too long to detail. Some *aikidoka* will take a *sutemi* whenever they get the chance, simply because it's fun and it looks great. It's not nearly as important to know when you can take a *sutemi,* as it is to be able to recognize when you *should.* This can only come with practice.

A final word about *sutemi.* It is very easy to injure yourself if you do not perform *sutemi* correctly. Because of the nature and dynamics of the *sutemi,* such injuries can be severe, ranging from a separated or dislocated shoulder, to a broken neck. For this reason, many schools do not teach sutemi until the student is *nikyu* (scond *kyu)* or higher, with at least a year of experience. **Do not** attempt a full *sutemi* for the first time in an unsupervised environment, or without adequate experience.

Nage *performs a dynamic, incorrect* kote-gaeshi, *taking* uke's *wrist to the outside. If* uke *takes a backwards fall, he risks spraining or breaking his wrist. Instead,* uke *takes a diving forward roll over his own wrist...*

...landing on his side and slapping out as he impacts. While he has "sacrificed" his body, he has saved his wrist.

SUTEMI (YAMA-ARASHI)

Nage *performs* yama-arashi, *but does not release* uke's *wrists.* Uke *cannot tumble out of the technique, so he instead somersaults, absorbing the impact with the side of his body and slapping out with his feet, so to speak. He has "sacrificed" his body in order to prevent greater potential harm.*

179

From a kneeling position, perform a forward tumble. However, instead of returning to kneeling position, allow your body to unroll, as shown... (2)...slapping out with your outside hand as you impact. Notice that since uke *tumbled over his right shoulder, his right leg is raised and bent, and his left is tucked beneath it. The force of the* sutemi *is absorbed by the left side of* uke's *body. Also notice that, while* uke *keeps his head raised, his shoulders are in contact with the mat.*

STANDING

Perform a forward roll from a standing position, and finish as in step two, above.

One of the easiest ways to practice taking a full *sutemi* is to do it with a partner, from *kote-gaeshi*. In the following example, *nage* does not throw *uke*, but merely holds the *kote-gaeshi* lock in "pre-throw" position, and allows *uke* to take a *sutemi*. Make sure you're comfortable with taking a *sutemi* from kneeling and standing position before attempting a full *sutemi*.

Nage *holds* uke's *wrist in a* kote-gaeshi *lock, as if preparing to throw. (2)* Uke *takes a forward tumble over his locked wrist. Since it is* uke's *right wrist that is locked, he is essentially performing a right forward tumble.*

Uke *lands in* sutemi *position on the mat. Again, make sure that you keep your head tucked, that you land on your side and not your back, and that you slap out.*

You can also practice taking a full sutemi on your own. Be extremely careful, however. If you are hesitant, if you are inexperienced, or if you get sloppy, you can easily injure yourself, including separating or dislocating a shoulder or even breaking your neck.

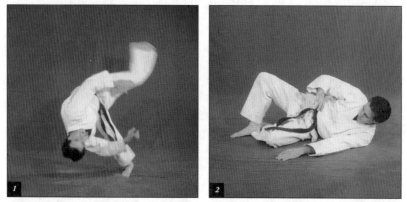

From a standing start, take a step forward and leap into the air. Tuck your body tightly as your feet leave the floor, and perform a mid-air somersault. (2) Unfold your body as you complete the somersault and complete the sutemi.

Because of its dynamism, the only way to truly polish your sutemi is to practice the fall itself. However, there is a specific *undo*, borrowed from judo, that will help you with the basics:

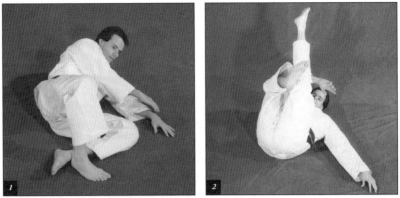

Begin on your left side. (2) Thrust your legs and hips into the air until only your upper back and shoulders are in contact with the mat. As you do so, switch your leg position and twist your body to the right, and...

...let your body fall to the right, in the exact reverse position as when you began, slapping out with your right hand as your lower body impacts the mat.

NOTE: *SUTEMI-UNDO* CAN BE PERFORMED IN SETS OF TWO—RIGHT-LEFT, RIGHT-LEFT—OR IT CAN BE PERFORMED CONTINUOUSLY—RIGHT, LEFT, RIGHT, LEFT, AND SO ON.

CHAPTER SEVENTEEN

AIKIDO EXERCISES

(AIKI-TAISO)

Aiki-taiso are basic exercises, performed without a partner. Like the Four Basic Principles, they were developed by Koichi Tohei, and are based on O'Sensei's teachings. *Taiso* are usually performed in unison with the rest of an aikido class before *waza* instruction. However, they are more than just warm-up exercises.

Much like karate *kata, taiso* are not techniques in themselves *per se,* but they embody many of the principles essential to the successful execution of aikido technique, such as centering, blending, balance, flexibility, hand and arm movement *(te-sabaki),* body movement *(tai-sabaki),* and footwork *(ashi-sabaki).* As such, *taiso* should be an integral part of your training, and not something to be "glossed over" or considered a chore. Some of the *taiso* may appear bizarre and without obvious purpose, merely a series of random movements. Once you begin executing aikido technique, however, their purpose can easily be seen. *Zengo-choyaku-undo,* for example, precisely embodies the initial movements of the *shomen-uchi kokyu-nage tenkan* technique. Thus, *taiso* can provide answers to problems you may be experiencing with your general *waza.* Similarly, failure to properly perform *taiso* can lead to problems with your *waza.*

Notice that individual *taiso* are called *undo. Taiso* and *undo* essentially mean the same thing—exercise. However, *undo* refers more to a particular movement. Thus, the individual *undo* are collectively known as *taiso.* To keep things simple, in this book, *taiso* and *undo* are used interchangeably. Also, there are *taiso* that specifically deal with *ukemi.* These *undo* are covered in the earlier chapter on that topic.

It's important, as it is while performing all aikido technique, to keep the Four Basic Principles in mind while performing *aiki-taiso*—keep one-point, relax completely, weight underside, and extend *ki.*

Refer to the previous chapter on the Four Basic Principles to refresh your memory.

Taiso are not generally performed in any particular order, although many of them are performed in groups, depending on their similarities. The following *taiso* have been grouped accordingly.

TEKUBI-UNDO (WRIST EXERCISES)

Tekubi-undo help develop wrist strength and flexibility, which is vital to *aikidoka*. The first four—*nikyo, nikyo* (b), *sankyo,* and *kote-gaeshi*—are actual locks, and teach proper *te-sabaki*.

Stretch your wrists as much as you can when performing *tekubi-undo,* but be careful you don't injure yourself by pushing the stretch past what is comfortable for you. Just go a little further each time, and flexibility will come.

NIKYO-UNDO (A) (FIRST WRIST EXERCISE/MOVEMENT)

Standing in hidari-hanmi *(left foot pointed forward with the right foot placed behind and perpendicular), extend your left hand in front of you, with the thumb pointing down and the fingers together, as shown. Your weight should be centered, as shown. (2) Grasp your left hand with your right, wrapping the fingers of your right hand over the top of the left and the right thumb below it, keeping the left thumb free. Make sure you grab the palm, and not the fingers. Your grip should be firm, but not crushing.*

Bring your hands into your one-point, rotating the left hand downward. (4) Bring your left wrist up to your chin, maintaining pressure with your right hand. You should feel the stretch in the top of your left wrist and hand. Make sure you keep your shoulders down and relaxed, and your elbows in close to your body. As you do so, shift your hips forward, again taking care to remain centered.

Release the stretch, returning your hands to your one-point as you shift your hips back to the starting position. (6) Pivot on the balls of your feet to migi-hanmi *(right stance). Change your grip so that you now grasp your right hand with your left, and repeat.*

Standing in hidari-hanmi, *extend your left hand before you, with the thumb down and the palm facing to the outside. (2) Grasp your left hand with your right, and bring your left wrist in to your chin. As you do so, press your left hand so that the fingers point towards your left elbow, while simultaneously rotating your fingers upwards, towards your head. You should feel your wrist stretching in two directions—to the left, and upwards. Make sure you keep your shoulders down and relaxed. Shift your hips backwards as you bring in your wrist, as shown, taking care to remain centered.*

Slowly release the stretch as you shift your hips forward and return to the starting position, as shown. (4) Pivot on the balls of your feet to migi-hanmi. *Change your grip from your left hand to your right and repeat.*

Standing in hidari-hanmi, *extend your left hand in front of you, with the thumb down and the palm facing to the outside. (2) Grasp your left hand with your right, as shown. Notice that the grip is similar to* nikyo-undo, *but the fingers of the right hand are reaching down to the bottom of the left palm, while the right thumb is pressing into the back of it. Again, make sure you grab the palm, and not the fingers.*

Twist the left hand upwards, so that the palm rotates outwards and up. You should feel the stretch throughout your entire wrist, all the way up to the elbow. Shift your hips forward as you perform the stretch, taking care to remain centered. Make sure your shoulders stay down and relaxed. (4) Release the stretch as you return to the starting position. Pivot to migi-hanmi, *change your grip from the left hand to the right, and repeat.*

Standing in hidari-hanmi, *hold your left hand so that the fingers are just below your chin, and the palm is facing outwards, to the left. Keep your left thumb in and your elbow down. (2) Grasp your left hand with your right, wrapping your fingers around the base of your left thumb, and pressing your right thumb into the back of your left wrist, just below the second and third knuckles, as shown.*

Bring your hands down to your one-point. You should feel the stretch along the back of your left wrist and forearm. Make sure you keep your shoulders down and relaxed, and your elbows in close to your body. As you stretch, shift your hips forward, taking care to remain centered. (4) Release the stretch and return to starting position. Pivot to migi-hanmi, *change your grip from your left hand to your right, and repeat.*

Standing in shizentai *(natural posture), hold your hands down by your sides. (2) Shake your wrists, keeping them as loose as possible. Take care to keep your weight down, and your body relaxed. You shouldn't feel yourself stiffening or "coming up on your toes."*

Shake your entire body, keeping it loose and relaxed. Again, make sure your weight stays down. (4) Stop shaking and relax completely. Close your eyes and breathe deeply as you let your weight and your ki *settle—imagine a bottle of Italian salad dressing, with all the herbs slowly settling to the bottom.*

Standing in shizentai, *swing your arms outward. Notice that the palms are relaxed, but slightly cupped. (2) Let your arms fall naturally downwards while bringing your hands together, crossing one before the other, just below your one-point. While your arms and hands should be relaxed, you should maintain control, and be able to stop them at once, smoothly, if asked.*

Swing your arms outward and upward, alternating the hand position—one before, then the other, etc. When you end the exercise, however, bring one hand to rest just above the other, maintaining the same cupped hand position.

Standing in shizentai, *swing your arms upward. (2) Cross your hands in front of your face, at eye level. At the apex of the movement, you should be able to see just beneath the inverted "V" formed by the intersection of your crossed hands. Again, stay relaxed, but maintain control.*

Let your arms swing back down to your sides and repeat, alternating the hand position.

UDE-UNDO (ARM EXERCISES)
UDE-FURI-UNDO (ARM SWINGING EXERCISE/MOVEMENT)

Beginning in shizentai, *with your arms hanging loosely by your sides, twist your upper torso to the left, allowing the energy generated by the movement to swing your arms in that direction. As in* tekubi-kosa-undo *and* tekubi-joho-kosa-undo, *your arms should be relaxed, but not lifeless. (2) Once your arms have reached the apex of their movement, twist your upper torso to the right, allowing your arms to swing in that direction. Repeat.*

A variation of ude-furi-undo. *Instead of allowing your arms to swing to the natural apex of their movement, bring them to a gentle but controlled stop before your one-point and just beside your hip, as shown. Your hands should be relaxed, but charged with* ki.

NOTE: UDE-UNDO ARE EXCELLENT FOR DEVELOPING THE FREE-FLOWING ARM AND BODY MOVEMENT ESSENTIAL TO AIKIDO WAZA, IN PARTICULAR BLENDING AND TENKAN TECHNIQUES.

Standing in shizentai, *twist your hips to the left, allowing your arms to swing in that direction, as in* ude-furi-undo. *(2) As your arms swing to the left, slide your left foot to the rear while pivoting on your right foot, keeping your weight down and centered. When you finish the movement, your arms should be wrapped loosely around your body, with your hips facing to the left, and your feet positioned in* migi-hanmi. *(3) Twist your upper torso to the right. As your arms swing, slide your left foot in a 180-degree arc while pivoting on your right foot, until you reach the starting position. Without pause...*

NOTE: THIS TECHNIQUE CAN BE PERFORMED SEVERAL TIMES IN EACH DIRECTION—FOR EXAMPLE, SPINNING FROM ONE SIDE OF THE DOJO TO THE OTHER, AND THEN BACK AGAIN.

...slide your right foot behind you while pivoting on your left, until your arms are wrapped loosely around your body on the right, and you are standing in hidari-hanmi. *Let your arms swing freely before you as you move. Repeat. (5) A variation of* ude-furi-choyaku-undo, *similar to photo 2a of* ude-furi-undo. *In this case, both hands are held before your one-point, as shown.*

GENERAL EXERCISES/MOVEMENTS

IKKYO-UNDO (FIRST EXERCISE/MOVEMENT)

Begin in hidari-hanmi, *with your arms down by your sides and your hands positioned by your hips, as shown.*

Shift your hips forward, taking care to remain centered. As you move, raise your arms in front of you, as shown, until your hands are roughly level with your face. Keep your arms relaxed but charged with ki, *your elbows in, and your hands open and facing slightly forward, as shown. Think of raising your arms to catch a basketball.*

Shift your hips back while simultaneously lowering your arms to the starting position and closing your fingers. Notice how the hands form a loose fist, fingers slightly extended, when they return to the hips. Repeat several times, then pivot to migi-hanmi *and begin again.*

196

Stand in hidari-hanmi *and perform* ikkyo undo *once.*

As you return your arms to the starting position, pivot to migi-hanmi.

Perform ikkyo-undo, *then pivot to* hidari-hanmi *and repeat.*

Stand in hidari-hanmi *and begin* ikkyo-undo. *(2) As you raise your arms, pivot on your left foot and slide your right foot 180-degrees behind you... (3) ...until you are standing in* hidari-hanmi, *but facing in the opposite direction. As you pivot, keep your arms raised in* ikkyo *position, lowering them as you settle into* hanmi.

Begin ikkyo-undo. *This time, slide your right foot forward as you raise your arms and then... (5) ...pivot on your right foot as you slide your left 180-degrees behind you until you are again standing in* migi-hanmi, *but facing in the opposite direction. As you pivot, keep your arms raised in* ikkyo *position, lowering them as you settle into* hanmi. *Repeat.*

HAPPO-UNDO (EIGHT DIRECTIONS EXERCISE/MOVEMENT)

Happo-undo is a superb *taiso* for developing *ashi-sabaki*. While essentially very simple in execution, this technique can be totally confusing when first attempted. To help you visualize the movement, picture an eight-pointed star on the mat, similar to this:

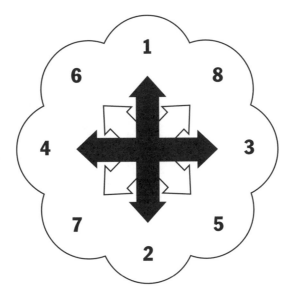

You begin in the middle of the star, facing position one. On moves one through four, you will be tracing a four-pointed cross. You will do the same on moves five through eight, except that the second cross will shift forty-five degrees to form an "X". The star is not static, but fluid, and its center passes through your one-point on every move of *happo-undo*. When executed properly, on move eight you will be facing forty-five degrees to the right of your starting position. If you're not you've made a mistake somewhere.

Stand in hidari-hanmi, *facing forward. Perform* ikkyo-undo, *then...*

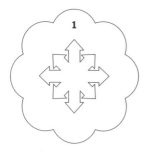

...pivot 180-degrees into migi-hanmi, *as if performing* zengo-undo. *Perform* ikkyo-undo *again.*

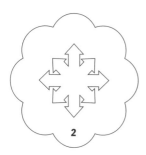

Pivot ninety-degrees and slide into hidari-hanmi *as you perform* ikkyo-undo, *then...*

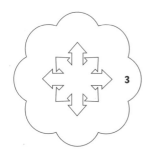

NOTE: YOU CAN ALSO PERFORM THIS TECHNIQUE BEGINNING IN *MIGI-HANMI,* BY SIMPLY REVERSING THE PATTERN.

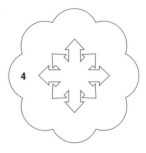

...again pivot 180-degrees into migi-hanmi *and perform* ikkyo-undo *once more. You should have just traced a cross pattern on the mat, and should be facing to the left, relative to step one. You're halfway there.*

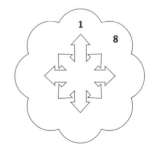

Now pivot to your left 135-degrees—that is, 90-degrees, then another 45 degrees—and slide into hidari-hanmi *as you perform* ikkyo-undo.

From this point, repeat steps two through four. On step eight, you should wind up in migi-hanmi, *facing forward and 45-degrees to the right of your starting point at the very beginning of* happo-undo.

Pivot forty-five degrees to your left and slide into hidari-hanmi, *and repeat* happo-undo.

Begin in shizentai, *with your arms hanging naturally by your sides. Look to your left and raise your arms, palms upward, as shown, while... (2) ...at the same time pivoting on your feet to* hidari-hanmi, *and then... (3) ...dropping your hips downwards, as shown.*

Move your hips back as you move your arms to the right, turning to look in that direction, and... (5) ...pivot into migi-hanmi. *When you arrive, drop your hips as before. Repeat.*

Begin in shizentai. *Look to your left and extend your left arm, palm down and fingers slightly cupped, as shown. Raise your right arm as you did in* sayu-undo. *(2) Slide your right foot in front of your left while simultaneously allowing your left hand to drop downwards. The left hand position is essentially the same as in the first half of* kokyu-ho-undo. *(3) Plant your right foot and slide your left foot* hidari, *moving back into* hidari-hanmi. *As you move, raise your left hand in front of you, moving in an oblique oval pattern, until…*

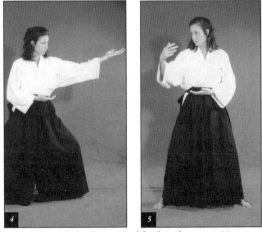

…you return to hidari-hanmi, *and finish in the same position as* sayu-undo. *Drop your hips as before. (5) Look to your right and repeat as before.*

NOTE: SOME PEOPLE FIND IT HELPFUL WHILE PERFORMING THIS TECHNIQUE TO THINK OF SCOOPING AN APPLE UP WITH YOUR EXTENDED HAND, RAISING IT BEFORE YOUR FACE, AND THEN EXTENDING IT OUTWARD TO SOMEONE BEFORE YOU.

FUNE-KOGI-UNDO (ROWBOAT EXERCISE/MOVEMENT)

Begin in hidari-hanmi. *Place your hands beside your hips, as shown. Notice how the wrists are bent, thumbs in, and the fingers slightly cupped. (2) Shift your hips forward, allowing the energy generated by the movement to move your arms forward and slightly downward, as shown.*

(3) Shift your hips backwards, allowing the energy generated by the movement to move your arms back to starting position. Repeat several times. (4) Pivot to migi-hanmi *and repeat as before.*

FUNE-KOGI-ZENGO-UNDO
(BACKWARDS AND FORWARDS ROWBOAT EXERCISE/MOVEMENT)

Begin in hidari-hanmi *and perform* fune-kogi-undo, *as before. (2) When you complete the movement, pivot to* migi-hanmi *and repeat.*

Begin in hidari-hanmi, with your left hand extended before you, as shown. The fingers should be relaxed, but not limp. Rest your right hand lightly on your one-point. (2) Slide your right foot 180-degrees behind your left and pivot. As you move, you should have the feeling of pivoting around your left hand. Imagine it is resting atop a pole stuck into the mat and can move freely up and down the pole, but very little in any other direction. Allow your left hand to drop as you move into hanmi.

As you settle into hidari-hanmi, extend your left hand before you, palm upward. Now the imaginary pole has vanished, and you should have the smooth, balanced feeling of sliding your right foot backwards as you extend your left hand forwards. (4) Rest your left hand lightly over your one-point as you extend your right arm before you, as shown. Repeat as before.

Begin in shizentai. *Slide your left foot forward as you open your arms, rotating your elbows upwards and extending your hands forward and slightly downwards. Imagine someone attempting to grab you from behind in a two-armed "bear hug." This* te-sabaki *will loosen or break the attacker's grip, while the* ashi-sabaki *(the slide forward) will lead him forward and make it harder for him to grab you.*

Without pause after completing step one, bend forward and twist your body down and to the left, taking care to keep your weight centered so you won't topple forward. Simultaneously sweep your left arm in a downward, inside arc, while sweeping your right arm upward and back, as shown. This movement will sweep your attacker off of your back and off to your left. Make sure you keep your back in a straight line with your rearward leg, with your buttocks tucked in—otherwise, the attacker will be pulled on top of you. Give him room to fly.

Return to starting position and perform ushiro-tori-undo *to your right. Repeat, alternating left and right.*

Begin in shizentai. *Imagine your attacker grabbing both of your wrists from behind. Keeping your elbows in and your shoulders down and relaxed, raise your hands to eye-level, as shown. The movement should be natural—as if you were attempting to scratch your nose, for example.*

As you raise your hands, slide your left foot before your right, taking care to remain centered. As your body moves to the right, rotate your wrists until your palms face the floor. Begin to bend at the waist, and...

...complete the movement by bowing low, as shown, and fully extending your arms forward and down. Your attacker will be led past you on your left and thrown forward. Return to shizentai *and repeat on the opposite side.*

USHIRO-UNDO (REARWARD EXERCISES)

You may have already begun to imagine defensive applications for many of the *taiso* you've seen so far. *Ushiro-undo* are more obvious. They're exercises that presuppose an attack from behind—in the following cases, either a "bear hug" attack or a grab to both your wrists. Imagining such attacks as you move will help you to correctly perform *ushiro-undo*.

USHIRO-TEKUBI-TORI-KOTAI-UNDO (REARWARD TWO-HAND WRIST GRAB FOLLOW-THROUGH EXERCISE/MOVEMENT, MOVING TO THE REAR)

The above description probably looks confusing—"rearward" versus "moving to the rear." *Ushiro* refers to the nature of the attack, while *kotai* refers to the direction of the defense. *Ushiro-tekubi-tori-kotai-undo* is basically the same as *ushiro-tekubi-tori-undo,* with one exception, as follows:

Repeat step one and two of ushiro-tekubi-tori-undo. *However, instead of placing your left foot before your right, slide your left foot backwards, as shown. (2)Plant your left foot and skip backwards on your right, while completing the* ushiro-tekubi-tori-undo *movement. You're basically giving your attacker more room to fly, by taking a deep skipping slide to the rear, out of his way. Return to* shizentai *and repeat on the opposite side.*

Begin in shizentai. *Keeping your left hand by your left hip, begin pivoting to your right while raising your right hand.*

Slide your right foot forward, crossing it before your left while moving into migi-hanmi. *As you move, continue to extend your right hand upward, rotating it until the palm is facing down as shown, while simultaneously extending your left hand hand downward and rearward, palm up, as shown, until...*

...you're standing in complete migi-hanmi. *You've basically turned your body 180-degrees, so that you would be facing your attacker, ducking under his right arm and holding him stretched out and suspended in front of you, at which point you could complete the throw. Return to* shizentai *and repeat to the opposite side.*

気

の

体

操

CHAPTER EIGHTEEN

KI EXERCISES

(KI NO TAISO)

Ki-no-taiso fall under the umbrella of *aiki-taiso*. However, while they too have some "physical" applications like *aiki-taiso*, *ki-no-taiso* are more specifically designed to develop and focus *ki*. (Of course, properly executed, *aiki-taiso* help develop *ki* as well, but let's not split hairs).

Unlike previous *aiki-taiso,* the *ki-no-taiso* which follow are designed to be performed with a partner. It is very easy to "set" on your partner, to drop your weight or resist them, while performing *ki-no-taiso,* to make it very difficult or impossible for them to perform the exercise. That's not the point—would you give a weightlifting partner more weight than they could move? Just as the goal of weightlifting is to gradually develop muscular strength, your goal in *ki-no-taiso* is to help your partner develop his or her *ki,* and for your partner to help you develop yours. Give them no more resistance than they can handle. As their *ki* grows stronger, give them a little more.

A final note: *ki-no-taiso* are a bit esoteric. When you perform them, you shouldn't feel you are "muscling" your way through them. On the other hand, if you don't use a little muscle, how are you expected to move at all? Developing one's *ki* in large part involves finding that place between minimal muscular effort and maximum effectiveness. It involves a great deal of visualization, focus, and faith. The first *ki-no-taiso* which follows demonstrates this perfectly.

Stand in shizentai. *Have your partner grab your arm, with one hand beneath your wrist and the other on your biceps, just above your elbow, as shown. (2) First, make your arm as hard and stiff as you possibly can. Tense every muscle. When you've done so, have your partner bend it by pushing up on your wrist and down on your biceps. Unless you are very strong or your partner is very weak, they should be able to eventually bend your arm at the elbow.*

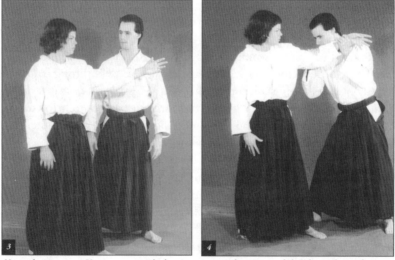

Now, relax your arm. Use no more muscle than is necessary to keep it extended. Relax and extend your fingers. Center your weight, and concentrate on your one-point. Breathe deeply and evenly. Visualize your ki flowing through you, like water, shooting through your arm and out of your fingertips and into infinity (or at least to the nearest wall). A good analogy is a high-pressure fire hose—the hose itself is flexible, yet the water rushing through it gives it tremendous strength. (4) Have your partner again attempt to bend your arm as before, gradually increasing the pressure as you continue to visualize your ki flowing through it. It's okay for your arm to bend a little; otherwise, it won't be relaxed. But don't concentrate on your arm, or your partner—concentrate on your ki. Your partner will have great difficulty bending your arm, more than expected. When a very experienced aikidoka performs orenai-te, it is usually more difficult to bend his arm when it's relaxed in this way than when it is tensed.

KI-NO-KOKYU-HO-UNDO-TENKAN
(BREATH BLENDING WITH KI EXERCISE/MOVEMENT)

Ki-no-kokyu-ho-undo is similar in execution to *kokyu-ho-undo*. It's an exercise to practice leading your partner. However, in order to physically lead your partner without muscling him or her—that is, without simply pushing or pulling them around on the mat—you have to capture and lead their *ki*.

Capturing someone's *ki* is very much like riding the crest of a wave. If you hit the wave too early, you'll miss it entirely. Too late, and it crashes into you. Hit it just right, and it's as if you and the wave are one. You have to ride the crest of the wave to capture your partner's *ki*. Move too early, and you'll leave them behind, ready to move in and attack you anew. Too late, and they'll crash into you or have time to set, and you'll find yourself using muscle to pull or push them where you want them to go while they resist. Capture your partner's *ki,* and you'll find yourself moving with them as if you both are of one mind and spirit—except that yours will be in control. (See next page for example.)

Standing in shizentai, *have your partner grab you* katate-tori migi-hansha *(his or her left hand on your right wrist).*

Move into your partner until you're standing shoulder-to-shoulder. As you move, extend your arm forward, as shown, leading your partner's arm, rather than pulling it. Visualize your ki *flowing through your body and your arm, as when you performed* orenai-te-undo.

Rotate in place by pivoting on your left foot and walking forward in a circle with your right. Keep extending ki *through your arm as you lead your partner in a circle around you. (If you're the one being led, keep a tight grip on your partner's wrist, even if you feel inclined to let go—remember, this is an exercise.) If you have captured your partner's* ki, *you should feel virtually no pressure on your wrist other than the grasp, while your partner should be whirling around you, as shown. If you find yourself walking backwards instead of turning, remember to keep your left foot in place and walk forward with your right in a tight circle. The sensation should be as if you're standing in the calm center of a merry-go-round, while your partner is clinging on for dear life to the fast-moving outer edge. After a few revolutions, switch hands and repeat.*

This exercise is essentially *kosa-sayu-nage-undo,* performed with a partner. The purpose is not only to develop *ki* extension and awareness, but centeredness and balance.

Standing in shizentai, *have your partner grab you* ryote-tori *(both of your hands with both of theirs). (2) Perform* kosa-sayu-nage-undo *to the left, extending* ki *through your body and both of your arms as you lead your partner, as shown.*

Slowly settle into the completion of the movement, as shown, being very conscious of your partner's body position relative to yours. If your partner is too far to your left, you won't be able to support them without using muscle, as their weight will be hanging from the end of your left arm. If they're too far to the right, you'll feel yourself being pulled in that direction. Your partner's body should be positioned directly in front of your one-point, so that their weight is supported by your center, down into the mat. Properly positioned, you should experience very little downward pull on your arms, and feel able to stand there for several minutes without becoming tired. Return to shizentai *and repeat, moving to the right.*

KI-NO-KOKYU-DOSA-UNDO
(KI/BREATH EXTENSION EXERCISE/MOVEMENT)

Ki-no-kokyu-dosa combines all of the principles contained in the preceding *ki-no-taiso—ki* extension, capturing and leading, and centeredness—and tests your command of all of them. As a partner, you must be especially sensitive, as *ki-no-kokyu-dosa-undo* can be rather difficult at first.

Begin with both you and your partner seated in seiza, facing one another with your knees about six inches (15 cm.) apart. Place your palms flat on your thighs, just above your knees, with your back straight and head erect. Concentrate on the Four Basic Principles as you settle your weight into the mat and breathe deeply and evenly.

Your partner will begin testing your ki and your centeredness by pushing against your chest, your shoulders, your arms, and your head—gently at first, and then with increasing pressure. Do not stiffen against the pressure or resist your partner's ki—rather, use your breathing to take it into yourself and make it yours, to further center and settle yourself. If you are resisting, when your partner releases the pressure, you will find your body briefly surging in that direction. If you are capturing your partner's ki, there will be little or no movement when the pressure is released, no matter how suddenly.

Your partner will finish by attempting to lift your knees off the mat, as shown. If you are truly relaxed and centered, it will be very difficult for your partner to lift you. If you are stiff or physically resisting, it will be easy.

Next, your partner will lift your arms. Rotate your wrists so that your palms are facing upwards, as shown. Keep your ki flowing through your body and your arms, as you did in orenai-te-undo. Your arms should feel heavy to your partner, yet if he or she releases their grasp on them, they should not drop or sag.

Moving from your hips, extend your ki through your arms and into your partner until he or she is tipped back off of their center, as shown. This is essentially the same movement as in ikkyo-undo. You should not feel as if you're pushing your partner backwards with muscle. As a partner, you should not set your weight or arbitrarily resist, but neither should you provide no resistance at all. Don't move until you are moved.

Once your partner is off-balanced, lead them to the side and onto his or her back by twisting your hips as you continue to extend ki, as shown. You should not feel as if you're pulling or pushing your partner over. If you're performing the exercise correctly, if your partner is truly off-balanced, you should feel very little resistance.

Have your partner return to seiza *and off-balance them again, this time to the other side. Repeat several times, alternating sides.*

Finally, when your partner is on his or her back, slide in close and position your hands over them, as shown. Your weight should be down and centered, and your posture erect. If your partner has been led to the right, then your right hand should be positioned just above their right wrist, and your left hand should be positioned just above their left shoulder. Notice how the fingers of the pinning hands are together, and how the outer edge of the hand effects the pin. Extend ki *through your body and your arms.*

When you feel ready, your partner will rise up against your hands, with increasing pressure. If you are centered and properly extending ki, *with your weight underside, you should be able to easily prevent them from rising. If you are stiff or using muscle to effect the pin, your partner will have little difficulty resisting you. After a few seconds, return to* seiza *and repeat on the right.*

REMEMBER: *KI-NO-TAISO* ARE EXERCISES, AND *KI* DEVELOPMENT IS A LIFETIME ENDEAVOR. AS A PARTNER, YOUR JOB ISN'T TO "PROVE" THAT *KI-NO-TAISO* DON'T WORK, BUT TO HELP YOUR PARTNER LEARN HOW TO **MAKE** THEM WORK.

CHAPTER NINETEEN

GENERAL TECHNIQUES

(WAZA)

There are fifty basic techniques in Suenaka-ha Tetsugaku-ho aikido. By basic, we mean that competence in the "fifty basic," plus variations, is the minimal physical requirement for upper kyu and dan promotion. When you add in all the possible variations—combination attacks, combination defenses, simultaneous multiple attacks (two or more *uke*), submissions, weapons defense, *jo-waza, keri-waza, shinke-waza, shime-waza, koshi-waza, suwari-waza, hanmi-handachi*, and so on—the list of techniques is infinite, just as there are an infinite number of aikido techniques in general.

Rather than show here each of the fifty basic, the following techniques were selected by Suenaka Sensei because they demonstrate the widest range of *waza*. Many of the techniques shown were taken directly from the fifty basic, while some are combinations of techniques from the fifty basic, and still others (such as *ryote-tori yama-arashi irimi*) do not appear in the fifty basic at all. Also, all of the techniques are single variations—for example, there is more than one way to perform *shomen-uchi ikkyo irimi*, dozens of techniques which fall beneath the umbrella of *katate-tori kokyu-nage*, many different *ude-osae*, and so on. What's more, a technique can be completed many different ways, with one of numerous submissions, throws and take-downs. In other words, the techniques you are about to see are not set in stone. Again, remember that aikido is fluid, and allows infinite combinations and variations. Likewise, the techniques are not presented in any particular order.

Unlike the chapters on *ukemi* and *aiki-taiso*, no English equivalents are given for the names of the techniques shown. As noted in the chapter on etiquette, it would simply be to cumbersome. However, you'll notice that a few techniques are accompanied by secondary names, such as in the first technique shown. These "nicknames," as it were, help to distinguish particular variations on a technique that may fall beneath a wide umbrella of similar techniques with the same designation. In other words, while there are many different variations on *katate-tori kokyu-nage tenkan,* "Classic Koke" refers to a specific variation. "Classic Koke" and *yama-arashi* are specific to Suenaka-ha Tetsugaku-ho aikido, and are not generally used.

The photo series for each technique is complemented by several photos illustrating common mistakes. Each of these photos is labeled with a dark bar across the bottom and the word INCORRECT so you can distinguish them easily from the photos illustrating proper technique. While these photos can't possibly cover everything that can go wrong with a technique, they should serve to point you in the right direction towards a solution if you encounter any problems in your own technique. Also, in the interest of brevity, INCORRECT technique examples are shown only once. For example, incorrect *ma-ai* while performing *ikkyo* is illustrated in the first *ikkyo* technique only, and not in subsequent similar techniques, even though the same caution may apply.

Finally, it should be self-evident that one cannot learn any martial art solely by studying photographs and descriptions in a book, and to attempt to do so is inviting disaster. All of the techniques you will see can cause crippling injury or even death if performed incorrectly. The techniques are meant to be an introduction to aikido, and to augment ongoing, responsible study as a member of an aikido class. **Do not** attempt to perform any of them if you or your partner are inexperienced, even if you have studied other martial arts.

GENERAL GUIDELINES WHILE PERFORMING WAZA

Although the following techniques are depicted in stages, for clarity, they should be performed fluidly, without pause. Don't stop between steps, "one, two, three," and so on, but think of performing the entire technique on a count of "one."

Notice that all defenses begin with nage standing in *shizentai,* rather than in *hanmi.* This is because *shizentai* is the most common and natural posture: most of us don't wait for a bus standing in *hanmi.* From *shizentai,* one can instantly and smoothly move into whatever *hanmi* is necessary to effectively answer an attack.

The *waza* descriptions rarely say that you "step" this way or that, but rather that you "move". As noted in the chapter on the Four Basic Principles, an *aikidoka* always keeps his or her weight underside, so that he or she can perform from a firm and stable base. As such, you should slide your feet across the mat as you move, rather than step or stomp. The feeling should be as if you are skating across the mat. This sliding feet technique is called *suri-ashi*. You should always move *suri-ashi* when performing any aikido *taiso* or technique.

Ma-ai, or proper distance between *nage* and *uke,* is vitally important when performing *waza.* Although occasional specific references to *ma-ai* are made throughout the following technique descriptions, pay close attention to *ma-ai* even when such references are absent.

Like *ma-ai,* great care should be taken in every technique to keep *uke* before your one-point, just as a swordsman always keeps his blade before him. In the following photos, pay close attention to how *nage* never allows the technique to "get away from him"—that is, to allow the *uke* to stray away from his control in any direction.

All techniques begin with nage delivering *atemi,* a strike to the *uke. Atemi* in aikido is used more as a distraction to the *uke* rather than as a technique in itself. However, in many cases, *atemi* is essential to the technique—for example, to cause *uke* to loosen his grasp on *nage,* or to prevent a counter-strike. Obviously, you should not actually strike your *uke* when practicing in the *dojo,* but you should always include *atemi* in your technique, so that it will become as much a part of your technique as the movements themselves, and will be there to come to your aid on the street.

With the exception of throws, where the *uke* is released from *nage's* control, all techniques end with a submission. Submissions are not always shown in the following techniques, but are covered in the following chapter.

In the martial arts in general, when a technique is executed to the point that the *uke* can stand no more, the *uke* signals submission by "tapping out" – that is, sharply slapping a part of their body, usually the chest or thigh, several times in quick succession. As a *nage,* this is your signal to immediately ease up on the pressure until the *uke* stops tapping. Depending on the situation, you can also slap the mat. Sometimes, when you find both arms immobilized, you can even tap out with your feet! As a *nage,* be sensitive to when your *uke* is signalling you to ease up. Otherwise, injury can result, not to mention frayed nerves and strained tempers.

Direction of defense is, of course, dictated by direction of attack. Where applicable, *nage* need not move in the direction indicated.

Uke *attacks* katate-tori hantai *(opposite hand wrist grab)*. *(2)* Nage *delivers atemi and moves* shikaku *(to* uke's *blind side) tenkan, out of range of a possible* uke atemi, *while leading the* uke. *Note how* nage's *right palm faces upwards.*

As nage *leads* uke, uke's *momentum leads his head into* nage's *right shoulder.* Nage *lays his hand alongside* uke's *head to hold it in place. Note the close* ma-ai *between* uke *and* nage. *(4)* Nage *reverses direction, stepping through with his right foot as he arcs his right arm upwards. Notice how* uke's *head is tilted upwards as* nage's *right shoulder rotates with the arm's motion.*

Nage *completes the step-through, throwing* uke *to the mat. It is* uke's *head, rather than his body, that is being thrown.*

Nage *pulls* uke, *rather than leading him. (3a)* Nage *grasps* uke's *collar with his left hand, forcing* uke's *head down. The wide, improper* ma-ai, *combined with* nage's *failure to lead* uke *off-balance, allows* uke *to easily turn and deliver a counter-strike or to* kaeshi *(reverse) the technique.*

Nage *pulls* uke's *body backwards using his grasp on* uke's *collar.* Uke *still has his balance. Further, if* uke *were shirtless, or if the collar were to tear, the technique would fail. (5a)* Nage *pulls* uke *to the mat, pushing* uke's *chest with his right hand.*

Uke *attacks* katate-tori hantai.
Nage *delivers* atemi *while moving
backward* migi-naname *(an
oblique angle to the right), leading
with his left hip, out of range of a
possible* uke atemi. *As he moves,
he leads* uke *with him.* Nage
*sweeps his right arm upwards as
he moves in* shikaku *to* uke's *left,
simultaneously grasping* uke's *right
arm at the elbow with his left
hand and grasping* uke's *right
hand in an* ikkyo *lock. Note the
close* ma-ai *between* uke *and* nage,
and how uke's *arm is bent and
held close to her head by* nage.

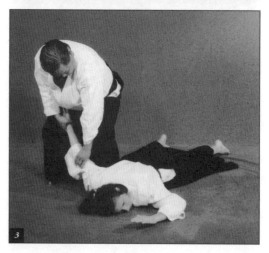

Nage *cuts* uke's *right arm downward until* uke's *head is below*
nage's *one-point. Note how* nage
keeps uke's *arm pressed close
against his own body.*

As he cuts downward, nage *slides
backwards on his right foot,
pivoting to his right and leading*
uke *off of her feet, to the mat.*

Nage *pushes* uke's *arm downward. Note the wide, improper* ma-ai, *and how* nage *does not have* uke's *head below his one-point, allowing* uke *to retain her balance.*

Nage *does not move* migi-naname, *but instead "muscles"* uke's *arm upwards.* Uke *is not led off-balance, and can easily counterattack.* Uke's *arm is stiff, not bent.*

Nage *drags* uke *to his right, rather than pivoting and leading her.*

Incorrect

Incorrect

Incorrect

Uke *attacks* katate-tori hansha *(same-side wrist grab)*. *(2)* Nage *delivers* atemi *and moves backwards* migi-naname, *leading with his left hip to lead* uke *off-balance. At the same time,* nage *lays his right* hand atop uke's *to hold it in position.*

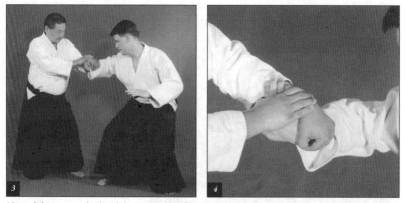

Nage *slides in towards uke while rotating his left wrist, laying the fingers and thumb of his left hand atop* uke's *right wrist. Note how* nage's *move inside bends* uke's *arm at the elbow and wrist, forming a* "Z". *(4) Detail of correct* nikyo *wrist lock and arm position.*

Nage *points the fingers of his left hand into his own one-point and drops his weight, rotating* uke's *wrist as he does so, completing the* nikyo. Uke *is forced to his knees by the pain. (6) Nage slides backwards, leading* uke *to the mat, where the* nikyo *lock is now a submission.*

Nage *has not moved* migi-naname *and has failed to lead* uke *off-balance. Uke can easily counterattack.*
(4a) Uke's arm is not bent, nor is nage facing uke. Uke *can easily counterattack or spin out of the technique.*

Nage *uses* shuto *(blade hand) to push down on* Uke's *wrist and arm. While this may be painful for some* uke, *it is not at all effective on many people.*

Uke *attacks* katate-tori hantai. Nage *delivers* atemi *and moves* migi-naname, *leading with his left hip.* (2) Nage *continues moving, leading* uke's *right arm in an upwards arc, as if preparing to execute* ikkyo. *As* nage *moves, he grasps* uke's *right hand with his left in a* sankyo *lock, completing the lock as he moves beneath* uke's *right arm, as shown.*

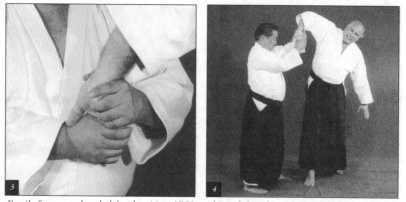

Detail of correct sankyo *lock hand position.* (4) Nage *drives* uke's *right arm upwards, pointing* uke's *elbow upwards and back* (naname-osae) *as he slides to the left, careful not to release the pressure delivered by the* sankyo *lock.*

Uke *is thrown backwards to the mat.*

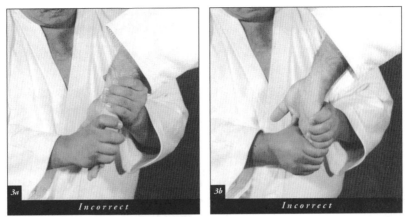

Nage *has grasped* uke's *hand too high.* (3b) Nage *has grasped* uke's *hand too low.*

Nage *pulls* uke *backwards, releasing the* sankyo *lock and allowing* uke *to escape or counterattack.*

Uke *attacks* katate-tori hantai. Nage *delivers* atemi. (2) Nage *moves* tenkan shikaku, *leading* uke *forward and off-balance. Note the close* ma-ai.

As nage *moves, he slides his left hand down* uke's *arm and employs the* kote-gaeshi *lock.*

Detail of correct kote-gaeshi *lock.*

With uke *sufficiently led, nage reverses his movement, sliding backwards* migi-naname. *Notice how this movement fully extends* uke's *arm and tightens the* kote-gaeshi *lock, while at the same time keeping* uke *off-balance and keeping* nage *out of range of an* uke *counter-strike. At the same time,* nage *lays his right hand atop* uke's *fingers, as shown.*

230

With uke *fully off-balance,* nage *twists* uke's *hand to the left.*

Detail of Correct kote-gaeshi *hand position. If* uke *has been sufficiently led and extended, this lock is always effective.*

Nage *cuts* uke's *wrist downwards and outwards while dropping his weight, throwing* uke *to the mat.* Nage *is careful not to deliver* kote-gaeshi *to the outside of* uke's *wrist, risking a sprain or break, but rather follows the curve described by* uke's *own fingers.*

Nage *does not keep* uke *in front of his one-point, and drags, rather than leads, him.* Uke *is not off-balance. (3b) Note change in* nage's *thumb position, providing insufficient control of* uke's *hand and wrist.*

Uke *is neither extended nor off-balance, and can counter-attack.*

Uke *delivers a* shomen-uchi *(overhead strike to the head) attack.*

Nage *delivers* atemi *while moving* migi-naname, *leading with his left hip. At the same time,* nage's *left hand blends with the* shomen-uchi *strike— resting on, but not grasping, the striking arm.*

Nage *sweeps* uke's *right arm in a downward oblique arc, into his right arm, which continues the sweeping motion, leading* uke's ki *in a tight circle.*

As the arm's arc continues, nage *moves* irimi, *placing his left hand alongside* uke's *face and leading* uke's *head into his right shoulder.* (5) Nage *steps through and throws* uke kokyu-nage.

The ma-ai *is too wide—uke is not led.* (4a) Nage *grasps* uke's *collar rather than capturing his head.*

Uke *attacks* shomen-uchi. Nage *moves* hidari-naname *(left oblique angle)* shikaku *and delivers* atemi. *As* uke's *strike descends,* nage *raises his arms, deflecting* uke's *strike. (Note how* nage's *move is similar to* ikkyo-undo. *For more details, refer back to the chapter on* aiki taiso.*) (2)* Nage *blends with and leads* uke *by pivoting to his right. Note that* nage's *hand position is identical to* katate-tori kokyu-nage tenkan.

Nage *throws* uke kokyu-nage.

Nage *blocks* uke's *strike, allowing* uke *to retain his balance.*

Uke *prepares to deliver a* shomen-uchi *strike.* (2) *As* uke *draws his arm back,* nage *delivers* atemi *with his left hand as he moves* hidari-naname irimi *and places his right hand on* uke's *wrist.* Nage's *movement continues leading uke backwards.*

After delivering atemi, nage *moves his left hand to* uke's *right elbow and grasps* uke's *left wrist, completing the* ikkyo *setup.* (4) Nage *executes* ikkyo, *cutting* uke's *arm down-ward as he slides forward on his left foot, moving uke off-balance and onto the mat. Note how* nage *stays upright and centered.*

Uke *attacks* shomen-uchi. Nage *delivers* atemi *and moves* migi-naname, *leading uke off-balance. (2) Nage moves his right hand smoothly to uke's right wrist while leading uke's ki as shown, moving uke even more off-balance.*

Detail of proper ikkyo *setup.*

Nage *pivots to the right as he cuts downwards.* Uke *is further off-balanced and led in a circle down to the mat, where a submission may be employed.*

Uke *attacks* shomen-uchi. Nage *moves* shikaku *and delivers* atemi, *as shown. (2)* Nage *lays his left hand atop* uke's *right arm, leading* uke *off-balance, as he moves his right hand to the back of* uke's *head.*

Nage *continues to sweep* uke's *right arm in a downward arc while leading* uke *and taking care to remain* shikaku. Uke's *arm is swept up and behind her, causing her to bend at the waist and off-balance even further. (4)* Nage *twists his hips to the right. The resulting leverage on* uke's *arm throws her forward,* kaiten-nage.

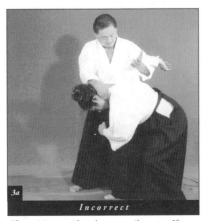

If ma-ai *is too wide*—uke *can easily escape. If* ma-ai *is too tight (as shown)*—nage *cannot get enough leverage on* uke's *arm to effect the throw.*

Uke *attacks* kata-tori, *grasping the* nage's *left lapel. As* uke *grabs,* nage *delivers* atemi *and moves* migi-naname, *leading* uke *off-balance.*

After delivering atemi, nage *reaches over the top of* uke's *right hand and grasps it, rotating it to* nage's *right into an* nikyo *lock, holding it snugly against his chest. Note that* nage *is still moving* migi-naname.

Detail of correct nikyo *lock hand position.*

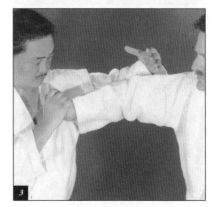

Nage *moves in towards* uke, *laying his left forearm atop* uke's *right. Notice how the combination of the* nikyo *lock and* nage's *move inwards causes* uke's *arm to form the "Z" that is essential to executing* nikyo. *(Refer to* katate-tori nikyo hansha.*) (5)* Nage *drops his weight, leaning slightly in towards* uke. Nage's *left arm does not press downward, but rather rotates inward in a scooping motion, as shown. The combined stresses execute* nikyo *and forces* uke *to the mat.*

Nage *has not rotated* uke's *wrist, nor is it held snugly against* nage's *chest.* Nage *has also not moved* shikaku, *and is vulnerable to an* uke *counter-strike. (5a)* Nage *pushes down on* uke's *arm with his forearm. While painful, it is not effective.*

Uke *attacks* kata-tori. Nage *delivers* atemi *while moving* migi-naname. *(2) After delivering* atemi, nage grasps uke's *right arm and leads it upwards and outwards as he moves* shikaku. Nage *must deliver* atemi *in order to loosen* uke's *grip so that it may be broken.*

Nage *moves into the classic* tenkan kokyu-nage *position as shown. (4)* Nage *throws* uke kokyu-nage.

Uke *attacks* kata-tori. Nage *delivers* atemi *with his right hand while laying his left hand atop* uke's *right elbow, as shown. (2)* Nage *moves* migi-naname irimi. *At the same time, he thrusts upwards against* uke's *jaw with the heel of his right hand while simultaneously dropping his weight on* uke's *left arm and pivoting to his left. Note how* uke's *balance is broken—his head is led backwards by the* ago-tsuki *(chin strike), while his body is led downward, backward and to the left by the pressure of* nage's *weight on his right arm.*

Uke *is thrown backwards to the mat.*

Incorrect

Nage *does not pivot or drop his weight. Since* uke's *balance is not broken, he does not fall, but can simply walk backwards.*

Uke *attacks with a* kata-tori. Nage *delivers* atemi *while moving* migi-naname. *(2) Nage grasps* uke's *right hand in a* nikyo *lock and sweeps* uke's *arm upwards, as if preparing to execute* ikkyo.

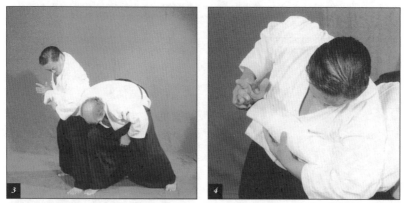

(3) Nage continues to lead uke *off-balance, allowing* uke's *arm to move into his chest. At the same time, he places his arm atop* uke's, *as shown, hugging it into his chest, and rotates* uke's *wrist outward while applying pressure inwards. (4) Detail of correct* ude-osae *(arm bar).*

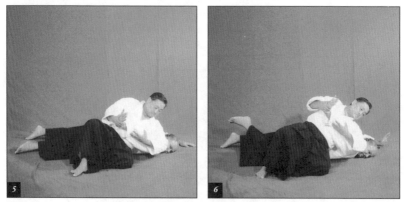

Nage *moves tenkan, to his right, leading* uke *off-balance and down to the mat, careful not to release the* ude-osae. *(6) Nage leans backwards into* uke, *putting pressure against* uke's *arm for the submission.*

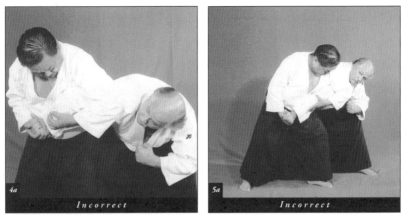

Nage *is not applying the* nikyo *lock. The* ma-ai *is also too wide.* Uke *can bend his elbow and escape.* (5a) Nage *moves forward rather than pivoting, and merely pulls* uke *forward.*

Nage *releases pressure on* uke's *arm, allowing him to bend his elbow and escape.*

Uke *attacks* yokomen-uchi. Nage *delivers* atemi *as he moves* migi-naname, *at the same time laying his left hand atop* uke's *right wrist.*

Nage *sweeps* uke's *left hand into his right, further leading uke off-balance. Notice how the combination of sweeping* uke's *arm and leading the* uke *results in* nage *moving naturally* shikaku. *As always,* ma-ai *must be close, as shown. As* nage *sweeps* uke's *arm, he grasps* uke's *right hand and rotates the wrist downward and outward, as shown, while bracing his left arm beneath* uke's *right* (sasae), *fully extending the arm and preventing a counter-strike. Note how the wristlock is positioned in front of* nage's *one point. Also,* nage's *left foot is positioned beside* uke's *right foot. It is this foot placement that defines the technique as* irimi.

Nage *begins pivoting to the right, taking care to maintain the pressure of the lock and keep* uke's *arm extended as he bends his knees and moves below* uke's *extended arm.*

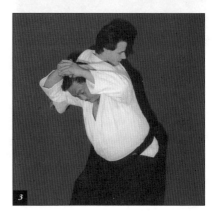

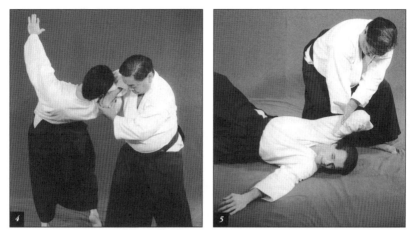

Nage *pivots 180-degrees and cuts* uke's *right hand tightly into* uke's *right shoulder as shown...*
(5) ...throwing uke *to the mat, where a submission may be employed.*

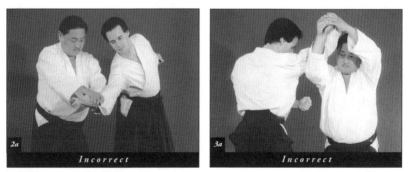

Ma-ai *is too wide, and* nage *has not braced* uke's *arm.* Uke *is not extended nor sufficiently led.*
(3a) Nage *has allowed* uke's *arm to rise over his head, rather than pivoting below it. This restores* uke's *balance.* Uke *may now escape, or merely pull downward on* nage's *arm to* kaeshi *the technique.*

Nage *cuts* uke's *arm outwards, where it can break the elbow and dislocate the shoulder.*

NOTE: *YOKOMEN-UCHI SHIHO-NAGE* IS EITHER *IRIMI* OR *TENKAN* DEPENDING ON *ASHI-SABAKI,* THE PLACEMENT OF *NAGE'S* FEET. IF *NAGE'S* INNER FOOT WAS POSITIONED BESIDE *UKE'S* (REFER TO STEP 3), IT WOULD BE *TENKAN.*

Uke *draws his right arm backwards, preparing to deliver* yokomen-uchi *(strike to the side of the head). (2)* Nage *moves* irimi *as* uke's *arm is moving backwards. This movement should not be a hard, clashing movement, but a smooth blending with* nage's *motion and* ki *(refer to* shomen-uchi ikkyo irimi*).* Nage's *right hand is placed against* uke's *right shoulder, while* nage's *left hand makes contact with* uke's *right wrist.*

Nage *sweeps* uke's *left arm backward and downward while continuing to move* irimi. *This movement, combined with the force generated by* nage's *movement against* uke's *right shoulder, leads* uke *off-balance and throws him backwards.*

Nage *has waited too long—what should be a smooth blend has become a block.*

246

Uke *attacks* yokomen-uchi. Nage *delivers* atemi *with his right hand and lays his left atop* uke's *attacking arm, leading* uke. Nage *simultaneously moves backward* migi-naname. (2) *As he moves, leading* uke, nage *lays his right hand beside* uke's *head and lightly grasps* uke's *right wrist, as shown, further leading* uke.

Nage *drops backwards* migi-naname, *allowing his motion to both lead the* uke *off-balance and apply pressure to* uke's *head.* Uke *is thrown* sumi-otoshi. *It is the drop backwards, and not the pressure on the head, that effects the throw. The pressure on* uke's *head only helps lead him.*

Nage *does not drop backwards* migi-naname, *but merely turns and pushes on* uke's *head.* Uke *is not led off-balance, and can easily escape.*

247

Uke *attacks* yokomen-uchi. Nage *delivers* atemi *while moving* migi-naname, *simultaneously laying his left hand atop uke's right arm, deflecting and leading the strike. (2) Nage continues to sweep uke's right arm, leading uke's right wrist into nage's right hand, as if setting up for* shiho-nage. *Instead,* nage *grasps* uke's *wrist* yonkyo, *as shown.*

Nage *moves naturally* shikaku *as he continues to lead* uke. Nage *reaches over* uke's *right biceps and beneath* uke's *right forearm, grasping his own right forearm, as shown.* Nage *must allow* uke's *wrist to turn within his grasp.*

Detail of correct "figure four" ude-osae.

Nage *pivots to his left, as shown, simultaneously cutting the* ude-osae *lock into* uke's *right shoulder, as if executing* shiho-nage, *throwing* uke *to the mat.*

Ma-ai *is too wide—there is not enough play in* uke's *arm to effect the* ude-osae. Uke *can easily escape or counter-strike.*

Uke *attacks* mune-tsuki *(a punch to the torso), as shown.* Nage *pivots to his right and moves forward, allowing the strike to pass him by, and delivers* atemi *while simultaneously laying his hand atop* uke's *right arm, to deflect the strike and lead* uke. *(2) While leading* uke tenkan, nage *slides his left hand down* uke's *arm until it stops at* uke's *wrist. Notice how* nage's *hand falls naturally into the* kote-gaeshi *lock (see* katate-tori kote-gaeshi hantai*). Also notice how* nage's *leading* uke *moves him naturally* shikaku.

Nage *reverses his movement, dropping back* naname-hidari *(refer to* katate-tori kote-gaeshi hantai*) and laying his fingers atop* uke's *to complete the* kote-gaeshi *lock and set up the throw. (4)* Nage *throws* uke *to the mat.*

249

Uke *attacks* mune-tsuki. Nage *moves* hidari shikaku *and delivers* atemi *while raising his left hand to parry* uke's *attack and lead* uke *past him, as shown.* (2) Nage *continues moving forward as he places his right hand to the side of* uke's *head, careful to continue leading* uke *as he moves.*

Nage *pivots to his right as he places his left hand behind* uke's *right shoulder, as shown. Notice how* nage's *pivot opens a space for* uke *to pass beneath* nage's *right arm, and how* nage's *right arm is raised to open the space.* (4) Nage *extends his right arm as he allows* uke *to pass by, while simultaneously dropping his weight and allowing the completion of his pivot to push* uke's *shoulder with his left hand.* Uke *is twisted off-balance to his right and thrown to the mat, while* nage's *completed pivot allows him to face* uke *as the technique is completed.*

Nage *places his hand behind* uke's *head. This could cause* uke's *head to be pulled into* nage's *right arm, and over-tightens the* ma-ai. Uke *could grab* nage *with his right hand and pull him in. (4a)* Nage *has not completed his pivot, and has pulled* uke *into him, rather than allowing him to pass by.*

Uke *attacks* nage mune-tsuki. Nage *moves* hidari shikaku *and delivers* atemi *while parrying* uke's *strike with his left hand. (2) Nage moves in, sliding his right arm up* uke's *chest as* uke *passes by, until* uke's *head is level with* nage's *right shoulder, as shown, and places his left hand against the back of* uke's *left shoulder*

Nage *points his right hand downward and drops his hips while simultaneously pressing his left hand into* uke's *shoulder. Note that* nage's *right arm has captured* uke's *head and* ki *and is re-directing them backwards in a very small circle.* Uke *is completely off-balanced and thrown to the mat.*

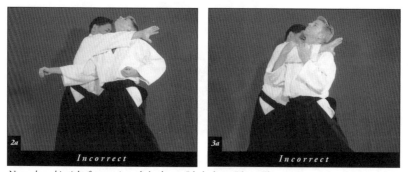

Nage *slams his right forearm into* uke's *throat, "clotheslining" him. This can cause serious injury to* uke, *and does not lead* uke *off-balance. (3a)* Nage *moves forward without leading* uke's *head and* ki *downward and without pressing his left hand into the back of* uke's *shoulder.* Uke *can merely walk backwards, or grab* nage's *right arm and destroy the technique*

Uke *attacks* mune-tsuki. Nage *delivers* atemi *and pivots out of the way of the strike while deflecting the strike with his left hand, as shown. (2)* Nage *grasps* uke's *right wrist with his right hand while simultaneously reaching over* uke's *right biceps and under* uke's *forearm, finally grasping his own forearm, as shown. Notice how, unlike the "figure four"* ude-osae, uke's *arm remains extended.* Nage's *left forearm applies pressure to* uke's *elbow,* kansetsu *(against the joint), completing the* ude-osae. *Note: Take great care—this lock can easily cause injury to* uke's *elbow.*

Detail of correct ude-osae.

While maintaining the ude-osae, nage *pivots* tenkan, *spiraling downward until* uke *is face-down on the mat.*

Nage *has not extended* uke's *right arm, allowing* uke's *to bend his elbow, destroying the technique, and allowing him to deliver a counter-strike.*

RYOTE-TORI YAMA-ARASHI ("MOUNTAIN STORM")

(also known as Ryote-Tori Kokyu-Nage Irimi)

Uke *attacks* ryote-tori *(grasping both of* nage's wrists). Nage *delivers* atemi—*in this case, a kick to* uke's *knee.*

Nage *rotates his wrists to the right, grasping* uke's *wrists. Notice how* nage *grasps* uke's *wrist on the inside. When you rotate your wrists, your hands will move naturally into this position.*

Detail of correct nage *hand placement.* Nage *has rotated his hand to the inside of* uke's *wrist, fingers on top and thumb below.*

As nage *grasps* uke's *wrists, he extends* uke's *arms and moves* hidari-irimi. *Note how this moves* uke *off-balance, and how* uke's *right arm is raised.*

Once behind uke, nage *pivots to his left, sliding into* migi-hanmi *as he moves backwards. (5) Uke is thrown head-over-heels to the mat.*

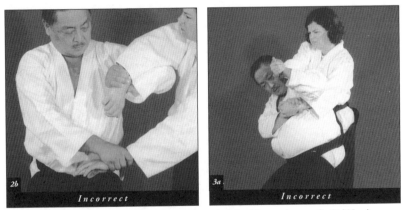

This hand placement will not allow you to move beneath uke's *right arm (see step 4). (3a)* Nage's *arms have collapsed, allowing* uke *to retain her balance and* kaeshi *or counter-strike.* Nage *cannot move beneath* uke's *arm.*

Nage *has not moved far enough behind* uke *to effect the throw.*

Uke *attacks* ryote-tori. Nage *delivers* atemi, *as shown.*

Nage *extends his left arm downwards and outwards at an oblique angle, to lead* uke *off-balance.* Nage *simultaneously raises his right arm, following the plane of* uke's *chest as he moves* hidari-naname. *Note how* nage's *extended arm and the movement combine to lead* uke *further off-balance, and how* nage's *right arm and hand controls* uke's *head.*

As uke *is led backwards,* nage *steps through with his right foot while dropping his weight and twisting his hips to the right, throwing* uke *to the mat.*

Nage *is leading* uke's *left arm to the side, allowing* uke *to retain his balance.*

Nage *has allowed his left arm to collapse as he moves, allowing* uke *to retain his balance.*

Nage *has allowed his left arm to drop, allowing* uke *to retain his balance.*

Uke *attacks* nage ushiro tekubi-tori *(grasping both of* uke's *wrists from behind), as shown.* (2) *Keeping his elbows in close to his body,* nage *extends his arms upward and forward, closing the* ma-ai, *as shown. Note how this movement is identical to* ushiro tekubi-tori zanshin undo, *in the chapter on* aiki-taiso.

As he extends his arms, nage *moves to his right and backwards, beneath* uke's *right arm. Note how* nage *delivers* atemi *(an elbow strike) as he moves.* (4) *Simultaneously,* nage *grasps* uke's *right hand with his left, beginning the* sankyo *lock. NOTE:* Nage *may move* migi *or* hidari, *as the situation dictates.*

Nage *emerges from beneath* uke's *arm, pivoting backwards to his left and complete the* sankyo *lock.* Uke *may now be thrown, or... (6) ...cut to the mat where submission maybe employed.*

Nage *raises his arms outwards, into* uke's *strength. Not only does this not close* ma-ai, *but* nage *must be very strong to make it work.*

Uke *attacks* ushiro tekubi-tori. Nage *extends his arms forward and ducks beneath* uke's *right arm, as in* ushiro tekubi-tori sankyo. (2) Nage *grasps* uke's *left hand with his right, beginning the* kote-gaeshi *lock.*

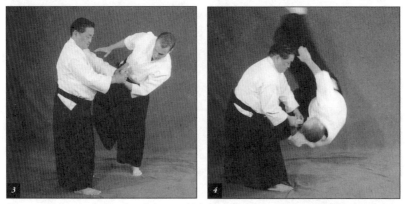

Nage *continues moving backwards as the* kote-gaeshi *lock breaks* uke's *grasp on* nage's *left hand, and...* *(4)...lays his left hand atop* uke's, *completing the* kote-gaeshi *lock. Uke is extended, led and thrown to the mat.*

CHAPTER TWENTY

Submission Techniques

(Katame Waza)

When you throw someone in aikido, the technique is over. In class, the *uke* rises and you begin the next technique. On the street, the attacker (hopefully) stays down or flees, or the throw buys you the necessary time to escape. But as you have already seen, not all aikido techniques are throws.

Aikido's jujutsu heritage shows itself in its numerous arm bars and joint and wristlocks. When you gain control of your attacker with a wristlock, for example, you are faced with several options. One of them is to simply let go. Obviously, this is not wise: it makes no sense to return the initiative to your attacker. Another option is to take the lock to the extreme, dislocating, spraining or breaking the joint to disable or cripple your attacker. While this option is one into which you may be forced in a street defense situation, remember that one of the goals of aikido is to gain control of a situation with as little harm to your attacker as possible. Also, depending on local laws, there may be legal repercussions should you decide to inflict physical damage. All joint locks allow you to throw your attacker in one way or another, but this is not always desirable, especially if you want to retain control of your attacker. All of these dilemmas can be answered with a submission.

Submissions allow you to retain complete control of your attacker while providing you with a wide range of options. You can hold your attacker in place until he or she cools down, and then release them, or keep holding them until the police arrive. Submissions also allow you to move smoothly back into technique. For example, you could drop someone to the ground with a *sankyo,* hold them there with an *ude-osae* submission, and then stand them back up on their feet with the same *sankyo* that put them down, so you can march them wherever you wish. Submissions can be merely painful, or, in life-or-death situations, they can be used to cause physical damage when taken to their extreme. Again, the key here is that submissions allow you to remain in control of your attacker, even after the technique proper is over.

Submissions become even more important when answering an armed attack. Obviously, if your attacker is using a knife, you want to relieve them of their weapon before releasing them. Submissions allow you to do so. A few examples of submissions against armed attack are shown below. Although the weapons shown are knives and *bokken,* keep in mind that they could just as easily be broken beer bottles, pool cues or other equivalents. You will note that there are no defenses shown against firearms. Although there are techniques for disarming an attacker threatening you with a firearm at close range, the potential for personal injury or death is too great to detail them in any situation other than as part of a class, and then at advanced levels only.

There are many different kinds of submissions, and even more variations on those submissions. However, as you train, you will probably find yourself encountering the same dozen or so basic submissions over and over. The more familiar with them you become, the more opportunities you will see for their employment, and the more variations you will discover. Thus, while the following submissions are demonstrated from a variety of basic techniques and both with and without weapons, their use is not limited to those techniques or against armed attack.

GENERAL GUIDELINES WHILE PERFORMING SUBMISSIONS

When practicing submissions in the *dojo,* be very careful. Give your *uke* time to feel the submission and tap out (see "General Guidelines While Performing Waza" in the previous chapter) when they are at their limit. Otherwise, injuries are certain to occur. When taken to their extreme, submissions can easily break bones and joints, tear muscles and tendons, and dislocate limbs.

As when practicing general *waza, ma-ai* is vitally important – *nage* must be very close to *uke* for submissions to work properly, and to prevent *uke* from escaping – so pay close attention to the *ma-ai* in the following illustrations.

Just as techniques are performed fluidly and without pause, submissions should flow from technique just as smoothly. Because of this, submissions are generally not practiced separately. In other words, even if your intent is to practice a particular submission alone, you should "lead into" the submission by first performing an appropriate technique that would lead you naturally into performng the desired submission.

When applying submissions, it is critical that you "take the slack out"—that is, to stretch the muscles, tendons and ligaments in *uke's* wrist and arm to the extreme. Otherwise, the submission will be ineffective.

Finally, note how *nage* releases the submission in step four of the first submission shown. For brevity's sake, this release is shown only once. However, unless otherwise indicated, all submissions end in this way.

From ikkyo, nage *slides forward, dropping* uke *to the mat. (2)* Nage *moves his left leg to the outside of* uke's *right arm. As he does so,* nage *transfers the* ikkyo *lock from his right hand to his left.*

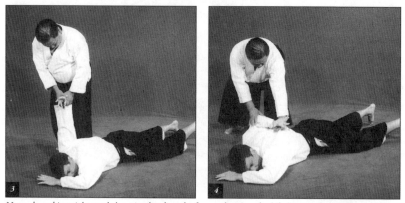

Nage *drops his weight on* uke's *wrist, bending the fingers downward while leaning slightly in towards* uke *and torquing* uke's *wrist to the right. This motion applies pressure to* uke's *wrist and shoulder, and keeps* uke *from spinning or flipping over and escaping. (4)* Nage *places* uke's *arm in the center of his back and then backs quickly away, taking the angle farthest away from* uke's *arms, as shown. This prevents* uke *from reaching out and grabbing* nage's *ankle, while putting distance between* nage *and* uke *in case* uke *rises and attacks again.*

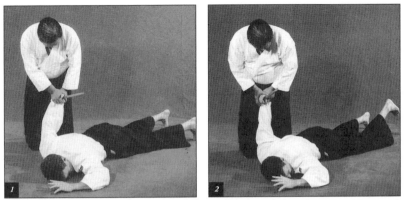

Uke is armed with a knife. Nage *has performed* ikkyo *and has dropped uke to the mat, retaining control over the weapon with the* ikkyo *lock. (2) Nage* slides forward on his left foot, as shown, wrapping *uke's arm around his leg and torquing* uke's *wrist to the right.*

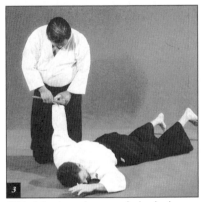

With uke's *grip on the weapon broken by the submission,* nage *disarms* uke.

NIKYO (A)

NOTE: THIS SUBMISSION CAN BE PERFORMED FROM *KATA-TORI NIKYO* AS WELL.

From katate-tori nikyo, nage *slides backwards while keeping the* nikyo *lock active.* Uke *is pulled forward, face-down on the mat.*

NIKYO (B)

From ikkyo, nage *slides forward and drops* uke *to the mat.* Nage *kneels beside* uke, *holding* uke's *arm at an upward angle, as shown, to help take out the slack. Notice how* nage's *left hand remains in place. (2)* Nage *presses* uke's *wrist in towards* uke's *elbow while torquing the wrist forward. At the same time,* nage *slides his left hand to* uke's *triceps and drops his weight, pinning the shoulder and completing the submission.*

NIKYO (C)

From kata-tori ikkyo, nage *quickly moves his left hand to grip* uke's *right elbow. (2)* Nage *slides backward on his right foot while pivoting to his right and executing* ikkyo, *as shown.* Uke *may now be dropped to the mat and a submission employed.*

266

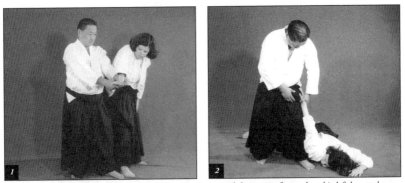

From sankyo, nage *cuts* uke *forward and down to the mat while moving forward on his left leg, as shown. This motion is not a downward pull nor an upward arc, but is taken forward and down, like a sword cut. Take care not to release the pressure of the* sankyo *lock. (2) With* uke *on the mat,* nage *slides his left leg next to* uke's *right arm and places the palm of* uke's *right hand flat against the outside of his thigh. Nage must release his right-hand grip to do so, but only after* uke's *hand is on position next to* nage's *thigh.*

Nage *leans his body slightly inwards while pivoting his body to the right.*

SANKYO (B)

From sankyo, nage *has cut* uke *down to the mat. Nage moves in on his left leg, wrapping* uke's *arm around it, as shown, and torquing* uke's *wrist to the right. Notice how* nage *keeps both hands in position.*

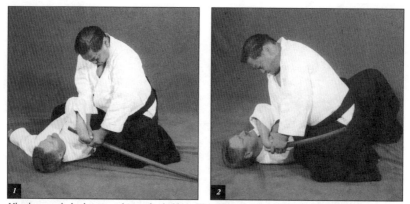

Uke *has attacked* yokomen-uchi, *with a* bokken. Nage *has answered* shiho-nage, *and is ready to throw* uke *to the mat. Instead,* nage *drops to the mat on his left knee, as shown, taking* uke *with him. Notice how the weapon is kept to the outside, while* nage's *right knee is on the inside of* uke's *right arm. (2)* Nage *places his right knee against* uke's *ribs and drops his weight on them. This knee placement is essential to prevent* uke *from rolling out of the submission. At the same time,* nage *tightens the* shiho-nage *lock by leaning forward and inward and torquing* uke's *right arm to the outside—that is, to* nage's *left.* Nage *uses his right forearm to help apply pressure and torque.*

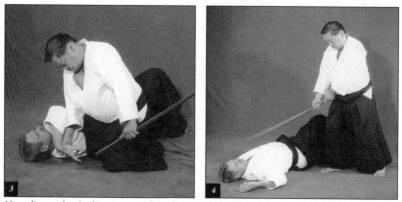

Nage *disarms* uke. *In this case,* nage *obviously is not able to place* uke's *arm in the center of his back. Instead,* nage *quickly rises, and…(4)…uses the* bokken *to hold* uke *at bay.*

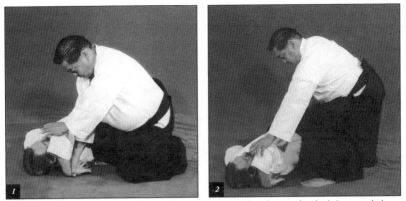

Nage *has submitted the unarmed* uke *as before.* Nage *places* uke's *right wrist beside* uke's *ear and places his left hand atop* uke's *elbow. (2)* Nage *rises while using his weight to hold* uke's *right arm in place, and backs away.*

NOTE: THIS SUBMISSION CAN ALSO BE USED AGAINST ARMED ATTACK, BUT IT IS A BIT CLUMSY TO EXECUTE WHILE HOLDING A WEAPON.

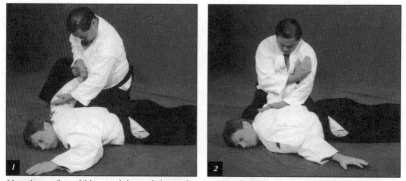

Nage *has performed* ikkyo *and dropped* uke *to the mat. Nage* kneels beside uke *while placing his left arm in-between* uke's *right arm and body, as shown, and allowing the* ikkyo *lock to slip away. Notice, however, how* nage's *close* ma-ai, *and the pressure of his body against* uke's *arm, keeps* uke *from escaping. Also notice how* nage's *open left hand lies against* uke's *left shoulder.*

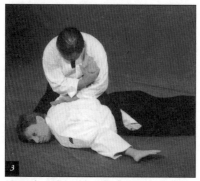

Nage *places* uke's *right palm flat against his left breast and holds it there while leaning inward and twisting his torso to the right, placing pressure against* uke's *right shoulder.*

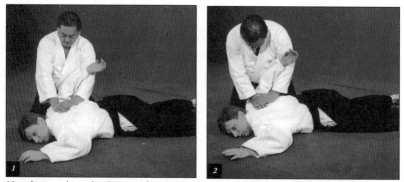

Nage *has moved into the* ude-osae *submission position, as in step 2 of* ude-osae(a). Nage *places* uke's *left palm against his left breast, then places both of his hands just below and to the left of* uke's *right shoulder, as shown, near but not on* uke's *spine. (2) Nage* leans in and drops his weight on his hands *while twisting his torso to the right.*

270

Nage *has locked* uke's *arm in the figure-four* ude-osae *position. (2)* Nage *drops* uke *to the mat as in step 1 of* shiho-nage *(a), while keeping the* ude-osae *lock in place.*

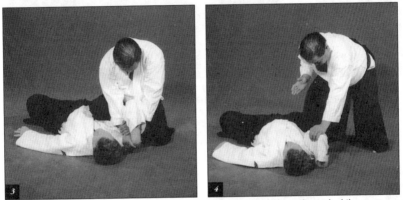

Nage *places his knee in* uke's *ribs and applies torque to the* ude-osae *lock, similar to the* shiho-nage *submission. Since* nage's *right arm is on the inside of* uke's *arm,* nage *can also press his elbow or forearm into* uke's *face. (4)* Nage *rises in the same manner as in steps 2 and 3 of* shiho-nage *(b).*

271

There is no special submission from *kote-gaeshi* – any of the submissions shown so far may be used. However, since *kote-gaeshi* ends with *uke* on his back, the only submission that may be immediately and effectively employed is *shiho-nage*. In order to employ any of the other submissions, *uke* must first be convinced to turn over onto his stomach. This is accomplished as follows:

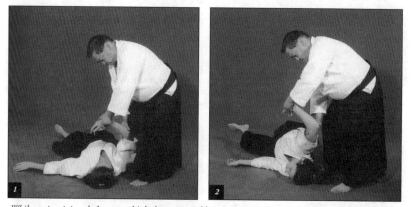

While maintaining the kote-gaeshi *lock,* nage *quickly moves to stand by the front of* uke's *head, as shown.* Nage *positions* uke's *hand above his face and holds it there with his inside hand, while grasping* uke's *elbow with his outside hand, as shown.* (2) Nage *moves to the inside while pushing* uke's *elbow in an arc around his head, clockwise. Think of using an auger, or a corkscrew – imagine there is a drill bit extending from* uke's *hand straight down through her head and into the mat, and* nage *is turning the bit by pushing the elbow. Take care to keep* uke's *hand above her face—otherwise, she can escape.*

Uke *turns over on her stomach to escape the pain that the torque places on her shoulder. Now a submission may be employed.*

NOTE: THIS TURN-OVER IS PERFORMED EXACTLY THE SAME ON THE OTHER SIDE, ONLY *NAGE* HOLDS *UKE'S* LEFT HAND IN HIS RIGHT, AND MOVES *UKE'S* ELBOW COUNTER-CLOCKWISE.

BY ROY SUENAKA

Many people who have written about Ueshiba O'Sensei and his aikido have never met him, yet profess to have significant knowledge of his teachings. Few have definitive knowledge of the true aikido that he meant to propogate to the world. As the saying goes, to understand the man, you have to know the man.

As a former student of Morihei Ueshiba O'Sensei, I observed many of his demonstrations and lectures. Despite my (at the time) limited understanding of the Japanese language, I listened patiently and critically with the hope that I could absorb with some clarity the true intention of his teachings. I have done my best to impart some of these teachings to you through this book. While *Complete Aikido: Aikido Kyohan* serves only as an introduction to Suenaka-ha Tetsugaku-ho aikido, I hope it has helped you to acquire the proper knowledge so that you can appreciate the intrinsic benefits one may achieve through the diligent and disciplined practice of aikido, and that it helps you to make a rational decision in selecting (if you are not presently enrolled in a class) an aikido style that meets your needs and expectations. Although aikido consists of highly complex and sometimes esoteric philosophical teachings, it has much to offer everyone, especially the deep understanding that we need of each other as human beings – as O'Sensei said, to integrate and communicate, so we may live together in peaceful harmony, as the word aikido implies.

A MARTIAL BIOGRAPHY OF
MOREHEI UESHIBA O'SENSEI

Aikido founder Morihei Ueshiba was born December 14, 1883 in Tanabe City, Wakayama prefecture on the main island of Honshu, Japan. A rather sickly child given to frequent illness, O'Sensei ("Great Teacher," as he is known by *aikidoka*) was more inclined towards academic and spiritual pursuits than physical ones, studying Shingon Buddhism beginning at age seven, then later Zen Buddhism, as well as demonstrating an aptitude for mathematics. Even at this early age, O'Sensei's spiritual bent was evident. Because of his frail nature, his father, Yoroku, a respected local businessman and political leader, encouraged his young son to engage in more physical activities, such as swimming and sumo.

When O'Sensei was twelve years old, Yoroku Ueshiba was roughed up by some local toughs employed by one of his political opponents. Intent on avenging his father's beating, young Morihei Ueshiba vowed to develop himself to the peak of physical power and martial prowess. To this end he traveled Japan, learning as much as he could from the masters he encountered before moving on. As a result, by his early twenties O'Sensei had studied arts as varied as kenjutsu (particularly the Yagyu Shinkage-ryu school of swordsmanship), jodo, Aioi-ryu jujutsu and Hozoin-ryu spear and bayonet arts. Many features of these diverse arts would later help to shape aikido. O'Sensei also saw active combat duty as a soldier during the Russo-Japanese war. As his martial prowess increased, so did his physical strength until in his prime, five-foot one-inch Ueshiba weighed nearly two-hundred pounds. Photographs of O'Sensei from the 1930's and 1940's show a solid, squarely-built man with massive shoulders and wrists and forearms thick as two-by-fours.

The most significant stage in O'Sensei's martial development occurred in 1912, when twenty-nine year old Ueshiba led an expedition of settlers to the frigid northern island of Hokkaido. It was here that he encountered Sokaku Takeda, acknowledged master of the unforgiving art of Daito-ryu jujutsu, whose fierce appearance and temperament were reflected in his martial technique. O'Sensei studied exclusively with Takeda, serving as the master's personal *deshi* and receiving his *menkyo-kaiden* teaching certificate some five years later. More than any other art, it is Daito-ryu that would most profoundly affect the development of aikido.

In late 1919, upon receiving news that his father was gravely ill, O'Sensei departed Hokkaido for home. This journey marks the most significant phase of the Founder's spiritual development. Along the way, he stopped in Ayabe to meet Onisaburo Deguchi, the flamboyant and charismatic leader of the eclectic and politically controversial Omoto-Kyo ("Teaching of the Great Origin") Shinto sect, known for its meditation techniques designed to unify one's spirit with the Divine. Though this visit lasted barely a month, Deguchi made a deep impression on O'Sensei and, upon his father's death the following January, O'Sensei returned to Ayabe and began a relationship with Deguchi and Omoto-Kyo that would last his lifetime. It was in Ayabe that O'Sensei established the Ueshiba Juku, his first formal *dojo*, and began active martial instruction.

In order to understand the origin of aikido's spiritual aspect, it is essential to note that as O'Sensei's study of Daito-ryu profoundly affected his martial technique, his study of Omoto-Kyo equally affected his spiritual development. In 1922, O'Sensei formally incorporated the two, the brutally physical and the transcendent spiritual, into a system he called aiki-bujutsu, which may be translated as "the martial system of spiritual harmony." Despite its forgiving name, the Daito-ryu influence was readily apparent in Ueshiba-ryu aiki-bujutsu, which relied heavily on the former system's excruciating joint immobilization techniques and bone-shattering throws. Wherein the aikido of O'Sensei's later years relied much on evasive, indirect *tenkan* (turning and blending) techniques now widely identified with the art, this infant version of aikido relied more on forceful, direct *irimi* (entering) techniques. Yet throughout it all, the physical and the spiritual were inextricably intertwined; rather than creating conflict, one served to illuminate and feed the other, like two flames burning atop a common candle.

Just as essential to the evolution of O'Sensei's *waza* was the inexorable changes in society during his life. Born less than twenty years after the start of Japan's Meiji Restoration, O'Sensei witnessed the rapid, forced decline of the militant feudal samurai state and the political rise of the mercantile classes. Although the samurai code of *bushido*, the way of the warrior, was still very much alive, ingrained as it was into the basal fabric of Japanese cultural consciousness, solving disputes and satisfying honor with the strike of the sword was no longer acceptable. The traditional *waza* were forced to re-define themselves, evolving with and adapting to the changing times, or perish. Thus, kenjutsu, the martial system of swordsmanship, became kendo, the way of the sword; the hoary roots of jujutsu bore the new fruit of judo, and so on. Likewise, as he studied under the martial masters of his day, gaining in physical ability and wisdom, O'Sensei recognized the necessity of this change. Daily practice of martial systems, even when great care was taken, often resulted in serious, sometimes crippling injury. O'Sensei saw this as self-defeating. Rather than viewing *uke* and *nage,* attacker and defender, as separate entities, he viewed them as a whole, for without one there was no need for the other. Thus, O'Sensei recognized the need for physical *waza* to evolve in a way that accommodated his evolving philosophy while remaining an effective martial system.

O'Sensei moved to Tokyo in the early 1920s and established a *dojo* there, giving many demonstrations to local police and military personnel, and cementing his reputation as a pre-eminent martial artist. In 1925, not long after he arrived, the third most profound experience of O'Sensei's life took place. Challenged to a *bokken* (wooden sword) duel by a visiting naval officer, O'Sensei declined, instead meeting the officer's challenge by merely moving out of the way of his increasingly more frantic strikes until the officer lay exhausted on the mat, defeated by his own aggression, while O'Sensei was victorious having never once landed a blow or injuring his opponent. Afterwards, O'Sensei walked out into his garden and, in his words, experienced a "golden light" descending on him from heaven, accompanied by complete clarity of thought and a unification of mind, body and spirit. It was then O'Sensei realized that 'The true nature of budo is in the loving protection of all things," a philosophy that to this day lies at the heart of aikido. To this end, in 1936, O'Sensei changed the name of his system from aiki-bujutsu to aiki-budo, "the martial way of spiritual harmony." Around 1942, O'Sensei began calling his system aikido, the way of spiritual harmony.

In 1942, prompted by both continuing government harassment because of his Omoto-Kyo connections and a growing sadness and despair over his country's increasingly militant stance, O'Sensei retired to his country home in Iwama, leaving the administration of his Tokyo *dojo* in the hands of his son and successor, Kisshomaru Ueshiba. In Iwama, O'Sensei waited out the war in prayer, meditation and practice, and established a shrine to the *Aiki O'Kami* (Great Spirit of *Aiki*), known as the Aiki Jinja.

In 1949, O'Sensei returned to his Tokyo *dojo* and began teaching again in earnest. Over the ensuing years, his reputation and skill spread, earning him great admiration and respect and drawing students and disciples from all over the world. In 1961, O'Sensei made a brief visit to Hawaii to build what he called a "silver bridge" of understanding and love between East and West. As a result of this trip, aikido quickly took root and spread throughout the United States. In 1964, he was decorated by the Emperor for his outstanding contributions to Japanese culture. Not long after, he again retired from active teaching, returning to Iwama and leaving instruction in the hands of his chief students and his son, though he made regular trips to Tokyo and traveled often to give demonstrations. Morihei Ueshiba O'Sensei died of liver cancer on April 26, 1969, aged 85. (O'Sensei's age at death is often listed as 86. This is because in the Orient in general, a person's age is reckoned from conception; therefore, a newborn is said to be a year old.)

This glossary is not at all meant to be a complete or definitive martial arts dictionary, but rather a basic reference aid for this book. As such, only elementary definitions are provided. Please note that, as in any language, many of the words, terms, and phrases that follow may have numerous meanings, depending on both general and martial context. For example, in karate, *keri-waza* would refer to kicking techniques, while in aikido, it generally means kick defense techniques.

Terms and phrases are defined here as they relate both to this book and Suenaka-ha Tetsugaku-ho aikido specifically, and aikido study in general. Japanese names are written in "Western" fashion, with the family name last, as in the text.

ago: Chin, jaw.

ago tsuki-age: A strike or push to the chin.

ai: To meet; love; unity; harmony.

ai-hanmi: To face one another in identical stance.

aiki: Unifying or harmonizing of *ki.*

aiki-budo: "The martial way of spiritual harmony." The name used by Morihei Ueshiba O'Sensei to describe his art, circa 1936-1942.

aikido: The Way to unify mind, body and spirit; the Way of peace; the Way to harmonize *ki.* Officially recognized as the name of O'Sensei's art circa February, 1942.

aikidoka: One who studies aikido; a practitioner of aikido.

aiki-en: Name of the martial art developed circa the 5th century a.d., and said to contain techniques from which daito-ryu jujutsu was created. The oldest known form of *aiki.*

aiki-in-yo-ho: The aiki system or doctrine of yin and yang, based on Taoist thought. Also written *aiki inyo-ho.*

aiki-jinja: The *aiki* shrine, located at the Founder's country home in Iwama, Japan.

aikijutsu: "The martial system of spiritual harmony." The name the Founder gave his art prior to 1936 (Ueshiba-ryu aikijutsu), derived from aiki-jujutsu. Aiki-jujutsu itself is often referred to as aiki-jutsu.

aikikai: The World Aikido Federation headquarters, located in Tokyo, Japan, and headed by the Founder's son, Kisshomaru Ueshiba Doshu.

aiki-ken: A sword used in accordance with *aiki* principles; swordsmanship in accordance with *aiki* principles.

aiki-nage: To throw an attacker without touching them, allowing the attacker's force to execute the throw (see also *sudori*).

aiki-no-kokoro: The spirit of *aiki* or aikido; the essential heart of *aiki* or aikido.

Aiki-O'kami: The Great Spirit of *Aiki*.

aiki-taiso: Basic aikido exercises performed solo, embodying *aiki* principles. Also *taiso*.

Aioi-ryu: An ancient system of jujutsu, one of many systems studied by the Founder, aspects of which he incorporated into aikido.

ashi: Feet; foot.

ashi-sabaki: Foot, feet or leg movement or placement.

atemi: A strike or strikes; striking.

ate-waza: Striking arts or technique(s).

bo: A cylindrical wooden staff, traditionally made of oak and roughly six feet long, often tapered at both ends.

bokken: A wooden practice sword.

bokuto: Another term for *bokken*.

bu: Martial spirit.

budo: The martial Way. *Budo* generally refers to the study of a martial system intended more for spiritual benefit rather than martial prowess.

budoka: A practitioner of *budo*.

bugei: The classical fighting arts.

bugeisha: A practitioner of the fighting arts; a *bushi*.

bujutsu: The martial arts. As opposed to *budo, bu-jutsu* generally implies a practical martial intent.

bushi: A warrior; a *samurai*.

bushido: The Way of the warrior; the martial Way.

chi-kara: Physical *ki;* muscular strength or force.

chi-no-kokyu: Breath of the earth.

choyaku: To step back and turn.

chuden: The second or middle level of mastery.

Dai Nippon Butokukai: Lit. "Greater Japan Association of Martial Virtues." A Japanese society dedicated to the preservation and promotion of contemporary Japanese martial arts. Also written Dai Nihon Butokukai.

Daito-ryu: A system of jujutsu founded circa 1100 A.D. by Minamoto Yoshimitsu. O'Sensei studied Daito-ryu under Sokaku Takeda and drew upon it extensively in creating aikido.

dan: Level; grade; rank.

do: The Way; the Path.

dogi: Martial arts practice uniform, usually referred to simply as *gi;* the uniform of the Way.

dojo: Martial arts training hall; the place of the Way.

doshu: A Grandmaster in a hereditary sense; a successor. Kisshomaru Ueshiba, son of aikido founder Morihei Ueshiba, is referred to as Doshu.

eri: Collar.

eri-tori: Collar grasp; to grasp the collar.

fudo-no-shisei: Immovable posture.

fudo-shin: Immovable mind.

fune-kogi: Rowing motion.

fune-kogi-undo: Rowing motion exercise. An *aiki-taiso.*

furi: To swing; a shaking or swinging motion.

furitama: Settling one's *ki;* a shaking motion used to settle one's *ki.*

gaku: The calligraphy or motto on the *dojo* wall.

ganmen: The face; the front of the head, as in an attack to that area.

ganmen-uchi: A straight attack to the face. Also *ganmen-tsuki.*

ganmen-tsuki: See *ganmen-uchi.*

gedan: Lower level of mastery.

gedan gaeshi: A low throwing technique; a low cutting motion with a sword.

geiko: Training. Also *keiko.*

genki: Good, health; vigor. Literally, good *ki.*

gi: Martial arts training uniform. Shortened from *dogi.*

giri: Honor; pride; a sense of duty and obligation.

go: Five; hard style.

godan: Fifth *dan;* a fifth degree black belt.

gokyo: Fifth classification or pinning/locking technique.

gyaku: Opposite; reverse.

gyaku-hanmi: Opposite stance; to face one another in opposite stance (ex: left *hanmi* facing right *hanmi*).

gyaku-te: Opposite hand; opposite side.

gyaku-yokomen: A strike to the opposite side of the head.

hachi: Eight.

hachidan: Eighth *dan;* an eighth degree black belt.

hakama: An ankle-length divided skirt worn by practitioners of many martial arts, including but not limited to aikido, kendo, iaido, and kyudo.

hanmi: A triangular stance where the leading foot is placed normal stepping distance in front and the rear foot positioned perpendicular to it. Weight is distributed equally on both feet.

hanmi-handachi: Two opponents facing off where one is kneeling or sitting and the other is standing; techniques practiced from this position.

hansha: Reflection; the same side (ex: grasping a person's right hand with your left).

hantai: Opposite; the opposite side (ex: grasping a person's right hand with your own).

happo: Eight directions.

happo-giri: To cut in eight directions.

happo-to: To strike or jab in eight directions.

happo-undo: Eight-directional exercise. An *aiki-taiso.*

hara: Abdomen; the tanden; the one point.

harai: A sweeping motion.

hazushi: The point at which *uke's* grip or grasp on *nage* is broken.

henka: Continuous; free-style (ex: *henka-waza* = continuous one-on-one *randori*).

hidari: Left.

hiden: Secret traditions, arts or techniques; the secret techniques within an art or style. (See also *kuden.*)

hiji: Elbow.

hiji-tori: Elbow grab; to grasp the elbow.

hombu dojo: The home or headquarters *dojo* of an organization. The Aikikai Hombu is in Tokyo.

Hozoin-ryu: A system of spear fighting founded in the 16th century. Studied by O'Sensei, aspects of which were incorporated into aikido.

iaido: The Way of perfection of the sword; the art of drawing, cutting, cleaning and sheathing the sword.

iaijutsu: The martial system of swordsmanship from which *iaido* was derived.

ibuki: A method of breathing; focused, controlled breathing practice.

ichi: One.

iki: Breathe; to breathe.

ikkyo: First classification or pinning/locking technique.

ikkyo-undo: ikkyo exercise. An *aiki-taiso.*

irimi: To enter; entering; an entering technique.

irimi-nage: An entering throw.

Itto-ryu: System of swordsmanship using a single sword, said to have been founded on the concept that a single technique *(kiri otoshi)* can be adapted to answer all situations. Studied by O'Sensei.

Iwama: Located in Ibaraki Prefecture, Japan. The site of O'Sensei's country home and *dojo,* and of the Aiki Jinja.

jinja: A shrine.

jo: A cylindrical wooden staff, roughly an inch in diameter and fifty inches long, traditionally made of oak.

jodo: The Way of the *jo;* a martial art.

jodan: The highest level; the upper level.

jodan-gaeshi: A high throw; a high cutting motion with a sword.

joho: High; upper.

jojutsu: The martial system of the *jo.*

jo kata: A choreographed series of movements and techniques using the *jo.*

jo-tori: To grasp the *jo; jo* taking techniques.

ju: Ten; gentle; soft; suppleness; the ability to adapt.

judan: Tenth *dan;* a tenth degree black belt. Generally the highest level of *dan* promotion.

judo: Lit. "The Gentle Way." A throwing and grappling sport founded by Jigoro

Kano in 1882, derived from jujutsu technique.

juji-nage: A crossed-arm throw or technique.

juji-waza: Crossed arm techniques.

jujutsu: A close-combat martial system emphasizing grappling, throws, locks and pins. O'Sensei drew heavily on jujutsu styles when creating aikido. Often written *ju-jutsu* and *ju-jitsu.*

kaeshi: To return; a reverse or counter; to reverse or counter a technique.

kaeshi-waza: Reversal or countering techniques.

kai: Headquarters or home organization.

kaiden: A master's license or teaching certificate.

kaiten: To open and turn; to revolve.

kaiten-nage: A revolving throw.

kama: A short-handled sickle.

kamae: Stance or posture; a combative stance.

kami: A deity; divine spirit.

kamidana: The altar or shelf supporting the *jinja,* where the *kami* resides. Often found on the front wall of a *dojo,* as part of the *kamiza.*

kamiza: Lit. "Upper Seat." A position of respect or veneration. *Kamiza* is usually employed to refer to a scroll, altar, photograph of a teacher or founder, or a combination of the three, placed on the front wall of a *dojo,* to which students bow in respect.

kan: A particular activity; a training hall, as in *budokan.*

kansetsu: Body joints.

kansetsu-waza: Joint techniques. Sometimes used specifically to refer to techniques executed against the natural range of motion of a joint.

kata: A fixed form; a choreographed series of sequential movements/techniques; the shoulder or lapel area.

katame-waza: Mat techniques. Often used specifically to refer to pinning or submission techniques.

kata-otoshi: Shoulder drop.

katate: One hand.

katate-tori: One-handed grasp; to grasp with one hand; to grasp one hand with one hand.

kata-tori: To grasp the shoulder or lapel; grasping the shoulder or lapel.

katsu hayai: Instant victory; to win quickly, with a minimum of effort, pain, or destruction.

keiko: Training; practice.

kempo: Sword techniques; fist way; a martial system emphasizing striking/fist techniques.

ken: A sword.

kendo: The Way of the sword; Japanese fencing using bamboo swords.

kenjutsu: The martial system of swordsmanship; sword techniques.

keri: Kick; to kick.

keri-waza: Kicking techniques. In aikido, *keri-waza* generally refers to kick defense techniques.

ki: Vital life energy; the energy of Creation; the vital life force of the Universe; spirit; energy.

kiai: Full of *ki;* life force; spirit meeting; spirit shout. A piercing cry used to focus *ki* during execution of a technique.

kiaijutsu: The martial system of *kiai;* techniques using *kiai* or intense mental concentration.

kiatsu: Pressure-point massage therapy utilizing *ki,* similar to accupressure.

ki-ga-nukueru: To lose *ki.*

ki-musubi: The linking of *ki;* to link *ki;* to unite one's *ki* with that of another.

ki-no-kenpo: Sword techniques with *ki.*

ki-no-kokyu-ho: Breathing meditation with *ki.*

ki-no-kokyu-ho-undo: A *ki-no-taiso.*

ki-no-nagare: Flowing *ki;* the stream of *ki.*

ki-no-taiso: *Ki* development exercises.

kio-tsuke: Attention.

kiri: To cut; a cutting attack.

kiri-otoshi: In swordsmanship, to cut from the top down. Fundamental technique of *Itto-ryu.*

kirikami: The first level of a system; first certificate; initial teaching license.

ki-shin-tai: *Ki* of mind and body.

kito: Rising and falling motion.

Kito-ryu: An ancient form of jujutsu, and one of the systems from which aikido was derived.

ki-wo-dasu: To pour forth *ki;* to extend *ki.*

ki-wo-kiru: To cut *ki.*

ki-wo-neru: To train one's *ki.*

ki-wo-totonoeru: To prepare one's *ki.*

kobudo: All classical martial and warrior arts. Most commonly used to refer to Okinawan weapons systems, such as *kama, bo, kusari-gama,* etc.

Kobukai: The name O'Sensei gave his Aiki Budo organization circa 1939.

Kobukan: The name of O'Sensei's original training hall, the present day Aikikai site.

kogeki: An attack.

koho: Backward (directional).

koho-kaiten: Backward tumbling.

koho-kaiten-undo: Backward tumbling exercise(s). An *aiki-taiso.*

koho-tento: Rising and falling method.

koho-tento-undo: Rising and falling exercise. An *aiki-taiso.*

koho-ukemi: Backward falling techniques.

kokyu: Breath; breath power; breathing with one's *ki* flowing.

kokyu-dosa: A *ki* extension exercise performed while kneeling in *seiza;* pinning with *ki.* An *aiki-taiso.*

kokyu-ho: Breathing method.

kokyo-ho undo: An *aiki-taiso.*

kokyu-nage: Breath throw; throwing with *kokyu.*

kokyu-ryoku: Breath power; controlling one's *ki* through breathing.

kosa: To cross; crossover; crossing.

kosa-sayu-undo: An *aiki-taiso.*

koshi: The hips or lower back.

koshi-nage: Hip throw; to throw *uke* over one's hips.

koshi-waza: Hip-throwing techniques.

kotai: A movement to the rear; to change.

kote: The wrist.

kote-gaeshi: Wrist-twisting or wrist-cutting technique or throw.

kote-gaeshi undo: Kote-gaeshi exercise; a wrist-strengthening exercise. An *aiki-taiso.*

ku: Nine.

kubi: The neck or throat.

kubi-shime: A choke.

kudan: Ninth *dan;* a ninth degree black belt.

kuden: Orally-bequeathed secrets or secret techniques. Also *hiden.*

kusari-gama: A *kama* (sickle) to which a chain, varying in length, has been attached. Also written *kusarigama.*

kuzushi: The point at which *uke* is off-balanced, and his or her momentum and *ki* are captured and turned to *nage's* advantage.

kyu: Lower, non-*dan* ranks. Unlike *dan* ranks, which proceed from *shodan* (first *dan*) up, *kyu* ranks "count down" as one is promoted, so that *ikkyu* (first *kyu*) is the last *kyu* rank before dan ranking.

ma-ai: Proper distance.

meijin: A true master; one who has attained perfection in an art. Often used as an honorific.

men: The face; the front of the head; forward.

menkyo: Teaching certificate; third license to teach.

menkyo-kaiden: Certificate of mastery. Awarded to one who has in the eyes of his or her teacher mastered all aspects of an art.

men-tsuki: A strike to the face. Also *men-uchi.*

men-uchi: A strike to the face.

migi: Right.

misogi: Ritual purification; methods for the purification of mind, body and spirit.

mochi: To grab; to grasp.

morote: Two hands; both hands.

morote-tori: A two-handed attack or grab, as when *uke* grabs *nage's* arm or wrist with both hands.

mune: The torso or abdominal area.

mune-tsuki: A strike to the torso or abdominal area.

mokuroku: A catalog of techniques; second level license or certificate.

mushin: No-mind; empty mind. See also *shin-no-mushin.*

nagare: Flow; to flow; flowing.

nage: A throw; one who is attacked; the defender.

nage-waza: Throwing techniques.

nana: Seven. Also *shichi.*

nanadan: Seventh *dan;* a seventh-degree black belt. Also *shichidan.*

naname: An oblique, angular movement or motion.

naname suri-ashi: Sliding one's feet at an angle.

ni: Two.

nidan: Second *dan;* a second-degree black belt.

nikyo: Second pinning technique.

nikyo-undo: *Nikyo* exercise; a wrist-strengthening exercise. An *aiki-taiso.*

nukite: A stiff-fingered strike using one or all of the fingers.

ojigi: Proper bowing.

oku: Inner; deep.

okuden: Inner secrets; certificate of mastery over inner secrets.

omote: The front; forward; towards. See also *irimi.*

Omoto Kyo: Lit. "Teaching of the Great Origin." A sect of Shinto founded by Onisaburo (Wanisaburo) Deguchi in the early twentieth century, and practiced by O'Sensei until his death.

orenai-te-undo: Unbendable arm exercise. A *ki-no-taiso.*

osae: A pin; a pinning method.

O'Sensei: "Great Teacher," or "Revered Teacher." Commonly used to refer to Morihei Ueshiba.

otoshi: A drop; to drop.

rei: Command for formal bowing; formal gesture to show respect and gratitude.

reigi: Etiquette. Also *reishiki.*

reiseishin: The state of unification of one's spirit with the Universe.

reishiki: Etiquette.

renshu: To train; to practice.

renzoku: Continuous motion of any kind.

riai: Proper timing.

roku: Six.

rokudan: Sixth *dan;* sixth degree black belt.

ryokata-tori: Grasping both of *nage's* shoulders.

ryote: Both hands.

ryote-mochi: To hold or grasp with both hands, as in grasping *nage's* wrist with both hands.

ryote-tori: To grasp both of *nage's* wrists.

ryu: A style; a school; a system; a lineage.

rondori: Continuous, freestyle practice, usually with two or more *uke* attacking *nage.*

sabaki: Free-flowing, natural movement.

san: Three.

sandan: Third *dan;* a third-degree black belt.

sankyo: Third pinning technique.

sankyo-undo: *Sankyo* exercise; a wrist-strengthening exercise. An *aiki-taiso.*

sasae: To support or prop.

satori: Enlightenment; a state of enlightenment.

sayu: To the side; left and right.

sayu-undo: Sideways motion exercise. An *aiki-taiso.*

seika-no-itten: The one-point. See also *hara, seika-no-tanden.*

seika-no-tanden: The one point. See also *hara, seika-no-itten.*

sensei: Teacher; respected teacher.

seigyo: Control; to control.

seiza: Proper sitting/kneeling.

shi: Four. Also *yon.*

shichi: Seven. Also *nana.*

shichidan: Seventh *dan;* a seventh-degree black belt. Also *nanadan.*

shihan: Master instructor.

shihan-bucho: Chief instructor.

shiho: Four ways or methods.

shiho-nage: Lit. "Four-directions throw."

shikaku: Blind side; behind and to one side.

shikko: Walking on bended knees, from *seiza;* "Samurai walking."

shime: A choke; to choke.

shime-waza: Choking techniques.

shin: The mind; new; spirit.

shindo: To vibrate/shake; vibrating or shaking.

Shindo Muso-ryu: A style of jujutsu founded by Muso Gonnosuke and studied by
    O'Sensei.

Shinkage-ryu: Lit. "Shadow Heart system." An older style of jujutsu studied by O'Sensei.

shinke: Nerve/pressure points.

shinke-waza: Nerve and pressure point techniques.

shinken-shobu: A challenge or fight to the death.

shin-no-mushin: Lit. "mind of no mind." The state of empty-mindedness, existing in
    the moment.

shin-shin: Mind-spirit; mind-body.

Shin-Shin Toitsu aikido: Lit. "Aikido with Mind and Body Coordinated." Founded by
    Koichi Tohei, and drawing heavily on the teachings of Shin-Shin Toitsu-do
    founder Tempu Nakamura, emphasizing *ki* development.

shizentai: Natural posture. Also *shizen-tai.*

sho: First or lower level; writing.

shodan: First *dan;* first-degree black belt.

shoden: First level of mastery.

shodo: The Way of Writing; Japanese calligraphy.

shodo-o-seisu: To control the first move; controlling the first move.

shomen: Face or forehead; the front.

shomen-uchi: An open-hand strike to the face or front; an overhead strike.

shuchu-ryoku: To concentrate all of one's energy on one point at a given moment.

shugyo: Hard, disciplined practice or training, as in total devotion.

Shuren Dojo: O'Sensei's Iwama *dojo.*

soto: Outside; outward.

soto-kaiten: Outside turning motion. Also *soto-mawari.*

soto-mawari: Outside turning motion. Also *soto-kaiten.*

suburi: Single or individual movements with the *bokken* or *jo,* as in a *kata.*

suburito: A heavy or weighted *bokken* used primarily for training while performing *suburi.*

sudori: When *uke* throws himself or herself with the force or their own attack. See also *aiki-nage.*

Suenaka-ha Tetsugaku-ho: Lit. "Suenaka Style, Philosophical Way." Style of aikido founded by Roy Yukio Suenaka, combining the teachings of O'Sensei and Koichi Tohei. Places equal emphasis on effective street defense and *ki*/spiritual development.

sumi-gaeshi: Corner throw; sacrifice throw, as in judo's *tomoe-nage.*

sumi-kiri: Clear mind and body; a state of purity.

sumi-otoshi: Corner drop.

suri-ashi: Sliding feet; to slide one's feet as one moves.

sutemi: Sacrifice fall; a somersaulting fall.

suwari: Sitting.

suwari-waza: Techniques performed with both *uke* and *nage* seated in *seiza.*

tachi: Standing; the Japanese sword.

tachi-tori: Sword-taking techniques.

tachi-waza: Techniques performed with both *uke* and *nage* standing; sword techniques.

tai: Body.

taigi: Lit. "body exercises." A series of techniques developed by Koichi Tohei, some modified from existing aikido techniques, which formed the fundamental *waza* of Shin-Shin Toitsu aikido.

tai-jutsu: Body arts; empty hand arts.

tai-no-henko: Blending practice; *nage* blending with *uke.*

tai-sabaki: Body movement; natural flow.

taiso: Exercise; exercises. See also *aiki-taiso.*

Takemusu-Aiki: Martial creative; excellent and infinite creativity in and through *aiki.* A state in which *aiki* principles are so manifest in a person that perfect techniques arise spontaneously from the energy of the moment. Takemusu-Aiki is the goal of all *aikidoka.*

Tanabe: Birthplace of O'Sensei, in Wakayama Prefecture, Japan.

tanden: Abdomen; *hara.*

tanin-su-gake: Multiple attacks simultaneously by two or more opponents.

tanren-uchi: Techniques or exercises to develop proper hip movement.

tanto: A wooden knife.

tanto-tori: Techniques to defend against knife attacks; knife-taking techniques.

te: Hand.

te-gatana: Sword hand.

tekubi: Wrist.

tekubi-furi-undo: Wrist-shaking exercises. An *aiki-taiso.* (See also *tekubi-shindo-undo.*)

tekubi-kosa-undo: Crossed wrist exercises. An *aiki-taiso.*

tekubi-joho-kosa-undo: High wrist-crossing exercises. An *aiki-taiso.*

te-sabaki: Proper hand/arm movement or placement.

tekubi-shindo-undo: Wrist-shaking exercises. See also *tekubi-furi-undo.*

ten: Heaven.

tenchi: Heaven and Earth.

tenchi-nage: Heaven and Earth throw.

tenkan: Turning away; leading away in an outward circular motion.

ten-no-kokyu: Breath of Heaven; a state of meditation.

tensho: Breathing exercises.

tepo: Pistol.

tepo-tori: Pistol defense; pistol-taking techniques.

tokon: Fighting spirit.

tori: To grasp; to take. In judo and some aikido styles, the *nage.*

tsubame-gaeshi: Swallowtail movement or throw, used to describe the movement or
    point in a technique where the *uke's* energy is brought into oneself and then
    directed outward in the defense.

tsuki: A thrust or strike; the attacker.

uchi: A strike.

uchi-deshi: Live-in student; a direct disciple or student.

uchi-kaiten: Inside turning motion. See also *uchi-mawari.*

uchi-komi: To step forward and strike.

uchi-mawari: To turn in. See also *uchi-kaiten.*

ude: Arm.

ude-furi: Arm shaking.

ude-furi-undo: Arm shaking exercises. An *aiki-taiso.*

ude-furi-choyaku-undo: Arm shaking exercises while moving *choyaku.* An *aiki-taiso.*

ude-kime-nage: Arm focus throw.

ude-osae: Arm bar or pin.

ude-tori: Grasping the arm; to grasp the arm.

Ueshiba, Morihei: The founder of aikido, referred to by *aikidoka* as O'Sensei. (Also
    written Uyeshiba.)

Ueshiba Juku: O'Sensei's first *dojo,* located on the grounds of the Omoto-Kyo
    compound in Ayabe, Japan.

uke: The person receiving a technique; the attacker.

ukemi: Protective, controlled falling techniques.

undo: Exercise or movement.

ura: The rear, as in a rearward entry technique.

ura-waza: Rearward entry techniques; turning techniques.

ushiro: Behind *nage's* or *uke's* back.

ushiro-hiji-tori: Grasping *nage's* elbows from behind.

ushiro-katate-tori: Grasping one of *nage's* hands or wrists from behind.

ushiro-katate-tori kubi-shime: Grasping one of *nage's* hands or wrists from behind and applying a choke to *nage* with the other arm.

ushiro-kata-tori: Grasping *nage's* shoulder from behind.

ushiro-kubi-shime: Applying a choke to *nage* from behind.

ushiro-ryokata-tori: Grasping *nage's* shoulders from behind.

ushiro-tekubi-tori: Grasping both of *nage's* hands or wrists from behind.

ushiro-tekubi-tori-kaiten-undo: An *aiki-taiso.*

ushiro-tekubi-tori-kotai-undo: An *aiki-taiso.*

ushiro-tekubi-tori-zenshin undo: An *aiki taiso.*

ushiro-tori: Wrapping both arms around *nage* from behind; a "bear hug."

ushiro-tori-undo: *Ushiro-tori* exercise. An *aiki-taiso.*

ushiro-ude-tori: Grasping both of *nage's* arms from behind.

ushiro-waza: Techniques to defend against a rearward attack.

Wadokai: Lit. "The Association of the Way of Peace." The governing organization of Suenaka-ha Tetsugaku-ho aikido.

waza: Technique; techniques.

Wakayama: The Japanese prefecture in which O'Sensei was born.

Yagyu Shinkage-ryu: A style of swordsmanship studied by O'Sensei.

yama-arashi: Lit. "mountain storm." An aikido technique.

yoko: Side, as in "the side of."

yokomen: The side of the head or face.

yokomen-uchi: A strike to the side of the head or face.

yon: Four. See also *shi.*

yondan: Fourth *dan;* a fourth-degree black belt.

yonkyo: Fourth classification or pinning technique.

yuki: To be brave; bravery.

Yagyu-ryu: A style of swordsmanship studied by O'Sensei.

zanshin: Continuous concentration or focus of *ki;* a ready mind; follow-through.

zazen: Seated meditation.

zengo: Backwards and forwards; backwards and forwards motion.

zengo-choyaku-undo: An *aiki-taiso.*

zengo-ikkyo undo: An *aiki-taiso.* Also *zengo-undo.*

zengo-undo: *Zengo* exercise. An *aiki-taiso.*

zenpo: Forward.

zenpo-kaiten: Forward tumbling.

zenpo-kaiten-undo: Forward tumbling exercise(s). An *aiki-taiso.*

zenpo-ukemi: Forward falling techniques.